Learning to Succeed

Learning
to
Succeed

REPORT OF THE
PAUL HAMLYN FOUNDATION
NATIONAL COMMISSION ON EDUCATION

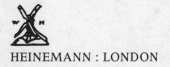

HEINEMANN : LONDON

William Heinemann Ltd
an imprint of Reed Consumer Books Ltd
Michelin House, 81 Fulham Road, London SW3 6RB
and Auckland, Melbourne, Singapore and Toronto

First published 1993

A CIP catalogue record for this book
is held by the British Library
ISBN 0 434 00035 3

Typeset by Falcon Graphic Art Ltd., Wallington, Surrey
Printed and bound
by Cox & Wyman Ltd,
Reading, Berkshire.

CONTENTS

Preface

This book contains the report of the *Paul Hamlyn Foundation* National Commission on Education.

The book is aimed at the general reader and not at the 'educational establishment', if there is such a thing. Like most subjects, education has its own jargon. We have sought to avoid it. The subject is of great practical importance to millions of people, and we want as many of them as possible to feel that we have written for them.

The background to the establishment of the Commission is as follows. It was set up in July 1991 following Sir Claus Moser's presidential address to the annual meeting of the British Association for the Advancement of Science in August 1990. In his speech Sir Claus drew attention to serious shortcomings in this country's education and training provision, and identified the need for:

> an overall review of the education and training scene: a review which would be visionary about the medium and long-term future facing our children and this country; treating the system in all its inter-connected parts; and, last but not least, considering the changes in our working and labour market scenes.

His call for a Royal Commission to carry out this review was immediately turned down by the Government, but it was clear that it generated much support both within and outside the world of education. The British Association therefore decided itself to set up an independent inquiry, with the support of the Royal Society, the British Academy and the Fellowship (later the Royal Academy) of Engineering. The Paul Hamlyn Foundation generously agreed to fund the work of the Commission.

The establishment of the Commission was welcomed by the Prime Minister and by the leaders of the opposition parties. Mr Major assured us that he looked forward 'to a constructive and no doubt robust contribution from the National Commission towards identifying and tackling the key issues that lie ahead in education and training'. I must stress that it is not our purpose in this report to comment specifically on the educational policies of the day. Our stance is consciously independent and non-political. It is our aim to promote a consensus about the needs of the future and to bring about the convergence of views which at present diverge.

The Commission was invited to consider all phases of education and training throughout the whole of the United Kingdom and to identify and examine key issues arising over the next twenty-five years. The membership of the Commission, which includes men and women from a wide variety of backgrounds from both inside and outside education, has reflected the far-reaching nature of this remit. The full terms of reference and a list of members are set out in Appendix 1.

We selected seven key issues for special study and appointed Working Groups to examine each of these. They were:

1   Effective schooling
2   Schools, society and citizenship
3   The teaching profession and quality

Each Working Group contained two Commissioners, one an expert in the field which the Group was invited to examine, the other (the Chairman) being chosen deliberately from Commissioners not professionally involved in the relevant area of education or training. We also established a Research Committee to ensure that all work of the Commission was underpinned by suitable research evidence. A total of twenty-four men and women accepted invitations to help us by becoming additional members of these bodies and were co-opted as Associate Commissioners. Their names also are listed in Appendix 1.

We owe a great deal to our staff. Our Director, Sir John Cassels, has been a tower of strength throughout, as has our Deputy Director, Barry Wakefield. We were fortunate in being able to recruit Janice Robins and Denise Eacher as joint secretaries to the Commission on temporary secondment from the Employment Department. They, together with our research officers, Sue Taylor and Josh Hillman, our consultant on higher education, Gwynneth Rigby, and all the other staff listed in Appendix 1 have formed a team which has served us with exceptional ability and efficiency.

I wish to record our particular gratitude to Paul Hamlyn himself for his enthusiastic commitment and backing. We also owe much to the Director of the Paul Hamlyn Foundation, Catherine Graham-Harrison, and to the Executive Director of the British Association, Dr Peter Briggs, for their wise advice and practical help. We are similarly indebted to British Telecom for its support in providing accommodation for the Commission's office and to others too numerous to list for help unstintingly given to us in the course of our work.

The Commission issued a general invitation to those wishing to do so to submit evidence to it. That invitation elicited a vigorous response and we received written evidence from some 250 institutions and individuals. The Commission and Working Groups took oral evidence from over 50 of these.

The Commission and its Working Groups have held conferences and seminars and have visited a variety of educational institutions in different parts of the United Kingdom. We have also studied various aspects of education and training in many parts of the world, and Commissioners have visited several countries, including, notably, France, Germany and the USA, to study such provision at first hand. Details of the conferences and seminars are also given in Appendix 1.

We must express our thanks to the Council for Industry and Higher Education, which jointly sponsored with us a series of six lectures on Universities in the Twenty-First Century. We are grateful also to the Franco–British Council which, with our help, organised a seminar on technical and vocational education and training for 16–19-years-olds in France and the United Kingdom. In addition, we benefited greatly from an international symposium on education at Leeds Castle most ably organised by the America–European Community Association Trust, whose Chairman, John Raisman, is also our Deputy Chairman.

Finally, the Commission has published a series of Briefings in which authoritative authors analyse and discuss important issues affecting education and training. We owe much to the many experts who prepared these invaluable documents for us and to the Editor of the series, Josh Hillman. All were subjected to scrutiny and editing prior to publication by myself, John Raisman and Sir Claus Moser.

The Briefings are contained in a single volume published alongside this report. In addition, we shall be publishing early in 1994 a further volume containing additional supporting evidence together with a number of lectures, papers and articles which we consider deserve a wider audience.

Wherever possible in our report, we say what we believe to be relevant and applicable to the whole of the United Kingdom. But we have always borne in mind that education in the United Kingdom is the responsibility of no fewer than four Secretaries of State, to whom a fifth – the Secretary of State for Employment – must be added when training is taken into account. Northern Ireland, Scotland and Wales each have distinctive arrangements for education and training, and a distinctive culture or approach. In each country, certain key aspects of provision have long been determined at a United Kingdom level, but other aspects, some of them also of key importance, have been determined by the countries themselves in ways that reflect their differing histories and circumstances. To an extent, our thinking has been driven by considerations in England. We think this appropriate in that the largest partner is inevitably a major influence elsewhere and the four countries have a common interest in standard provision for certain important areas. We acknowledge, however, that we have not always been able to give the attention we would have wished to the problems and achievements that are unique to each country.

For several reasons, therefore, our report at some points concentrates solely on provision in England or in

England and Wales. We do not, however, think that our report would have been radically different had we started from a different vantage point. This is because, in our membership, visits and other deliberations, we have tried always to recognise the circumstances of each country and to learn from each. Indeed, as later chapters show, those searching for ways of improving education in one part of the United Kingdom often need look no further than to other parts of the United Kingdom for useful models. As a result, we believe that our analysis and principles have application throughout the United Kingdom and that our major recommendations either reflect current developments in one or more of the four countries, or can be properly adopted or adapted by each. We hope, therefore, that the reader in Northern Ireland, in Scotland and in Wales gets just as much from our report as the reader in England.

To have had the privilege of chairing the Commission has been for me a demanding, challenging, but invariably rewarding experience. John Raisman, my wise and assiduous Deputy Chairman, Claus Moser, the thoughtful and perspicacious Chairman of our Research Committee, John Cassels, our skilful and dedicated Director, and all of the Commissioners and Associate Commissioners have worked together as a superb and cohesive group throughout. I am very grateful to them all and trust that this report and its innovative recommendations will have a major and increasingly beneficial influence upon education and training in the United Kingdom in this century and, even more, in the next.

In order that the objectives which we have defined shall be achieved, we earnestly invite the endorsement and collaboration in pursuit of our aims of present and future Governments, of all those involved in the provision of education and training and, indeed, of the public as a whole.

Walton of Detchant

JOHN WALTON
Lord Walton of Detchant,
Chairman of the National Commission on Education

September 1993

The Commission's Vision

1 In all countries *knowledge and applied intelligence* have become central to economic success and personal and social well-being.

2 In the United Kingdom much higher achievement in education and training is needed to match world standards.

3 Everyone must want to learn and have ample opportunity and encouragement to do so.

4 All children must achieve a good grasp of literacy and basic skills early on as the foundation for learning throughout life.

5 The full range of people's abilities must be recognised and their development rewarded.

6 High-quality learning depends above all on the knowledge, skill, effort and example of teachers and trainers.

7 It is the role of education *both* to interpret and pass on the values of society *and* to stimulate people to think for themselves and to change the world around them.

The Commission has adopted this vision for the future development of education and training in the United Kingdom. It has also defined seven goals which must be achieved to make a reality of the vision. Both the vision and the goals are discussed in Chapter 3 of this report.

1
Where We Are Today

Education and Training in 1993

It is possible to summarise the results at present achieved by education and training in the United Kingdom quite briefly. A minority of academically able young people receive a good, if narrow, education and, for them, provision is well suited and efficiently run. For a majority of young people, education is of more variable benefit. The talents of many are not valued enough and not developed enough; and, once they start work, the same is true in terms of training. In addition, an uncomfortably large minority of young people leaving school have trouble with literacy and numeracy and seem to have benefited all too little from their education.

This is not a flattering picture. One way of checking its accuracy is to seek to make comparisons with other countries.

Some international comparisons
It emerges clearly that those who are *academically* the most able fare well in the United Kingdom today (as they have in the past).

According to the Organisation for Economic Co-operation and Development (OECD), in 1988 we had a higher proportion of young people (16.3%) becoming graduates than any other country in central and western Europe except Ireland (17.2%).[1] Moreover, a very high proportion of entrants to universities in this country succeed in graduating – in sharp contrast to the experience of students in some west European countries including, for example, France where many discontinue their studies after one or more years of higher education.

It is true that in some countries elsewhere in the world, including the United States and Japan, higher percentages of young people become graduates than here, but our own rate has been rising very quickly in recent years. The Government predicted in 1991 that about a third of our young people will go on to higher education (university education, or the equivalent, leading to a degree or higher level diploma) by the end of this decade, and it already looks likely that in practice the proportion by then will be a good deal higher.

The most serious shortcoming of education in the United Kingdom is to be found elsewhere. It is its failure to enable not just a minority but a large majority of young people to obtain as much from their education as they are capable of achieving.

This can be illustrated in various ways. A report published by the National Institute of Economic and Social Research (NIESR) in 1993 looks at the percentages of young people achieving comparable school qualifications at the ages of 16 and 18 plus in four countries.[2] Both at 16 and at 18 plus the percentages for England are far below those for Germany, France and Japan. Students in Scotland and Northern Ireland (but not in Wales) probably do rather better than those in England, especially after age 16, but are generally much nearer in achievement to English students than those of the other countries mentioned. With regard to Northern Ireland, for example, recent research has highlighted a pattern of low achieve-

ment among boys leaving Catholic secondary schools.[3]
The figures are shown in Tables 1.1 and 1.2.

Table 1.1 Sixteen year olds in certain countries reaching equivalent of GCSE grades A–C in mathematics, the national language and one science, 1990–91.

Country	Percentages
Germany	62
France	66
Japan	50
England	27

Source: Green, A. and Steedman, H., 1993.[2]

Table 1.2 Young people in certain countries obtaining a comparable upper secondary school qualification at 18+, 1990.

Country	Percentages
Germany	68
France	48
Japan	80
England	29

Source: Green, A. and Steedman, H., 1993.[2]

International comparisons of this kind are not at all easy to make with precision, and there must inevitably be some room for argument about how fair the comparisons in these tables are. Nevertheless, we see no escape from the conclusion that the NIESR comparisons point to a substantial gap in performance between England and the three other countries listed, especially at the age of 18 plus.

Vocational qualifications

It might be thought that our young people do better when it comes to vocational qualifications. The authors of the NIESR study go on to compare the vocational qualifications of young people in France, Germany and Britain. They say in the case of Germany that in 1978 no fewer than two-thirds of the German labour force held a certificated, recognised craft qualification compared to one-third of the British labour force at a similar level; and that since 1978 the gap has actually widened because in Britain numbers have not increased significantly whereas very large numbers of young people are undergoing apprentice training in Germany.

The situation in France is different. In the 1960s a smaller share of the French workforce had vocational qualifications compared with the British. Since then France has made vigorous efforts to improve the availability of qualifications at craft level, and France overtook Britain in the early 1970s. In the 1980s France increased the numbers holding craft-level qualifications in its workforce by a quarter, at a time when in Britain numbers were barely rising.

These are disturbing figures. There is no refuge in suggesting that perhaps even without formal qualifications British workers are just as productive as German and French; detailed studies in various parts of industry by NIESR have shown that they are not by any means as productive and that a key reason is precisely their lack of adequate training. Productivity studies have shown that, in spite of a sharp rise in the rate at which British productivity was improving in the 1980s, German and French manufacturing productivity is still about 20% higher than British. Many factors contribute, but labour productivity plays its part.

Literacy and numeracy

Finally, it is clear that there are many young people in Britain who have reached only low levels of literacy and numeracy at school. A survey of trainees in the Youth Training Scheme showed in 1989 that over a quarter of the trainees were in need of help with numeracy and more than a sixth needed help with literacy.

More recently, surveys were carried out for the Adult Literacy and Basic Skills Unit into literacy and numeracy among 21-year-olds and further education college students. The Unit reported as follows:[4]

> A major survey into the attainment of a representative group of 21-year-olds has revealed that almost 15% have limited literacy skills and 20% have only very limited competence with basic maths. A further larger group will need some additional help because the skills they have are not likely to be good enough to cope with changing requirements and demands.
>
> We have also demonstrated the major effect that poor basic skills have on job prospects, unemployment, housing and health and the inter-generational transfer of reading difficulties. Screening of 10,000 students in further education colleges revealed that almost 4 in 10 would need some additional help with basic skills if they were to get a qualification at NVQ Level 2 [i.e., a National Vocational Qualification at craft level].

Arbitrary Factors Affecting Education

Looked at from the point of view of individual children, it is clear that another factor in the British scene is its arbitrariness. In a truly fair society, everybody would have an equal chance of a good education. That is not of course to say that all would achieve equally good qualifications,

since it is obvious that people's natural abilities and motivation differ. In practice, however, how well people are
educated and trained in the United Kingdom depends on
many factors beyond their own or their parents' control,
including, for example, geography, social class, gender
and ethnic origin.

Under-5s

A child's chances are already affected before the age of 5
by the fact that good quality early childhood care and
education services, which may have a marked effect on
the subsequent success of children in education, are very
unevenly distributed and also receive varying amounts of
public funding. Much of what is provided is in the private
sector and therefore depends on the parents' ability to
pay. The United Kingdom has one of the lowest levels of
publicly funded pre-school services in Europe.[5]

School

As to school itself, children's chances are greatly affected
by where their parents live. The gulf in outcomes
between our best schools and our worst is big, much bigger than in most countries. For example, the OECD
study mentioned earlier found that differences between
English schools in levels of mathematical achievement
were far larger than in any of the ten other countries
studied, including Scotland, with the single exception of
Switzerland.[6]

At present many primary schools are not necessarily
able to give all their pupils the help they need to master
the basics of reading and writing successfully. Successive
reports by HM Inspectors have also shown that children
of average and higher ability are often not sufficiently
challenged by the teaching they receive in the later years
of primary school: instead of making good progress they

become bored.

At secondary school level the design of the curriculum has been dominated by the needs of the minority who are being prepared for further study at an intensive academic level. The pre-eminence of 'A' levels in England, Wales and Northern Ireland has cast a shadow on studies of a technical, practical or vocational nature. Scotland has done rather better with its broader Highers.

It is clear that children often have a better chance of doing well if their parents can afford to send them to a good independent fee-paying school and decide to do so. About 7% of our children are in private sector schools. The level of resources put into independent schools is usually much higher than that available for schools maintained by the State so that, apart from anything else, pupil-teacher ratios are much lower and pupils can receive more individual attention from teachers. Facilities are also usually more favourable.

Many State-maintained schools achieve excellent results by any standards. On the other hand results in deprived areas are sometimes disappointing. This may not be any fault of the schools, and in fact there are many schools which do well in discouraging circumstances. The fact is that the dice are loaded against any school in such areas. As a result, a cycle of failure may set in which is self-reinforcing; abler pupils and more active parents seek places elsewhere, resources decline as funds follow pupils away and good staff are increasingly hard to recruit.

Higher education
As noted earlier, young people who go on into higher education are likely to do well and have a very good chance of obtaining a degree in 3 years (3 or 4 years in Scotland). They are joined by a growing stream of mature students – students aged 21 or more – who enter higher

education after an interval. Of today's 18-year-olds, perhaps 40% will have degrees by the time they are 35.

Other young people

For other young people, things are much more problematic. By the age of 17 many have left full-time education. Typically they have little to show for their education in terms of qualifications. A minority stays on at school or college full-time to 18 but only some of these young people go into jobs where they receive further training and are encouraged to obtain a vocational qualification.

Finally, an uncertain outlook indeed awaits those young people who have left full-time education at 16 or 17. Some 90,000 young people of 16 and 17 were unemployed in the winter of 1992–3. About 400,000 were in full-time jobs but only about a quarter of these were receiving training. Given that workers with no qualifications are much more likely to find themselves unemployed than others, it is unacceptable that so many young people start their working careers in so unpromising a way.

Other factors: social class

Social class is among the arbitrary factors which most affect the quality of education in the United Kingdom. Children from social classes 1 and 2 of the Registrar-General's classification, on average, do better in examinations at 16, are likely to stay on longer in full-time education and are more likely to go to university than those from classes 3 to 5. There has been little change over the years in the proportion of entrants to higher education who come from working-class families.[7]

Equal opportunity between the sexes

On the other hand, there is much greater equality between the sexes in education than formerly. Girls do better on average than boys in GCSE examinations and achieve about the same number of 'A' level passes as boys do. The numbers of women going into higher education are now about equal with men, having been much lower in the recent past. Nevertheless, cultural factors still stand in the way of full equality of opportunity. It is still too readily assumed, for example, that girls will not want to study subjects such as engineering which have long been male strongholds, and girls themselves often accept too readily that such subjects are not for them. And when young women enter work, their training opportunities are not always as good as men's and often tend to lead to jobs with lower pay and status.

Ethnic minorities
When one examines how young people from ethnic minorities fare in education, it becomes clear that these young people are much more likely than young whites to stay on in full-time education after the age of 16, as Table 1.3 shows.[8]

Table 1.3 Sixteen to nineteen year olds in full-time education, 1982 and 1988–90, by ethnic origin, Great Britain.

Percentages

Ethnic group	1982		1988–90	
	Men	*Women*	*Men*	*Women*
White	25	24	36	38
Afro-Caribbean	26	37	39	48
South Asian	58	51	60	53

Source: 1982 PSI Survey; 1988-90 Labour Force Surveys. In: Jones, T., 1993.[8]

In 1982 Afro-Caribbean and South Asian people were less likely than whites to have formal qualifications, but this is gradually changing; among young people aged 16–24, people from ethnic minorities are more likely than whites to have a degree or other higher education qualification.[9] There is no marked difference in the availability of job-related training for people from ethnic minorities as compared with whites, though in general people from ethnic minorities are more exposed to unemployment.

Special educational needs
Many children have special educational needs (SENs) either at some point in their education or throughout it. During the 1970s and up to the late 1980s there was a rapid development both in understanding children's SENs and in providing for them with suitable education.[10] There is some fear that recent legislation may make it more difficult to maintain the quality of such provision; on the other hand there are many examples of good practice which give promise, if adopted more widely, of still further progress.

Other groups
Finally, there are some groups whose circumstances may make special consideration necessary, for example, members of HM Forces. We ourselves helped to fund a study by the Open School of education for children who are in hospital or sick.[11] This shows that there is no satisfactory framework of law laying down who is responsible for what; the education which sick children actually receive varies a great deal in quality and quantity.

The Importance of Aspirations

Much has been written in recent years about the poverty of our aspirations. Many pupils and parents do not aim high enough. Some teachers expect too little of their pupils.

Employers may respond in kind, looking for too little from their recruits, providing training that is often inadequate, and hoping that they will continue to be able to sell products of relatively low added value. The problem is long-standing, with roots deep in our industrial and pre-industrial past.

But the situation is changing, and that change can, and must, be accelerated. The fruits of fifty years of free and compulsory secondary education and of twenty-five years of widespread comprehensive schooling are now being seen among today's parents. We are witnessing a steady rise in the numbers of parents who have continued in school after 15 or 16 years, who want more for their own children's education, and who can give more to it. The school attainments of these children benefit substantially. We can confidently expect their numbers to grow and their demands on provision to press yet more strongly as attainments rise.

It is not enough, however, for us simply to sit back and welcome this change, very welcome though it is. It reminds us of education's power to transform, and of the critical role of the family. But this alone is not enough. Though levels of attainment and continuation in education are improving as a result of this sort of social change, we are starting from too low a base for trends of this sort to do much to close the gap in attainment between us and our major competitors. And, as we point out elsewhere, such trends also bring with them risks, in particular the risk that other groups in our society will be left behind, and will find their opportunities pre-empted by those whose start in life was more fortunate.

Indeed, it is the creation of opportunity that holds the key for the fortunate and less fortunate alike. If attainment does not open up opportunities, then aspirations will suffer. If aspirations suffer then so, too, will subsequent attainment. We must therefore increase opportunities.

Conclusion

Excellence can certainly be found and is not rare in British education and training. Nevertheless, there is much that needs to be improved and it is encouraging that education has risen high in the political and public agenda and that much effort in recent years has been spent in pursuit of reform. Before considering the future, however, it is necessary to understand the present context and the paths by which provision has developed in recent years; we examine both in the next chapter.

Notes

[1] Centre for Educational Research and Innovation, 1992. Education at a Glance. OECD Indicators. Organisation for Economic Co-operation and Development. Table R2.

[2] Green, A. and Steedman, H., 1993. Educational Provision, Educational Attainment and the Needs of Industry: A Review of Research for Germany, France, Japan, the USA and Britain. National Institute of Economic and Social Research.

[3] Cormack, R.J., and others, 1992. Secondary Analysis of the School Leavers Survey (1989). In: Seventeenth Report of the Standing Advisory Commission on Human Rights. HMSO, pp. 60–75.

[4] In: Dearing, R., July 1993. The National Curriculum and its Assessment: An Interim Report. National Curriculum Council and School Examinations and Assessment Council.

[5] Sylva, K. and Moss, P., November 1992. Learning Before School. NCE Briefing No 8. National Commission on Education.

[6] Centre for Educational Research and Innovation, *op cit*, Table R9(e).

[7] Halsey, A.H., August 1992. Opening Wide the Doors of Higher Education. NCE Briefing No 6. National Commission on Education.

[8] Jones, T., 1993. Britain's Ethnic Minorities. Policy Studies Institute, p. 42.

[9] Jones, T., *op cit*; Table 3.5.

[10] Wedell, K., May 1993. Special Needs Education: The Next 25 Years. NCE Briefing No 14. National Commission on Education.

[11] Tait, K., December 1992. The Provision of Education for Children in Hospital or Sick at Home. Open School.

2
The Context and Background

Education and training both mirror change and help to cause it. This chapter shows how in the last fifty turbulent years change has revolutionised many aspects of national life and how education and training have been affected and have responded.

The Economy

It is not always as well understood as it should be how fundamental the performance of the economy is to the well-being of the country. If industry and commerce flourish they provide the basis for a good standard of living. Jobs depend on wealth creation, and hence the well-being both of individual people and of families and communities. The standard of public provision, including the quality of health services and care for the old, depends on how well the economy works. And so of course does the quality of education. The extent to which education and training in turn affect the economy is a question central to this chapter.

This connection – between the economy and education and training – did not seem important earlier in the century. In the early 1900s we were at the centre of the biggest empire in world history, and as the first industrialised nation we still had a very powerful trading position.

Our industrial success had not depended on education and training. As recently as 1913 our exports were dominated by textiles and clothing, iron and steel, and coal, and we relied greatly on Third World markets. The education of the workforce was scanty and its training mostly took the form of new recruits 'learning by doing' under the supervision of experienced workers. Despite various national inquiries, the commonsense view was that industry had no need for a better or differently prepared workforce, and no attempt was made to create one.

The 1918–1939 years were dominated by the depression and recovery from it. Our traditional industries contracted sharply. There was some movement towards 'new' industries such as chemicals, vehicles and electrical engineering, but no parallel advance in scientific and technical education.

Since 1945 the economy has grown by some 2.4% a year on average; taking into account population increases – about 0.4% a year – people in the United Kingdom have, on average, been better off by about 2% each year. In some years the growth has been faster, but there have also been times when it has slowed down or even, as very recently, declined for a time. By our own previous standards, the rate of economic growth since 1945 has been rather rapid.

International trade and innovation

International trade has been transformed by the steps taken to open up free competition. There could hardly be a greater contrast with the inter-war years, when protectionism and industrial cartels were rife. We have become part not merely of a European economy – though trade within Europe has grown particularly quickly – but of a global economy. People who want to buy goods in Britain are able to choose among the products of firms competing on an equal basis from all over the world. The result is that the quality and price of goods are determined in international marketplaces, not just a British one, and that customers have more choice and more power than ever before.

Meanwhile, scientific knowledge has been expanding apace and there have been rapid developments in the technologies for putting it into practical use. Most dramatic and far-reaching has been the advance in the use of information technology (IT), and with it the rapid evolution of computers and computer software and also a transformation in telecommunications. But in many other fields – for example biotechnology and the development of new materials – advance has been hardly less striking.

Our relatively poor economic record
Amid all this, our economic record has in many ways been disappointing. Above all, our own progress has been overshadowed by the success of others. In living standards, by 1991 we were eighteenth among the 24 countries in membership of the Organisation for Economic Co-operation and Development,[1] and eighth among the 12 countries of the European Community. And we are uneasily aware of the rapid progress of various newly industrialising countries.

We have not been as successful as most competitor nations in taking advantage of opportunities to develop and expand industry. We have had no 'economic miracle' and successive economic policies have had mixed fortunes. We have struggled to keep inflation in check and in recent years success in this has been bought at a grievous cost in unemployment and lost output.

Too many of our companies have wilted in the face of foreign competition and too many managements have been made to look inadequate in the process. With some exceptions, manufacturing industry has not done well, especially in meeting customers' demands on quality. The trade unions have contributed their share; they have had too much power and too often it has been used negatively. Studies of productivity have confirmed our poor showing.

This is a gloomy recital, in some ways too gloomy. It does not for example pay tribute to those companies which have thrived in the bracing climate of world competition, especially, for example, in energy, chemicals and pharmaceuticals. Our financial and retailing sectors have also done well. It does, however, underline a truth which cannot be evaded. The nation's future well-being cannot be separated from the performance of our economy. Before examining how much that in turn depends on education and training, we look at how the organisation of work is changing in the modern world and note some fundamental trends in the development of British society.

The Organisation of Work

There has been a transformation in the way in which work is organised since the 1940s.

The old style of organisation
Well into the 1960s, companies of any size typically relied on rigid centralised structures in which there were many layers of management. Such structures were meant to ensure that orders from the centre were passed on correctly and that they were properly complied with. They did not encourage enterprise or initiative, and they did not help companies to react swiftly to change. Innovation was painfully slow, and the whole apparatus was expensive.

Management in our companies was in many ways amateur. Relatively few members of boards were graduates, and among the professionals lawyers and accountants, rather than scientists or engineers, commonly held sway.

Lower down, most workers learned their jobs by doing them, whether they were white-collar workers or on the shop-floor. Some shop-floor jobs, for example those of maintenance craftsmen, were designated 'skilled'. Young entrants acquired the right to do these jobs by serving apprenticeships, typically 5 years in length, not by undergoing training or obtaining qualifications.

Such arrangements were suited to a 'Taylorist' approach, so called after F.W. Taylor, once the leading exponent of 'scientific management' in the USA. Work was broken down into clearly-defined segments which workers could easily master with a minimum of training. The system did not require initiative. On the contrary, independent-mindedness and a readiness to take the initiative were unwelcome, as being likely to disrupt production.

Arrangements of this kind did not encourage people to take individual responsibility. Nor did they promote a feeling of common purpose. Rather they led to a perception that the interests of managements and of workers were separate, or even opposed. Manual workers were organised in various unions, or sections of unions, which defended the privileges of workers with defined skills, or in unions which upheld the interests of the less skilled workers and had no interest in their becoming skilled (which would mean transferring to another union). Change which might upset the balance between different groups of workers was liable to be resisted.

The impact of international competition
International competition and technological change have been sweeping aside companies clinging to this model.

Successful companies today are highly market-oriented and therefore highly adaptable. They have 'flat' and flexible management hierarchies and depend on employees working together in teams to develop and make new products or provide services.

Everywhere, and at all levels, professionalism is required. Senior managers are highly trained professionals and many graduate specialists are employed. Leading international companies invest heavily in training the whole workforce, and bring pressure on their suppliers to do the same. All employees are expected to be aware of their contribution to the business, to take responsibility for the quality of what they do and to be both self-disciplined and ready to take the initiative when circumstances require it.

Rapid change and the pressures of competition have made it far more difficult for employers to offer secure jobs for their employees. Jobs which are not part of the 'core business' have in any case very generally been hived off to contractors who specialise in providing particular services. The safe assumption for people starting work today is, generally speaking, that they will change employer – and sometimes occupation – several times in their working lives, and that this will often need to be accompanied by further learning by way of education and training.

Self-employment has been gaining steadily in recent years and by 1992 there were 3.2 million self-employed people, the great majority being men.

The proportion of the population aged over 16 which is economically active, i.e. in employment or looking for work, is the highest in the European Community except for Denmark. Our overall proportion is 64%; among men the proportion is nearly 76%, and among women 53%. Most men work full-time, but 45% of women are part-time workers.[2]

Society

The post-war era began with a great expansion of the 'welfare state'. Mass provision was seen as the means of improving the general standard of living of people: it included the National Health Service; National Insurance; local authority housing; and State-funded education. Basic industries – coal, electricity, gas, the railways – were nationalised. It was the norm for pay and conditions of work to be settled by industry-level collective bargaining. Full employment, it was thought, had come to stay, and it was underwritten by the Government.

This vision has lost much of its power.

Higher standards of living, together with the increasing power of consumers, have placed greater emphasis on individualism. Rising educational standards have had the same effect. So have the changes at work already noted; trade union membership has fallen greatly. Many more people own their own homes. Government policies have both followed and reinforced this trend.

People's horizons have widened; television, increased leisure and holidays abroad have helped the process. The English Channel no longer seems to divide us from the Continent as it once did. Since we joined the European Economic Community in 1971, Europe has rarely been out of the news. Where their elders hesitate and debate, more and more young people relish the opportunities open to them to travel and work in Europe.

Life expectation has risen. The proportion of the population over the present pensionable age (60 for women, 65 for men) has risen to 10.6 million and will rise steeply in the early decades of the next century. Increasingly people in the 'Third Age', now defined as people in the 50–75 age bracket, will both need and want to work, though not so much in full-time paid jobs as they grow older but in a range of part-time and voluntary activities.

The total population is now about 57½ million and is predicted to rise to 59 million by the start of the next century. Young people represent a smaller proportion of the total than 20 years ago: in 1971 there were 14.3 million people under 16, but by 1988 the figure had fallen to 11.5 million and it is set to fluctuate around 12 million in the early decades of the next century.[3]

Emerging trends

A number of emerging trends pose important challenges for education.

In recent years differences in income between the least well off and those with higher incomes have widened, as Table 2.1 shows. Over the period covered, the real income of the bottom fifth of households did not change at all, whereas it increased by 23% for the middle fifth and by 40% for the top fifth. Altogether, society is more unequal and more polarised.

Table 2.1 Median net real income after housing costs by quintile group, 1979 and 1988–89, United Kingdom.

£ per week at 1992 prices

| Year | Quintile group of individuals | | |
	Bottom fifth	Middle fifth	Top fifth
1979	81	143	253
1988-89	81	176	355

Source: Social Trends 23, 1993 Edition, Table 5.18.

The reappearance of high unemployment has shattered any illusion that everybody prepared to work is assured of a job. In April 1993 the number of people claiming unemployment benefit in the United Kingdom was 2.9 million, which represented 10.5% of the workforce. Over a million had been unemployed for over a year, and a further 600,000 for over 6 months.

Some parts of the country and some localities have much higher than average unemployment. Thus the proportion unemployed in Northern Ireland in April 1993 was 14.1% and in Londonderry the figure was 19.4%. High concentrations of unemployment existed also, for example, in South Tyneside (19.4%), Liverpool (15.5%), Middlesbrough (15.4%), Merthyr and Rhymney (14.3%) and in parts of conurbations such as Glasgow and Manchester. Some housing estates have had much higher levels of unemployment still. Concentrated unemployment has aggravated problems of poverty and given rise to fear of the emergence of an underclass. Such conditions have a particularly sharp impact on the outlook of children and young people affected.

Another, and a very important, negative factor for the young has been the effect of the decline of marriage as a stable institution. Since 1971 marriages have fallen by a fifth, while divorces have doubled. The number of births outside marriage has been increasing fast and now three in ten out of all births are outside marriage. It is, nevertheless, the case that 82% of dependent children in 1991 were in households headed by a married couple. Moreover, despite the increases in births outside wedlock, there is evidence that many of the parents involved may be in stable relationships; three-quarters of these births are registered by both parents and a half are registered by parents living at the same address.[4]

A further factor of importance is that 43% of women with a child aged 4 or less now go out to work; women who are doing so are usually working part-time (30%) but 13% have full-time jobs.[5]

These developments in the family are particularly significant, given how important the home is for the development and learning of children, especially in their earliest years. There are many difficulties for a single parent in bringing up a family, among which poverty often ranks highest; but some of the difficulties also arise in two-parent families in which both parents are wage-earners. This underlines the importance of child care facilities of good quality for children below school age. Once children start to attend school the difficulties are not at an end; there is often a gap between the end of school hours and the time when a parent returns home from work.

Another factor has been the advent of TV, which has deeply affected home life and tended to undermine the social life of communities and neighbourhoods. In 1991 people were watching TV on average for 26 hours a week.[6] Television tends to encourage indiscriminate passive viewing. On the other hand, children learn from watching TV and videos, and are much better informed in many ways than before. There are important positive aspects to TV and radio to be exploited.

Finally, children and young people are increasingly exposed to the dangers of drug abuse and crime, including violent crime. The number of drug offenders in the United Kingdom climbed in 1991 to 47,600, of whom 40% were under 21, mostly male.[7] A third of all men born in England and Wales in the early 1950s had a conviction by the age of 31, and 1 in 14 had been convicted of a violent crime.[8] These are examples of social problems critically affecting the lives of many children in school and outside.

Education

Provision in England and Wales before 1944
As noted earlier in this chapter, education and training did not seem important for industrial success in the 1900s.

It is true that there had already been several Royal Commission reports in Victorian times arguing the necessity for developing scientific and technical education and drawing attention to the strides being made in other countries. Thus the Royal Commissioners on Technical Instruction said in a report of 1884:[9]

> Your Commissioners cannot repeat too often that they have been impressed with the general intelligence and technical knowledge of the masters and managers of industrial establishments on the Continent.

And again:

> . . . the one point in which Germany is overwhelmingly superior to England is in schools, and in the education of all classes of the people . . . the dense ignorance so common among workmen in England is unknown . . .

Such reports had little practical impact; as noted earlier, the commonsense view, held in industry as well as in governing circles, was that our domination of international trade proved that nothing much needed to be done.

Of far greater significance for the future direction of education in Britain was the way in which independent schools – the 'public schools' – developed in the Victorian era. These schools improved and extended provision for a comparatively small élite which included in its number most of those responsible for governing the country and its empire. The schools aimed to provide a 'liberal education' suitable for a gentleman, one which inculcated moral values and was heavily biased towards the Greek and Latin classics and away from practical or 'instrumental' studies.

Compulsory free elementary education for children was introduced in 1890. Under the Education Act of 1902 secondary education was greatly expanded. The recently established Board of Education modelled the type of education to be given on the ideas for a liberal education developed by the independent schools in the nineteenth century, and no room was found for scientific or technical education.

The Education Act 1944 and after

By the time the Education Act of 1944 was passed, despite various efforts to accelerate the introduction of technical and scientific education, our provision was much less well developed than that of most European countries. But even after 1944, when secondary education was made compulsory for all up to the age of 15, we held to the approach we had hitherto adopted. Although the 1944 Act provided for three sorts of secondary school – grammar, technical and secondary modern – in practice, technical schools at their peak never catered for more than 2% of the school population and there was no clear idea about the role of secondary modern schools. In retrospect the 1944 Act can be seen as having particularly benefited the academic minority through the growth of grammar school provision and having confirmed the labelling of the rest as 'also-rans'. For the latter, no educational goals were set in the form of examinations which they were expected to sit.

This outcome following the 1944 Act was broadly acceptable to both employers and trade unions. It was still the exceptional employer who deplored our slowness to develop educational provision relevant to industrial needs – and indeed industry did not seem to have many needs which went unsatisfied. The trade unions were also content with the status quo. So too were young people; we had full employment and those who chose to leave school at 15 – the majority – had no difficulty in getting jobs. So was there really a problem?

Indeed there was. As Dr David Finegold has pointed out,[10] the economy was trapped in a low-skill equilibrium in which the majority of enterprises were staffed by poorly trained managers and workers produced low-quality goods and services. Our national approach both to the running of industry and to the provision of education suited each other well enough, but international competition was about to prove it to be thoroughly inadequate for a leading industrial nation in the last quarter of the twentieth century.

Selection for grammar schools was made customarily by means of an '11 plus' examination, which therefore determined the educational fate of children for years. Nevertheless, there was no clear national standard by which success and entry to grammar school was to be achieved. Different Local Education Authorities (LEAs) provided widely varying numbers of grammar school places and it was impossible to pretend that there was equality of opportunity to gain places in different areas. It also became very clear that a single exam at a particular age could not reliably separate 'sheep' from 'goats'. The remedy sought was to introduce comprehensive schools in the late 1960s and 1970s.

In Scotland, which had followed a path in some ways similar to that in England and Wales after 1945, all education authority schools became comprehensive. In Northern Ireland, however, the traditional pattern of selective schooling survived largely intact and few comprehensive schools were subsequently created.

Studies had shown that, in addition to 2% of pupils who received their education largely in special schools and units, a further 18% of pupils might require some form of special needs education at some time in their schooling. The Warnock Report of 1978 stated that the aims of education were the same for all children and that special educational needs were not caused solely by deficiencies within a child but rather by the relationship between the child and the environment. An Act of 1981 dealt specifically with special educational needs, and current SEN provision has been built on that foundation.

Higher education

Meanwhile, expansion of university education followed the Robbins Report in 1963. Full-time students in universities rose in number from 119,000 to 295,000 over the following twenty years. Provision for the study of science and engineering was greatly expanded. There was also a rapid growth in higher education provided by polytechnics and colleges. Whereas in the 1930s fewer than 3% of young people entered higher education, by 1990 the figure was already 19% and had reached 28.3% by 1992.

Industry and manpower

So far as industry was concerned, some progress was made towards making management more professional by the founding of business schools from 1965 onwards. With continuing full employment, however, skill shortages gave rise to frequent complaints. When these could not be solved on a voluntary basis, a statutory system of Industrial Training Boards was introduced in 1964 to put things right. The Boards had powers to raise compulsory levies from their industries and use them to make grants to encourage companies to train. The system had some success but in time it was first modified and then largely abandoned, so that only two Boards (in construction and in engineering construction) remain today. The Boards were accused of bureaucracy and ineffectiveness. Perhaps a more serious failing was that they gave more pain than pleasure: employers who got back less in grants than they paid in levy felt the pain, whereas those who, on balance, benefited were content to attribute it to their own meritorious conduct.

The Manpower Services Commission was established to pursue 'an active manpower policy' under an Act of 1973. The setting up of the Commission coincided with rapid increases in unemployment, and dealing with the effects of it occupied much of the Commission's energy. It is possible however to discern in the Youth Opportunities Programme and later the Youth Training Scheme attempts to move towards a new form of apprenticeship which would have helped to put the supply of skills to industry on a more solid long-term basis. However, the Commission was a tripartite organisation to which both employers and trade unions nominated Commissioners; such organisations became stigmatised as 'corporatist' in the 1980s and the Commission was wound up following the 1987 general election.

The 'Great Debate' on education
In a speech in 1976 at Ruskin College, Mr James (now Lord) Callaghan as Prime Minister launched what became known as the 'Great Debate' about education. Many aspects of education were opened up for discussion, including education as a preparation for work, teaching methods and the curriculum, and teachers and their professionalism. Among possibilities aired were a more interventionist role for the Department of Education and Science and HM Inspectorate, more lay influence through governing bodies and a new deal for 16–19-year-olds.

What gave a sense of importance to the 'Great Debate' was the rapidly growing understanding that Britain was not competing successfully enough in world markets and that to a large extent this had come about because our workforce was not professionally managed, was not well enough educated and did not receive adequate training. The example set by foreign subsidiaries in Britain bore this out most tellingly.

Moreover, it was no longer true that young people who left school at 16 (the minimum leaving age since 1973) could always count on getting a job. The old system was breaking down, and far-reaching changes were needed to modernise industry and make it efficient. These included adapting education and training in ways which would help to meet its needs, while also preparing young people for a very different world than was earlier assumed to await them.

Recent reforms
The 'Great Debate' could not go on for ever. It eventually resulted in the fundamental changes set in train by the Education Reform Act of 1988. For the first time there was to be a national curriculum for schools in England and Wales, supported by assessment and testing. The powers of school governing bodies were to be strengthened. There would be City Technology Colleges, set up with sponsorship from industry, and grant-maintained schools; neither would be under the control of LEAs.

The Act aimed at ending a 'producer' dominance in education and substituting for it more of a 'market' or 'competitive' element. It also played an important part in a political drive to reduce the status and powers of local authorities. There was a similar drive in parallel legislation for Scotland.

The 1988 and subsequent Acts also made fundamental changes in higher and further education. The polytechnics were taken out of LEA control and were later turned into universities. The further education sector was also detached from the LEAs and, like the universities, given its own funding councils. The Education Act 1993 provided for a Funding Agency for Schools for England and a Schools Funding Council for Wales, and these bodies will be responsible for financing grant-maintained schools in England and Wales. Over a five-year period, therefore, there has been a profound shift in power from local to central government in education.

Attitudes of industry

These developments in education have been matched by fundamental changes in the stances adopted by both employers and trade unions. The Confederation of British Industry published in 1989 a report by a Vocational Education and Training Task Force which stated: 'A quantum leap is needed in Britain's education and training performance.'[11] It went on:

> To maintain and improve Britain's position in an increasingly competitive world nothing short of a skills revolution is needed . . .
> Individuals are now the only source of sustainable competitive advantage. Efforts must be focused on mobilising their commitment and encouraging self-development and lifetime learning . . .

The Trades Union Congress declared its position no less clearly in its report 'Skills 2000', also published in 1989.[12] The report stated:

> Britain is facing a skills challenge greater than any since the Industrial Revolution. Major changes in work, in the workforce, and in the global economy are creating the need to tap the potential of all our workers. By the year 2000, we will be either a superskills economy, or a low-skill, low pay society.

The Need for a Vision for the Years Ahead

On many occasions in the past it has seemed that there was a national lack of willingness to face radical change in education. Attempts to move the emphasis of provision at least some distance from the notion of a liberal education rooted in the past, towards the needs of industry and the demands of work in the future have repeatedly been frustrated. The events of the last few years have shown that things can change after all. In fact they have changed at a headlong speed, so that many people in education believe that the pace of change has become altogether too rapid and that too much is being attempted too quickly.

One effect is that the present is a good time to step back from the rush of current events and look more clearly at where we should be going and how. This is exactly what we seek to do in this report.

We start in the next chapter by defining a vision by which we believe the country's policies and actions should be guided in the years ahead.

Notes

[1] Living standards are measured here in terms of gross domestic product per head at purchasing power parities.

[2] Central Statistical Office, 1993. *Social Trends* 23. Employment, pp. 55–58.

[3] *Ibid*, Population, pp. 14–15.

[4] *Ibid*, Households and Families, pp. 25–35.

[5] *Ibid*, Table 4.8.

[6] *Ibid*, Table 10.7.

[7] Home Office Research and Statistics Department, September 1992. Statistics of Drug Seizures and Offenders Dealt with, United Kingdom 1991, pp. 12–13.

[8] Central Statistical Office, *op cit.* Crime and Justice, p. 172.

[9] Second Report of the Royal Commissioners on Technical Education, C 3981, 1884.

[10] Finegold, D., July 1992. Breaking Out of the Low-Skill Equilibrium. NCE Briefing No. 5. National Commission on Education.

[11] Confederation of British Industry, 1989. Towards a Skills Revolution. CBI.

[12] Trades Union Congress, 1989. Skills 2000. TUC.

3
A Vision for the Future

The Need for Knowledge and Skills

Our country is now firmly a part of the European Community. The European Community's future, and within it our own, must be seen in a global context.

Among the most certain predictions about the future is that the world's population will continue to grow rapidly and that wealth will be very unevenly spread between countries. Already the billion people constituting the poorest fifth of humanity have only 4% of the world's wealth, whereas the richest fifth has about 58%. Over the next two decades it is predicted that the world's population will grow by more than 90 million a year – an increase of a quarter of a million a day. The population of Third World countries will in that time increase by more than a half – about 2 billion people. By AD 2025 there will be about 8.5 billion people on earth. By comparison Western Europe will be a small and relatively rich region. Our own population in the United Kingdom will be a fraction of 1% of the population of the world.

It is certain, too, that scientific and technological advances will continue apace. Information will be transmitted cheaply and instantaneously more or less anywhere in the world. It is foreseen that it will be possible to store the entire contents of the US Library of Congress on a silicon disc thirty centimetres across. It will be possible also to produce computers small enough to go in a pocket which will be as powerful as the largest supercomputers of today. More immediately, it is already being taken for granted that we may within a few years have the choice of 200 or more television channels for viewing, and that people at home may be able to call up at the touch of a button any film they choose to see, or any recording they want to hear.

The biological sciences hold out great potential for advance in the years ahead and the benefits to mankind and to human health from biotechnology are already emerging. Some of these have given rise to debate about the ethics of releasing genetically modified organisms but all the available evidence suggests that anxieties on this score are largely unfounded. Less controversially, where plants are concerned, there is the possibility of developing crops that yield new products and can resist the most extreme climates and the worst attacks of pests. This could transform not only agriculture but also the food and chemical industries and revolutionise the means of preventing famine and starvation.

These are only examples of the impact that science and technology are likely to have in a relatively short period. Many more could be cited, in medicine, for example, and in the field of new materials. It is therefore clear that change is not going to slow down; on the contrary, all the evidence indicates that it will continue to accelerate. Moreover, the interval between a new advance and its widespread application is being continually shortened.

It is also likely, and certainly to be hoped for, that growing internationalism will cause the spread of cultural strengths from country to country, thus adding to the quality of life through the arts and humanities.

There are obvious risks of conflict in a world in which

so much is changing and where there is so much inequality, even if the danger of a catastrophic East-West nuclear conflict has receded with the collapse of communism. The environmental problems which confront the world will also become more pressing as time goes by; their solution will demand much political as well as scientific attention and may perhaps exact a high economic price.

Supposing however that no major threat to world peace and economic advance materialises, it is certain that we in the United Kingdom will rely more and more on our knowledge and skills if we are to improve our standard of living and play a constructive part in the world. We shall want to share in the continuing expansion of trade between developed countries. We can go further and contribute to easing the problems of other countries which need to make the best use of their natural resources and enable their own people to acquire the knowledge and practical skills on which their survival and hopes for the future will depend.

The 'Knowledge Revolution'

For us, knowledge and skills will be central. In an era of world-wide competition and low-cost global communications, no country like ours will be able to maintain its standard of living, let alone improve it, on the basis of cheap labour and low-tech products and services. There will be too many millions of workers and too many employers in too many countries who will be able and willing to do that kind of work fully as well as we or people in any other developed country could do it – and at a fraction of the cost. There are several examples today of insurance companies which have their clerical back-up work done in countries where education is adequate and labour is cheap. Computer software is already often written in countries far distant from where it is to be used. These are pointers to the future.

The example of Japan's economic success in the postwar years shows what can be achieved despite a lack of natural resources or geographical advantages. That success is being emulated by other countries on the Pacific rim – Korea, Hong Kong, Singapore, Taiwan and now mainland China – and they are sure to be followed in due course by countries elsewhere in the world. In all these cases, progress is based on well-designed high-quality products made at competitive prices and marketed world-wide. The key to success is a national will to succeed coupled with the application of knowledge and skills of a high order and the availability of an industrious workforce happy in the early years of development to accept wages which, by Western standards, are very low.

Spurred in part by the pressure of competition like this, society and the world of work in industrialised countries are already undergoing profound change. As change progresses, it will produce what more and more thinkers and writers studying future trends have come to view as a revolution – a 'knowledge revolution'. That revolution will be of profound importance for education.

Much has already been written on this theme. A powerful exposition of it is put forward by Peter Drucker.[1] He takes the view that the basic economic resource already is and will in future be knowledge (not capital, natural resources or labour). According to this analysis, the leading social groups of the knowledge society will be 'knowledge workers'. Knowledge workers will consist of 'knowledge executives' – people who know how to put knowledge to productive use, much as capitalists know how to use capital productively – 'knowledge professionals' and 'knowledge employees'. Forty years ago people doing knowledge work and skilled service work (the latter being a lesser form of knowledge work) were still less than one-third of the workforce but by now they already account for three-quarters, if not four-fifths, of the workforce in all developed countries.

The economic task of the future, according to Drucker, is to raise the productivity of knowledge work. He cites this country as an example of low productivity of knowledge:

> According to its production of scientific and technical knowledge, Britain should have been the world's economic leader in the post-World War II era. Antibiotics, the jet engine, the body scanner, even the computer, were British developments. But Britain did not succeed in turning these knowledge-achievements into successful products and services, into jobs, into exports, into market standing. The non-productivity of its knowledge, more than anything else, is at the root of the slow and steady erosion of the British economy.[2]

There may be debate about the terms in which Drucker's argument is stated. Nevertheless, the message that the central ingredient in economic success has become knowledge – to which we would add *applied intelligence* – is clearly correct. The way that jobs which need a high degree of knowledge and applied intelligence are growing, while those which need less are disappearing, confirms this.

During the period 1971–90, according to the Institute of Employment Research at the University of Warwick, jobs in our country grew by nearly 1.8 million to 25.9 million.[3] During the same period the kinds of jobs people do were changing fast. There was an increase of 3.1 million in the number of managerial, professional and technical jobs. At the same time 1.1 million skilled manual jobs disappeared, as did no fewer than 1.8 million jobs for machine operatives and other less skilled workers.

The Institute's projections for the present decade, which are based on fairly modest estimates for growth in the economy and in jobs, are shown in Figure 3.1. Again strong growth in managerial etc. jobs is projected, and once more many manual jobs, whether skilled or not, are expected to disappear. By the year AD 2000 it is foreseen that there will be some 10.5 million managerial, professional and technical jobs in all, whereas manual jobs (skilled, machine operative and less skilled) will be down to 7.3 million. The reversal compared with twenty years ago – when manual jobs outnumbered managerial etc. jobs by 5.7 million – is very striking.

Figure 3.1 Projected changes in occupational employment, 1991–2000, United Kingdom.

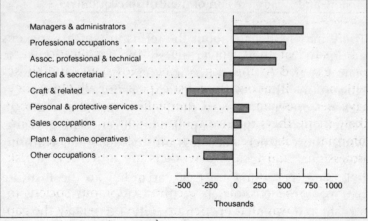

Source: Wilson, R.A., February 1993.[3]

This trend in jobs has been accompanied by a widening of the gap between the pay of the most skilled and that of the least skilled, as Table 3.1 shows. The table gives men's earnings; much the same pattern has emerged with women's earnings. It shows the weekly earnings for a man at the highest decile point and for a man at the lowest decile point. The former will have 10% of men earning more than himself and 90% earning less. For the latter the proportions are reversed. The gap between the level of earnings at the two points was £144 in 1982; by 1992 the gap had widened to £374. It meant that earnings at the top decile point were 3.2 times greater than those at the bottom decile point by 1992 (as compared with 2.6 times in 1982).

Table 3.1 Gross weekly earnings for adult men, 1992, Great Britain.

			£
	Man at highest decile point	Man at lowest decile point	Difference
1982	234	90	144
1992	544	170	374

Source: New Earnings Survey 1992.

It is also clear that people with lower qualifications are more exposed to the risk of unemployment, and those with no qualifications the most exposed of all. Once they have become unemployed, unqualified people are more likely than others to remain out of work for long periods. Information about redundancies shows that managers and professional and technical workers are much less at risk than manual workers.

It would be possible in the future for our society to develop in a way that opened up still more widely the gap between 'knowledge workers' and the rest. Those whose education had enabled them to become 'knowledge workers' and who, as people owning the resource most vital for success in the marketplace, were able to command relatively high salaries and safe jobs would be in a position of remarkable power and privilege. Those denied such an education would be excluded, and the exclusion would become more painful with the passing of time as the less skilled jobs continued to disappear and pay in the jobs that were left fell further behind.

The threat to social cohesion is obvious. It is not one that any democratic country would willingly accept. The risk is greater, however, in our case than it is for other countries which have been more successful in developing education and training for the great majority of their young people, as Chapter 1 shows. It makes it all the more important and urgent therefore that we should develop educational and training provision suited to the needs and capabilities of the whole population and not only those of the academically more able members of it.

The need to improve provision for all applies regardless of age. In an era in which change takes place so quickly, continuous learning is an essential at work. The need for it is obvious enough with professionals – doctors, say, and engineers – because of the constant flow of new processes, techniques, products and materials which directly affects them. It is no less true of other workers as new technology, innovation and changed working patterns are introduced. Constant adaptation to change is the order of the day and will remain so in the future. The fact that the average age of our workforce will be rising in the years ahead underlines the need for all people at work to have the opportunity to go on learning, to acquire new skills and to adapt continually to change.

The Wider Purposes of Education

Economic success will underpin the prosperity of the country and therefore our ability to improve life for everybody. Nevertheless, education, vital as it will be to our future economic success, involves far more than the pursuit of material rewards.

The first section of the Education Reform Act 1988, in referring to the curriculum of schools, speaks of promoting 'the spiritual, moral, cultural, mental and physical development of pupils and of society' and of preparing pupils for the 'opportunities, responsibilities and experiences of adult life'. Education provides the means whereby society transmits its values from one generation to another. Those values include truthfulness, respect for other people, a sense of the obligations due to the community in which we live (as well as the rights derived from being members of that community) and a caring attitude towards others. They also include the ability to enjoy and contribute to the richness of our cultural heritage in music and drama, in the arts, in sporting and outdoor pursuits and in the wealth of other activities which flourish so abundantly in our country.

It is clear then that children at school should learn about the society in which they live and how they can contribute to it. They should come to understand how decisions are made in a democratic society and how they can learn to take part in them through discussion and the ballot box. They need to know how Parliament and other democratic institutions work, and the place of the law in safeguarding our rights and freedoms. They need to understand how wealth is created. They need also to learn how they themselves can become active members of society. They must know what rights they have, but also what responsibilities they must bear as good citizens.

The role of education does not end there. Good teaching will foster in students a spirit of inquiry about the world around them. It will encourage them to think for themselves, to be critical and to be self-critical. It is people who make the world what it is and every young person has the opportunity to change it; Einstein and Churchill were students once (one a more apt learner at school than the other, it seems). Freedom is preserved only if enough people care about it and are ready to be active in defending it. The cause of racial or religious tolerance demands positive commitment if it is to prevail; passive acquiescence will not do. Nor can social cohesion ever be taken for granted. All these things are the concern of education; education is about empowerment as well as the transmission of knowledge.

Schools are required to provide for religious education for all their pupils, and the Education Reform Act lays down requirements for acts of collective worship which are to be of a broadly Christian character unless the nature of the school community makes that inappropriate. Beyond this, pupils learn profound lessons from the ethical character of the school itself, a character which is determined by the attitudes and behaviour of the head-teacher and the staff. If teachers are enthusiastic, well-prepared for lessons, thorough, helpful, businesslike and friendly, and above all if they have high expectations of pupils, then they provide an example to which young people will respond and which is likely to influence their future lives permanently for the good. Very many adults looking back at their school days feel a debt of gratitude to particular teachers who inspired them and helped them to become the people they are.

The question of high expectations is central. As Professor Peter Mortimore and his co-authors wrote in *School Matters*: 'If teachers believe that pupils can change and that learning can become easier in the right climate, then they will transmit that positive view to their pupils.'

They also wrote: 'What our data illustrate is that children's performance changes over time. Given an effective school, children make better progress. Greater progress leads to greater capability and, if handled sensitively, to greater confidence. In this way children's ability grows.'[4]

Effective schools can also have a most positive effect on children's behaviour, not least the behaviour of those unfortunate children for whom school is a welcome escape from home. Professor Mortimore and his colleagues devised a scale to measure the effect on behaviour of the fifty schools which they studied, and found that the best school measured by this scale scored 32% higher than the average. The worst school's score was 15% below.

Every person is capable of developing. In thinking of schools, it is easy to concentrate on logical and linguistic skills, but this gives too narrow a focus. Professor Howard Gardner at Harvard has put forward the attractive idea of 'multiple-intelligence', described as a 'capacity to solve problems or to make something that is valued in at least one culture'.[5] He suggests that there may be seven intelligences: linguistic, logical-mathematical, musical, spatial, bodily-physical, interpersonal, and relating to internal self-knowledge. Professor Charles Handy, author of the *Age of Unreason*, has suggested that there may be as many as ten.[6]

What these ideas do is to reinforce a simple truth that everybody knows: that different people are good at different things. Not only are they born with different kinds of ability or intelligence, but what they choose to do with them is much influenced by home and the community in which they grow up and mature. An effective school encourages and helps its pupils to develop their capabilities; as a result they gain confidence, their self-esteem rises and they achieve more.

It is above all this pattern of success – of *learning to succeed* – that is at the heart of a good education. It is central to our vision for education in the next century that all children should from a very early age learn to succeed and go on succeeding. Children who reach the end of primary education feeling enthusiastic about learning and confident of their ability to learn are already well on the way to making a success of the whole of their schooling and going on further in life with a ready habit of learning.

Conversely, it is difficult for children who have become used to failing, who are denied the joy of learning and who have come to think of themselves as 'failures' to recover confidence in their ability and worth and to make the progress of which they are capable later on: difficult, though not impossible – and many people who did poorly at school discover only later that they are able to learn, to enjoy learning and to benefit from the experience. One of the strengths of this country is the variety of 'second chances' which it offers to those who did not do themselves justice earlier at school. It is a strength we must not only preserve but develop and exploit to the full. Half of today's workforce will still be at work in AD 2020, and many of them will need educational opportunities in the years ahead in order to fulfil themselves in a changing society.

It follows that the opportunities for learning offered to children should never be too narrow and should become broader with time. Some children find it easier to express themselves through song, dance and drama; others have physical skills which they can develop in the gymnasium or on sports fields. Others, again from an early age, are drawn to practical skills, and many find computing and IT skills exciting and excel at them. Yet others are drawn into voluntary activities in the community. All of these offer valid and important routes by which young people can learn to fulfil themselves. We do not do young people a service if we appear to treat pursuits of these kinds as of minor importance or if we fail to give them a range of opportunities for developing their talents. Our education system should be rich and varied enough to offer real opportunity to all. It is true that there are some things which all children need to learn; but it is also true that there is a great range of other worthwhile studies and pursuits among which children as they grow up should be able to choose, led by their own talents, interests and ambitions.

Our Vision for the Future

We are led by all these considerations to adopt the following vision for the future of education and training.

The Commission's Vision

1 In all countries *knowledge and applied intelligence* have become central to economic success and personal and social well-being.

2 In the United Kingdom much higher achievement in education and training is needed to match world standards.

3 Everyone must want to learn and have ample opportunity and encouragement to do so.

4 All children must achieve a good grasp of literacy and basic skills early on as the foundation for learning throughout life.

5 The full range of people's abilities must be recognised and their development rewarded.

6 High-quality learning depends above all on the knowledge, skill, effort and example of teachers and trainers.

7 It is the role of education *both* to interpret and pass on the values of society *and* to stimulate people to think for themselves and to change the world around them.

We now put forward seven goals for achievement in the years ahead in order to make a reality of this vision. We recommend that Governments and all those who have a responsibility or a stake in education and training work together to reach them.

Goal No 1: High-quality nursery education must be available for all 3- and 4-year-olds.

Learning starts from birth. Parents are key educators. Nursery education reinforces learning in the home. All children benefit from it, and for many it is essential if they are to learn to succeed. We recommend that it should be made available to all 3- and 4-year-olds.

Goal No 2: There must be courses and qualifications that bring out the best in every pupil.

The framework of curriculum and qualifications for pupils aged 5–18 must offer attractive routes to success. The full range of pupils' abilities must be recognised and their development encouraged and rewarded. There must also be paths forward into further or higher education or into work in accordance with individuals' choices and abilities. We recommend an improved curricular framework and a new General Education Diploma at Ordinary and Advanced level.

Goal No 3: Every pupil in every lesson has the right to good teaching and adequate support facilities.

Every pupil has the right to be taught the curriculum offered by the school or college. That means that every pupil is entitled to be taught every lesson by a highly professional teacher competent to teach that lesson. The supporting facilities – the classroom itself, for example, books and the learning technology – must be at least adequate. We recommend a new deal in the classroom to bring this about.

Goal No 4:   Everyone must be entitled to learn throughout life and be encouraged in practice to do so.

Learning does not stop at 16, at 18, at 21 or at any other age. Everyone must have the entitlement to go on learning whether for employment purposes or to fulfil other personal goals. There must be real opportunity to use the entitlement, and incentive and encouragement to do so. We make recommendations in order to bring this about.

Goal No 5:   The management of education and training must be integrated, and those with a stake in them must have this recognised.

Within the past few years the power of central government in education and training has grown by leaps and bounds. Management of education and of training must be integrated both at the centre and at local level. All those with a major stake in the system must have a place in its management, and full accountability at each level is essential. We recommend robust and adaptable arrangements for the future.

Goal No 6:   There must be greater public and private investment in education and training to achieve a better return.

There must be continuing efforts to cut waste and raise productivity and quality through innovation and the use of technology. Nevertheless, greater public investment will be required as economic circumstances permit. At the same time there is a need to achieve a better balance in resourcing. More of the costs need to be borne by beneficiaries, both employers and students. We make recommendations for better resourcing, better directed.

Goal No 7:   Achievement must constantly rise and progress be open for all to examine.

The country is faced by a massive and continuing challenge in a fast-changing world. Targets for achievement are already demanding, but they will go on rising and we must therefore constantly seek higher levels of performance. We recommend measures to enable progress to be checked and made the subject of searching and well-informed debate.

The rest of this report examines how these goals can be achieved and effect given to the vision which we have set out for the years ahead.

Notes

1   Drucker, P.E., 1993. *Post-Capitalist Society*. Butterworth-Heinemann.
2   *Ibid*, p. 170.
3   Wilson, R.A., February 1993. Review of the Economy and Employment 1992/93: Occupational Assessment. Institute of Employment Research, Warwick University.
4   Mortimore, P. and others, 1988. *School Matters: The Junior Years*. Open Books. pp. 286 and 264.
5   Gardner, H., 1983. *Frames of Mind*. Basic Books.
6   Symposium, Leeds Castle, Kent, 19–21 March 1993. Education: Direction of Future Policies. The America-European Community Association Trust in conjunction with the National Commission on Education, p.15.

4
A Framework for Learning
Curriculum, Assessment and Qualifications

A Framework for Success

The search for higher achievement in education must begin with the framework for learning which is laid down for the compulsory years of education by the basic curriculum in schools, the arrangements for assessing pupils' progress and the qualifications towards which they will be working.

The national curriculum for England and Wales appears in terms of the law as a duty: State-maintained schools are bound to teach it; by inference, pupils are bound to learn it; assessment provides a means of checking whether they are doing so.

A framework of real value rises far above so prosaic a prescription. It makes sense only when the full reality of learning and teaching is taken into account. Thus an excellent framework:

- will motivate pupils towards learning and promote enjoyment in learning. It will do this by such means as challenging pupils and arousing their curiosity, by helping them both to acquire and to use the basic tools of communication, by opening out aesthetic and other experiences to which they can respond, by providing learning which individuals perceive as relevant to their own present or future needs and by helping them to mature as confident and self-reliant members of society;

- will challenge the acceptance of low expectations and low aspirations too often found in our system. Thus it will offer schools and teachers support and encouragement, and will in particular give them scope for creativity and innovation. It is the task of teachers to provide schemes of work best suited to the range of abilities and needs represented in any group of pupils;

- will aim to be appealing to all pupils, and will therefore be varied enough to enable each to develop his or her own range of 'intelligences' or abilities;

- will provide for progression, and will therefore follow naturally on from nursery education and will lead naturally on to further or higher education or employment and training;

- will provide a basis for measuring the attainment of young people;

- above all, will offer to all pupils a means of succeeding and having that success recognised.

In this chapter we put forward such a framework, one which is designed with the needs of future decades in mind. We deal in turn with the national curriculum, with assessment and with qualifications. The discussion in this chapter centres around provision in England and Wales; it will in many ways provide a guide also for Northern Ireland. Arrangements for Scotland are rather different, and we refer to them in a concluding section.

The National Curriculum

The Education Reform Act of 1988 provided for the introduction of a national curriculum in England and Wales for the first time. Up to this point, decisions about the curriculum had rested nominally with Local Education Authorities but had in practice largely been in the hands of schools themselves.

The change has been very widely welcomed both by schools and by teachers and by the wider public, including parents. We have found no desire on the part of anybody to go back on it.

The Act both guides schools about what is expected of them and makes it easier for outside inquirers – parents, say, or employers – to judge whether schools are providing it. It introduces a degree of order and clarity which before was lacking.

The change, however, has another side to it. In effect it confers an entitlement on every pupil to be taught what is in the national curriculum. This is a development of great importance and potentially of great benefit. The State has, by implication, undertaken to see that children receive the teaching to which they are entitled; and, for that undertaking to have force, it follows that the teaching itself must be of a satisfactory standard and that it must be carried out in circumstances that enable each child to profit from it. It therefore has implications relating to the quality of teachers, to class size and to other factors affecting learning which we take up in later chapters.

The development of a national curriculum takes time, and rightly so. The national curriculum is not the private property of the Secretary of State for Education of the day, any more than it is of any group of advisers, whether they are Department for Education (DFE) officials, government-appointed advisory bodies, political researchers or educational experts. It is the property of the nation, and it is right that in framing the national curriculum there should be wide and thorough consultation with teachers, with members of school governing bodies, with employers and above all with interested members of the public, especially parents and – so far as possible – with pupils themselves. Only if this happens can the curriculum that results lay claim to real legitimacy and be generally accepted as possessing it.

It is not surprising if the complex and difficult business of introducing the national curriculum and attendant arrangements for assessment for the first time has generated heat as well as light. It is not our task to comment on the processes which have taken place so far, still less to apportion blame for such difficulties as have arisen. We do not consider that these give any evidence of a lack of will to implement a national curriculum of high quality. Our task is rather to consider how the national curriculum might be developed in the future to the maximum benefit of young people. In doing so we have to bear in mind the clear and urgent need identified in the previous chapter to raise achievement in schools to much higher levels.

Principles embodied in the national curriculum
The design of the national curriculum must embody principles enabling it to meet a number of requirements. We would particularly mention the following:

- there should be a core of the subjects or areas of study judged essential for the learning of all young people laid down for each stage at school;

- areas or fields of study should be identified within which all young people will be able to select subjects or specialist courses for study, so offering choice;

- the basis for choice of subjects or specialist courses should require breadth but not to the detriment of depth of study in any particular chosen subject;

- in each subject or specialist course it should be made clear what those following the curriculum will be expected to know, to understand and to be able to do;

- the basis for assessing progress in relation to what is prescribed should be provided.

Within these principles, a crucial issue is that of the basis on which the components of the curriculum should be formed in order to provide both a balanced and a relevant curriculum for all pupils. There is an extensive literature bearing on this.[1] We have examined a number of practical examples, including the Scottish model, and, for the post-16 years, the International Baccalaureat, the proposed British Baccalaureat[2] and the proposals put forward by the Royal Society for the post-16 years.[3] In doing so, we have constantly borne in mind the importance that *knowledge and applied intelligence* are assuming, and will increasingly assume, in our society.

Our conclusion is that, on balance, the best practical approach is to lay down a relatively small number of basic areas within which there is a wide choice of specific subjects. The areas which we put forward as the basis of our proposals are the following:

- language;
- mathematics;
- natural science and technology;
- expressive arts (including physical education);
- humanities (including social science).

Included within 'expressive arts' above will be art, music, dance and drama; and included within 'humanities' will be history and geography.

Before developing our ideas concretely, we wish to stress a number of important points that need to be taken into account.

Points of importance in developing the curriculum
The first point we wish to emphasise is that the national curriculum has been pre-empting too much time in schools. It is highly desirable for schools to have greater flexibility in the use of time. In part this is necessary to make possible teaching which is essential to reinforce learning by pupils who are finding the going hard in some respects and to provide remedial teaching as soon as the need for that is identified. In part it is desirable in order to encourage studies which will extend those who have already mastered what is required in the curriculum. And in part it is necessary to allow schools to develop their own provision and to innovate in ways which will enhance the education which the school provides and take account of local needs and circumstances. The opportunity for creativity by schools and by teachers is most valuable and must be fostered.

We welcome Sir Ron Dearing's proposals for slimming down the requirements of the national curriculum,[4] but we wish to go further. In our view the national curriculum should not compulsorily pre-empt more than 50% of the available time in the earliest years of schooling (Key Stage 1, ages 5–7) or 70% in the next two stages (ages 7–14). We consider that the compulsory element in Key Stage 1 should concentrate on basic skills such as literacy and numeracy and that at Key Stages 2 and 3 more room should be made by specifying the essential core of knowledge, skills and understanding in those subjects appropriate at these stages. Schools would have the opportunity to develop further specific parts of the curriculum in the light of their own circumstances and to introduce courses of their own.

Secondly, it is essential to take heed of the need to develop the kind of 'life skills' whose importance employers have strongly emphasised. These are in no way narrow technical skills in which employers themselves should be expected to instruct their employees; nor are they to be dismissed as accomplishments which are relatively easily learned on the job or elsewhere in adult life. The life skills concerned include: working in teams; effective communication, which involves the use of the ability to read, write, speak, listen and apply numbers to achieve practical ends; problem-solving; and personal effectiveness, coupled with self-discipline, in thinking and acting.

Much of the curriculum in later years emphasises personal achievement and runs against the grain of acquiring 'life skills'. The latter involve themes which cut across the curriculum. For that very reason they tend to be squeezed out by it. Careful development work is needed to establish how 'life skills' can best be inculcated at school. The field of study we have termed 'citizenship' offers some opportunities for relevant work. We have noted also the approach adopted in Scotland, which relies on a mixture of 'permeation', curriculum inserts/enhancement and special short courses; there may be lessons here which could be applied elsewhere in the United Kingdom.

Thirdly, it is perfectly clear that a national curriculum which assumes that formal education comes to an end at age 16 is already inadequate by international standards and will become more and more obviously so as time goes on. All young people need to continue formal learning to age 18 as a minimum. This does not mean that it is desirable that compulsory education should be extended to the age of 18 by law. It does however suggest that a further voluntary stage of the national curriculum should be added covering the years 16–18 (which for convenience we call Key Stage 5). Students will have an entitlement to receive education in accordance with Key Stage 5 if they so choose, but they will be free to pursue other studies to the extent that they wish.

It is important that educational provision for young people aged 14–18 should be planned as a single whole. This leads us to our fourth and final point. It is welcome that the Government has set up a single body, the School Curriculum and Assessment Authority (SCAA), to advise it on the future development of the curriculum and assessment in place of two previous separate bodies, but this still leaves another important national body concerned with qualifications operating separately, the National Council for Vocational Qualifications (NCVQ). We are certain that for the future vocational studies must be seen as part of the mainstream of educational provision from age 14 onwards. This will never be completely achieved while these two separate national bodies have responsibilities impinging on the curriculum, and we therefore propose that the two should be brought together to form a single body which we would term the Education and Training Development Authority.

The content of the national curriculum

Pre-school provision – We argue in this report that nursery education for children aged 3 and 4 should be progressively extended until it is available to all children whose parents wish them to have it. This raises the question of what children should be learning at this stage. We note that the Rumbold Committee, which reported in 1990 on education in the early years, proposed that there should be 'a broad, balanced curriculum which provides children with a successful bridge from home to school, promotes their all round development and prepares them for later learning. In practice this entitlement would be delivered through structured play and opportunities to experience situations such as shopping or making things which bring together a number of skills in an integrated way'.[5] We broadly agree with this approach.

Key Stage 1 (ages 5–7) – The essential need at this stage is to ensure that the basic skills of literacy and numeracy are firmly established and that a start is made with learning the rudiments of science and technology (seen as a single subject). Accordingly, we envisage the structure of the curriculum as follows:

Compulsory core: English (and Welsh in Wales), mathematics, natural science/technology. Together these will occupy 50% of the total time.

Other areas of study: These will be chosen at the discretion of the school to include early experience of the expressive arts and humanities. For this, national guidelines on content and objectives should be available for introduction as part of the total curriculum adopted by the school.

Key Stage 2 (ages 7–11) – At this stage some broadening of the compulsory element of the curriculum should take place, to include citizenship and a modern foreign language. Special attention is needed to ensure that the teaching challenges all children in the age group. The curriculum will now be as follows:

Compulsory core: English (and Welsh in Wales), mathematics, natural science, technology, citizenship, a modern foreign language.

Other areas of study:　　As a minimum, one subject
each from the expressive arts
and humanities.

The above will require 70% of the total time available.
Again, national guidelines on content and objectives will
be available for the non-core subjects for introduction at
discretion as part of the total curriculum adopted by the
school. The school will be free to use the remaining 30%
of time, after provision for religious education, as it may
decide, reinforcing the teaching of some aspects of the
national curriculum courses, or introducing other national
curriculum courses or courses of its own.

Note in particular the following points:

1　We consider the teaching of citizenship of great
importance. We define the subject in a broad way to
concern the relationship between individuals and the
world they live in. It relates not only to this country
but to the European Community and the world as a
whole. It concerns the institutions of democracy and
the rights and responsibilities of individuals in a
democratic society; the creation of wealth; the role of
public and private employers and voluntary organisations; and the opportunities which people have to
shape or play a creative part in the life of the community. In this regard we note with interest the incorporation of two community relations cross-curricular
themes, Education for Mutual Understanding and
Cultural Heritage, in the Northern Ireland common
curriculum.

2　The learning of a modern foreign language will begin
in Key Stage 2. It will seem increasingly odd as time
goes on for the learning of a second language to be
deferred until later, and this will contrast with practice in other European countries. For most children a
start will now be made on learning another language

in use in the European Community, but the choice should not be compulsorily restricted to those languages. It is impossible to make the teaching of a second language compulsory at present because of the shortage of suitably qualified teachers, but the Government should ensure that the shortage is remedied as quickly as possible – for example by employing qualified teachers from other parts of the European Community.

3 We note that Sir Ron Dearing has said: 'Basic information technology skills must be located securely at the heart of the National Curriculum.'[6] We agree strongly. In our view teaching the basics of IT should form part of the technology syllabus but application of IT should be incorporated in the teaching of a wide range of subjects.

Key Stage 3 (ages 11–14) – At this point independent learning should be reinforced. Careers education and guidance becomes increasingly necessary. We envisage its being within the scope of 'citizenship' as defined earlier. More frequent advantage will be taken of links with local employers and the opportunity taken to make planned workplace visits.

Core and other subjects will remain as for Key Stage 2.

Key Stages 4 and 5 (ages 14–18) – At Key Stage 4 (ages 14–16) there will continue to be the same compulsory core subjects as before. There will be a wide choice of subjects outside the compulsory core, but it will be a requirement that the subjects chosen must include at least one each from the two basic areas of study not included in the core, namely expressive arts and humanities.

We particularly wish it to be open to young people who are interested in starting vocational courses to be free to do so from age 14 onwards. We hope that vocational courses will often reinforce and be reinforced by a course under the national curriculum. Thus, food science and catering are natural companions.

The curriculum at Key Stage 4 will thus be as follows:

Compulsory core: English (and Welsh in Wales), mathematics, natural science, technology, citizenship, a modern foreign language. Together these will occupy 50% of the total time.

Other areas of study: Apart from religious education, these will be at the discretion of the school, provided that at least one subject each is chosen from the fields of expressive arts and humanities. National guidelines on content and objectives will be available for introduction at discretion as part of the total curriculum adopted by the school. Vocational courses will be available for those who wish them.

At Key Stage 5 (ages 16–18) much wider choice still will be available. Students will be entitled to be taught any or all of the six subjects which form the compulsory core at Key Stage 4, but this will not be obligatory. Incentive and guidance to students as to their learning will be provided by the requirements of the new General Education Diploma, which we describe below in our section on qualifications.

We stress that at both Key Stage 4 and Key Stage 5 we envisage that the curriculum will be taught on a modular basis, that is to say that subjects will be broken down into 'modules', each of which will take between a term and a year to cover, depending on the nature of the subject matter.

A key aspect of our approach is that young people who decide to leave full-time education in order to undertake a traineeship, whether employer-based or college-based, at age 16 or 17 will still be working for a qualification within the national framework (see Chapter 10).

General

We emphasise that the curriculum needs to be so framed as to recognise the different needs, abilities, interests and circumstances of pupils. It should offer flexibility not only in the choice of programmes but in rates of progress.

Curriculum requirements will be framed on the basis of outcomes, that is to say that they will make clear what those following the curriculum will be expected *to know, to understand, and to be able to do*. Subjects or fields of study at the later stages will not be formally designated 'academic', 'technical', 'practical' or 'vocational': in all cases they will require outcomes with a mix of knowledge, understanding and practical ability, the balance of which will vary according to the subject.

Curriculum requirements will be defined in clear but relatively brief statements, not in exhaustive detail, and will be accompanied by illustrative examples to clarify what is required.

Governing bodies of schools (and other institutions involved post-16) must approve the whole curriculum which they offer, including the compulsory national curriculum elements, religious education and the optional elements. Parents and pupils will have a right to a clear statement about the curriculum offered and the entitlements and choices open to students.

Independent schools and the national curriculum

We recommend that the national curriculum should be made compulsory for independent schools as well as maintained schools. We explain earlier in this chapter that the national curriculum in effect confers an entitlement on every pupil to be taught what is in the national curriculum. We consider that that entitlement should apply whatever kind of school a child or young person attends.

It might be objected that parents should be free to send their children to any school, whatever is taught there, if they are paying; but this misses the point that the entitlement is the children's, not the parents'. Again it might be thought that all independent schools are obliged by the fact that they are charging fees to apply standards at least as demanding as those in the national curriculum; but in practice standards in independent schools are known to vary greatly and some of them are, frankly, poor.

A final objection might be that independent schools must be free to innovate and that an obligation to follow the national curriculum would inhibit that. We cannot accept the implication that innovation is the sole preserve of independent schools – an implication which is amply refuted by experience – but in any case we believe that any force this objection might have had will be removed by the greater flexibility with which the national curriculum will be applied in future.

Arrangements for Assessment

Current arrangements

The 1988 Act lays down requirements for the assessment of pupils' achievements in relation to the national curriculum. Assessment arrangements are clearly an essential part of the national framework provided by the Act. There is a wide range of possibilities as to how they might be organised.

The current assessment arrangements draw on a scheme originally devised by a Task Group on Assessment and Testing (TGAT) which reported late in 1987. The scheme put forward by TGAT envisaged a system of assessment drawing on teachers' observations as well as on 'standard assessment tasks' devised nationally. The intention was that this information would serve more than one purpose. It would in the first place provide a *formative* assessment of a pupil's progress, that is to say an assessment which would give a good picture of an individual pupil's current strengths and future needs and therefore be helpful in planning for the pupil's future progress. In addition, after being 'moderated' – adjusted as necessary as a result of scrutiny by outside assessors – and put in standard form, the information could be aggregated to produce *summative* information relating to class, school, local authority and national performance which could be presented to a variety of audiences, including, for example, current and prospective parents of pupils at individual schools.

With the intention of providing a form of assessment which emphasises progression, the scheme provides a ladder of ten levels through which a pupil might be expected to progress in studying a subject. At age 7, for example, most pupils would have reached level 1, 2 or 3 in a subject, and so on until at 16 most pupils would be at level 7, 8, 9 or 10. Teachers would record for every pupil in each 'strand' of each subject what progress they are making up the ladder.

The Government decided to introduce Standard Assessment Tasks (SATs) which would be used to determine the attainments of pupils towards the end of each Key Stage, i.e. at the ages of 7, 11 and 14, thus providing summative information about achievement. The General Certificate of Secondary Education (GCSE) would be adapted so as to provide the information in question at the age of 16. Schools' SATs results would be published in 'league tables'.

The assessment arrangements have turned out to be far more onerous than was expected or is desirable. We warmly welcome the steps now put in hand to make them less burdensome following recommendations by Sir Ron Dearing in the interim report on his review of the national curriculum and associated arrangements for assessment.[4]

Assessment arrangements in future

Our role requires us to consider the longer term. In so doing, the two basic purposes of assessment mentioned above – *formative* and *summative* – need always to be kept in mind.

The paragraphs which follow summarise our views.

First, while teacher assessment is of course essential for formative assessment it can also be used for summative purposes, especially when moderated by outside assessors. National tests provide summative assessments, but they do also provide teachers with a reliable contribution to an overall assessment of a pupil's performance and in that way provide an incentive and spur to higher achievement. We have no doubt that there is a place for national tests as well as teacher assessment.

Secondly, it is right to give special attention in assessment to certain core subjects at Key Stages 1–3, since these provide the building blocks for all other learning.

We would suggest that more use might be made of banks of tests nationally devised which are available to teachers to use when it is opportune in the classroom to check on the progress of pupils. This technique could go some distance to satisfying the need for summative as well as formative information. Its use might enable annual externally set tests to be further reduced in size or even dispensed with if experience shows that it yields reliable information.

Thirdly, we record that we are inclined to doubt whether the 10-point scale provides the best method of assessing progress for the future. An alternative might be to establish the range of achievements at present reached in each core subject at the end of Key Stages 1, 2 and 3 by means of sample surveys and to grade these on a suitable scale (say from A to G). In subsequent years pupils' attainments could then be assessed in relation to the grades so established. This might be done, either on the basis of teacher assessments combined with tests from a bank of externally-devised tests administered by the teachers, or, if this is judged essential, by external tests specially devised annually.

Fourthly, we take seriously the risk that the use of external tests may encourage 'teaching to the test'. The risk may be less at Key Stage 1 but increases as pupils grow older and the progress to be assessed becomes more complex. It must be guarded against very closely.

Aggregated information about pupils' achievements
The question arises of the use of aggregated information about the achievements of schools' pupils.

There is no serious case for saying that the information should not be aggregated – whether for LEAs, for schools, for departments within schools, for individual classes or for individual pupils. The information provides a valuable means whereby progress can be tracked and appropriate action taken to applaud success or investigate and remedy the causes of indifferent progress. We are particularly attracted by Sir Ron Dearing's recommendation that national test and teacher assessment ratings should both be shown separately in all forms of reporting and school prospectuses.[7]

Nor is there any sound case for saying that information about the achievements of a school's pupils should not be published. On the contrary, the governing body has a duty to ensure that it is published in an appropriate form to parents and available to prospective parents. We should in fact be in favour of developing the annual report further by requiring that it should be 'signed off' by the inspector for the school in question (see Chapter 13), acting much as an auditor does with a company's annual report.

There is then the further question of publishing schools' results in so-called league tables. The present Government's view is that this is an important part of stimulating healthy competition between schools, and that competition of this kind is essential to raising the level of educational achievement in this country – or at any rate in England and Wales.

This approach runs into difficulties on at least two counts. The first is that the position of a school in a league table of this kind is influenced by many factors which have little to do with whether it is a good school. A selective school will normally show up well, just because it is selective. The same can easily happen where there is no selection. It is well established, for example, that the children of parents with post-compulsory schooling are likely to do well at schoolwork. Conversely, poverty is liable to impact on a home in a way that holds a pupil back. Accordingly, it is not surprising if a school which draws many of its pupils from a relatively prosperous neighbourhood figures higher in a league table than one in a deprived working-class area, especially if significant numbers have English as a second language. There is no telling, however, whether it is a better school on that account. League tables can easily mislead, therefore, and it is not surprising if many teachers and governing bodies do not like them.

The second point is that, if schools come to believe that their position in a league table is vital to their prestige and to their future success, they may adopt practices which are not in the best interests of children in order to maintain or improve their position. If more children apply for places than are available, schools may be tempted to select covertly on ability or on the basis of parental attitudes. They may be wary of accepting pupils who they fear will prove hard to teach, and too ready to exclude those who prove disruptive. They may try to reduce the proportion of children with special educational needs at the school, even if those children would benefit from education there. In the later years of education, they may seek to discourage some pupils from staying on for fear that they would be likely to lower the average level of attainment in examinations.

It does not seem to us right to conclude that aggregated information about the performance of schools should not be published. We do, however, suggest that if the Government wishes to publish this information it should take good care to do so in ways which promote its proper use and warn against its shortcomings. Thus:

1 It should be made perfectly clear that information in this form is highly simplistic because it singles out certain performance measurements without providing any fuller context. It therefore cannot give a picture of any school in the round. For that, information must be sought from individual schools' annual reports and prospectuses, and also inspectors' reports on schools.

2 The information should always be presented in alphabetical lists rather than in the form of league

tables which invite the conclusion that the 'best'
school is at the top and the 'worst' at the bottom, and
newspapers should be discouraged from doing otherwise.

3 Information should always be included which
enables the value of the contribution of schools
themselves to be judged. How to do this is discussed
in a Briefing prepared for us by Professor Andrew
McPherson of Edinburgh University[8] and is the subject of developmental work by a number of LEAs. Sir
Ron Dearing has recommended that the School
Curriculum and Assessment Authority and OFSTED
(the Office for Standards in Education) should commission research into 'operational approaches' to
measuring added value.[9]

4 There is least value of all in publishing league tables
of results achieved at Key Stage 1, which throw more
light on pupils' backgrounds than on the primary
schools themselves.

Assessing national progress
We think it essential to monitoring the nation's progress
in educational achievement to set up a unit for that
express purpose. Its functions would be modelled on
those of the former Assessment of Performance Unit.
The reason why such a unit is required is that the objective measurement of a nation's educational progress
requires the collection of information over time on an
exactly comparable basis, and reliable results require the
conducting of large-scale sample surveys from time to
time. Such information is absolutely essential given the
importance of better educational performance for the
nation.

It is highly desirable that the unit should operate on a
United Kingdom basis. This might be achieved by co-
operation with the Scottish Assessment of Achievement

Programme if that course is deemed preferable to setting up a single unit with the whole of the United Kingdom within its remit (see the section on Scotland in Chapter 13). However it is achieved, it will be highly desirable for it to be possible to make accurate comparisons not only with the past but also between England, Wales, Scotland and Northern Ireland. Furthermore, the unit will be able to take part in arrangements for the international comparison of educational achievement. These are potentially highly illuminating but are also technically difficult to carry out with accuracy. It is our hope that an Educational Achievement Unit for the United Kingdom might take a leading part in a network of units concerned with the international comparison of educational achievement in countries round the world.

Qualifications: A New General Education Diploma

Chapter 3 lays stress on the importance of widening the range of opportunities for learning offered to pupils as they grow older. This needs to be reflected in the design not only of the national curriculum but especially of the system of qualifications.

It is high time that the confusion and shortcomings that have characterised qualifications in England and Wales were finally removed. Further piecemeal adjustment of what is already in place will not be sufficient, though much that already exists or is being developed can contribute to the design of new qualifications of high quality which can meet our needs for a long time to come.

We recommend the introduction of a new General Education Diploma which will be awarded at two levels: Ordinary level, normally reached at age 16; and Advanced level, normally at age 18. This will replace the range of qualifications, including GCSE, 'A' levels, BTEC and both general and more specific vocational qualifications, which is at present available or is being developed for 16–18-year-olds.

It is essential to have an award available to most 16-year-olds partly because this marks the completion of the compulsory curriculum and partly because, while it is still customary for so many young people to leave full-time education at that age, they should have a 'passport' based on their achievements up to then to take with them into the labour market. In time, as it becomes accepted that all young people will continue with formal learning at least to the age of 18, many young people may proceed direct to the Advanced level qualification without having entered formally for the Diploma at Ordinary level.

As we explain earlier, courses throughout Key Stages 4 and 5 will be organised on a modular basis. Achievement will be assessed at the conclusion of each module and credit points for that achievement awarded accordingly. Teacher assessment will play the major part in this, and must be subject to moderation to ensure rigour and uniformity of standards. It is relevant here to note that teacher assessment is already accepted in vocational qualifications and also makes a contribution towards the assessment of work for GCSE courses. Its use is also widely accepted in other European countries. There is no doubt that it can be used successfully here too, but it will be right to take every care to ensure that its more widespread use is closely monitored and can be clearly and publicly demonstrated to be working satisfactorily.

The Diploma will be a 'grouped award' at both Ordinary and Advanced levels, that is to say that achievement in a range of subjects will be required.

Awards will be graded according to the nature of the particular credits achieved.

The requirements for achieving the Diploma at the two levels are shown in Figure 4.1.

Figure 4.1 Requirements for award of the General Education Diploma.

For award of a Diploma at Ordinary level a student must obtain at least:

- the minimum total number of credit points pre-scribed; and these must include

- the minimum number of credit points prescribed in subjects within the compulsory core.

For award of a Diploma at Advanced level a student must obtain at least:

- the minimum number of credit points prescribed in a nominated major area of study; and in addition

- the minimum total number of credit points pre-scribed in subjects from at least 3 core areas not within the major area of study.

It is the intention that the Diploma shall achieve a proper balance between requiring breadth of study and encouraging the pursuit of particular subjects in depth, and the precise point at which it should be struck will require close examination coupled with wide consultation. We illustrate in Figure 4.2 a number of examples of the mix of studies which students might pursue in order to obtain an Advanced level Diploma.

Figure 4.2 Examples of studies for Advanced level of the General Education Diploma.

Student A (intending to study languages in HE)	*Student B* (intending to study engineering in HE)	*Student C* (intending to study sciences in HE)
French) M Spanish) IT Music History	Science* M Maths* Gujarati Theatre studies	Chemistry) M Physics) German Maths Philosophy
Student D (intending to study business studies in HE)	*Student E* (intending to enter employment at 18)	*Student F* (in traineeship)
Business studies) M Economics) Spanish IT European history	Motor maintenance and repair* M French Computing science Physical education	Leisure/tourism* M Italian Environmental studies Economics

M = major area   * developed out of GNVQs/NVQs at level 3

We envisage the Diploma as permitting great flexibility while retaining an essential underlying logic, but at the same time as enabling each student to be given a challenge and incentive of appropriate rigour. For example, we would want students to be able to pursue subjects in which they are strong by means of Advanced level modules before the age of 16, and to receive appropriate credit for these counting towards an Ordinary level Diploma.

All modules will be separately certificated and entered as they are achieved in pupils' records of achievement. This will be of particular value to students who for any reason fail to meet the requirements for the award of the Diploma at age 16 or 18 as the case may be. Many of these students may wish to go on studying, or to resume studies later on, so as to earn further credits and obtain a Diploma in due course; their perseverance deserves encouragement and recognition.

No age limits will be set for the award of a Diploma.

Some pupils may take it earlier than the normal ages of 16 and 18, and adults should be able to set themselves the goal of achieving the award of a Diploma at any age.

The Diploma will entail the disappearance of 'A' levels in their present form, but we see no reason why even those whose interests are most nearly met by 'A' levels need feel anxiety on that score. In taking evidence from representatives of the Headmasters' Conference, which has in membership many leading independent schools, we were told that they regretted that the debate about 'A' levels had suddenly been cut short by the Government's saying that it was totally committed to the 'A' level system; they did not want to stick to 'A' levels as such but would be very keen, whatever new system emerged, whether modular or not, to protect the interests of those who needed a very strong academic challenge at the highest level without having to plod their way through modules of a lower standard. That is a position which we fully understand and accept; we take it as a necessity that modules of the required rigour will be available under the new Diploma. We believe that *all* schools and colleges will see the Diploma proposed as in the interests both of young people and of the aims which they themselves stand for. It should certainly help to bring to an end the increasingly sterile debate about 'parity of esteem' between the different qualifications available at ages 16–18. It should also give a new dimension to the narrowly academic experience which 'A' levels force on so many academically able young people.

In the development of the Diploma close attention will need to be given to forming into a single whole elements which have rather different origins. Thus National Vocational Qualifications are 'criterion-referenced' – that is to say that there is a set objective standard against which the competence of candidates is judged – and there is no grading of success; only 'pass' or 'fail' is recognised. In 'A' levels, by contrast, grades are awarded, and the performance of candidates is largely 'norm-referenced' – that is to say, judged in relation to the performance of other candidates. We would wish to see moves to criterion-referencing to the maximum extent possible, because of its objectivity; but we are certain that it is desirable to award grades in accordance with the quality of students' achievements. It will also be essential to develop 'theoretical' elements to provide proper underpinning for the practical requirements of NVQs.

Later in this report we propose the development of traineeships requiring both training and further education; we envisage that young people entering traineeships will be working for the new Diploma, whether at Advanced or at Ordinary level. It is a great advantage of the arrangements we put forward that, while safeguarding quality, they permit flexibility in the way learning is pursued. This applies both to traineeships and to technical and vocational modules being taken at ages 14 or 15. It will often make sense, for example, for modules in a catering course to be provided for 14- or 15-year-olds in an appropriately equipped college of further education, just as students at a college might learn Italian or Spanish in the sixth form of a neighbouring school which counts the teaching of foreign languages as one of its strengths.

We believe that the Diploma we propose can be developed without excessive disruption out of the current and emerging array of provision for 16–18-year-olds. A crucial test will be whether it satisfactorily provides for and encourages onward progression for all students, whether through continuing full-time education or in employment. That is our aim. There is every reason to believe that it can be achieved, and that, when it has, a qualification will have been put in place whose quality will stand out internationally and which will do good service for generations of young people and the country itself well into the next century.

Personal records of achievement

We envisage that the work going into developing personal records of achievement will be continued and developed by the Education and Training Development Authority.

Records of achievement, like assessment, can serve both formative and summative purposes. Thus, it is desirable that students should each have records which include *all* their achievements as they pass through school or college, not only formal learning achievements, and which contribute to an annual review of their progress by teachers, parents and students themselves. The annual review will lead to an agreed 'personal development plan' for the next year. This is a valuable formative use.

Records of achievement need also to be developed in a way which makes it easy to present relevant information to somebody outside the school or college, for example, a prospective employer – a summative purpose. An employer will not be helped to reach a decision about recruiting a school-leaver by an unwieldy dossier of information, especially if much of it is out of date or excessively detailed.

A well set out record of achievement will be of special practical use to a student in crossing the divide from school to college or university or, even more, at the point of entering employment on leaving full-time education. We envisage that it will become more and more widely accepted that every employee should have a personal development plan, recording at annual intervals actions to be taken by both employer and employee so that the latter can pursue agreed performance and career goals at work. The records of achievement of school-leavers will form a natural starting-point for compiling personal development plans for them as they set out on their working lives.

The Position in Scotland

Earlier in this chapter we set out the principles which we think should inform a national curriculum. We believe that the system in Scotland is in general well placed to effect these principles. Especially at the post-16 stage, however, we see a need for some additions, and we recognise certain issues that require further consideration.

The curriculum in Scotland is not statutory, but it is national in the sense that primary and secondary schools work within national guidelines issued by the Scottish Office Education Department (SOED). SOED is advised by the Scottish Consultative Council on the curriculum and by Her Majesty's Inspectorate (HMI). HMI are key leaders of curriculum change, but widespread consultation has accompanied most of the major developments of the past twenty years, and this has helped to retain for the curriculum in Scotland a greater measure of legitimacy than has yet been won by the statutory national curriculum in England and Wales.

On occasion, the Scottish approach has also made it possible to change curricular arrangements very rapidly within the limits of consent. The Scottish Certificate of Education (SCE) Standard Grade reforms which came on stream in the mid-1980s were developed from deliberations that started almost twenty years ago, and have been widely welcomed. So too have Scottish Vocational Education Council (SCOTVEC) National Certificate modules, even though they were implemented from scratch in little more than two years. On the other hand, the Government's attempt to introduce national testing quickly into primary and secondary schools encountered immediate and sustained opposition across a broad front, and it achieved a measure of acceptance only after substantial modifications were made to the form and purpose of the tests.

There is always a danger that an unhealthy complacency nestles at the heart of consensus. In recent years, government ministers in Scotland, and sometimes their advisers, have been quick to voice such concerns in relation to issues of standards and the curriculum. It is not our purpose to discuss whether or not their worries are well-founded in particular cases. We do, however, have an equal and opposite concern for the effects of an ill-founded scepticism on schooling, not only in Scotland, but in all parts of the United Kingdom. Chronic mistrust of schools and teachers provides no basis for developing a national curriculum of high quality. It reduces the possibilities for swift and effective change, where that is desirable, and it curtails educational options for teachers and learners alike.

Schooling in Scotland in recent years has been subject to government policies similar to those in the rest of the UK. However, public confidence in schools and teachers, as distinct from ministerial confidence, has remained high. One indication of this is that no school in Scotland has yet opted out of the control of the local authority. There have been debates, vigorous debates, over issues of standards and values. Consensus has not precluded criticism, and weaknesses have been acknowledged. Indeed, the confidence that comes from consensus may even have made it easier to recognise weaknesses and to canvass remedies.

However, where faults have been recognised, the tendency in Scotland has been to search for specific explanations and specific remedial measures and not to doubt the fundamental integrity of the system that ministers are seeking to change. By contrast, the tendency in England and Wales has been to extrapolate explanations of specific problems to a general critique of school and teacher performance which has divided public and professional opinion.

The result in England and Wales has been much chopping and changing of reforms that are externally led, and that rely heavily on external, summative testing. By contrast, Scotland has been able to go further in directions we support since it has reached the following resolution of the issue of national testing. National testing is confined to only two curriculum areas, language (English) and mathematics. Banks of external tests devised by teachers in collaboration with the Primary Assessment Unit of the Scottish Examination Board are available at five levels. Teachers are free to choose which of a range of tests they will use, and to choose when they administer a test to an individual child. There are no fixed dates for administration. The purpose of testing is to confirm the teacher's judgement that the child has attained the level of the test. Results are not published, but are reported to parents and, in summary form, to the elected board for the school. National monitoring of standards is maintained by the Assessment of Achievement Programme (AAP) housed in the Scottish HMI. The AAP uses a light sampling approach to the reporting of trends in attainment in particular curricular areas.

These arrangements do much to leave initiative and responsibility where we want to see them, in the hands of teachers, whilst also providing a framework for supporting teachers in their grasp of national standards, and for reporting to parents and school managers.

Guidance on the curriculum of the primary school in Scotland and on the first two years of secondary school is provided under the Government's 5–14 Development Programme. Even before the Government's concessions on assessment and testing, the curricular elements of the 5–14 programme enjoyed a wide measure of public and professional support. This support continues, and we see no need to disturb it. The curriculum embodies our principles of a core, of choice and breadth, and of the assessment of clearly specified outcomes. However, it has a distinctive approach to flexibility of choice for the teacher, to the issue of citizenship and life skills, and to the application of knowledge (our 'applied intelligence'). Each of these three issues merits a brief comment.

In all three cases, the differences arise from the different approach that is taken in Scotland to the specification of the areas of the curriculum, and a preliminary word of explanation is therefore necessary. At the 5–14 stage, five substantive areas are recognised: language, mathematics, environmental studies, expressive arts and religious and moral education. For the two-year SCE Standard Grade courses at, roughly, 14–16 years, three of these areas continue, namely language, mathematics and religious and moral education; but environmental studies divides into three components (scientific studies and applications, social and environmental studies, and technological activities and applications) whilst expressive arts divides into two (creative and aesthetic activities, and physical education). Permeating these substantive areas are cross-curricular strands that relate to certain activities or skills, for example, those of knowing and understanding, of using evidence (activities which include the use of information technology), and of developing informed attitudes. There is also guidance on the contexts in which knowledge and skills should be acquired and applied.

Our first comment is that a curriculum that is specified in this way can give great flexibility to school and teacher, especially when national testing itself offers choice to the teacher and is not intrusive. In practice there are several ways in which many of the aims of the Scottish curriculum can be achieved. The extent of this flexibility should be borne in mind in any decision on the amount of time that should be allocated to work within national guidelines; current SOED advice to primary schools suggests 80%, a higher figure than those we recommend for England and Wales.

Secondly, although the curricular framework in Scotland does not use the language of citizenship and life skills, it is capable of delivering the outcomes we wish to see under this head. For example, they can be achieved at the 5–14 stage through the spheres of environmental studies and religious and moral education, with various enhancements during the course of secondary schooling along the lines of extant provision for careers education, guidance, and personal and social development.

Thirdly, explicit provision for the application of knowledge and understanding is made in the Scottish curricular framework. For example, health education is one of five components of the environmental studies area in the 5–14 curriculum and itself contains two strands: knowledge and understanding, and taking action on health.

Turning to the curriculum at 14 years of age and thereafter, we doubt whether most of our proposals would pose difficulties for Scottish principles and practice. The two that would require most consideration in Scotland are, perhaps, those for the post-16 entitlement and for the award of the Diploma at Ordinary and Advanced levels.

Again a preliminary word of explanation is necessary. In 1992 a Government Committee chaired by Professor John Howie recommended that the system of post-16 school qualifications in Scotland, principally the SCE

Higher, be replaced by a new qualification that would be awarded on a group basis. The qualification would come in two forms: a Scottish Baccalaureat (Scotbac) having an academic emphasis and awarded only after two years of post-compulsory schooling; and a Scottish Certificate (Scotcert) with a mainly vocational emphasis and awarded in two parts, respectively in the final year of compulsory schooling and in the first post-compulsory year. The Committee also proposed that courses for both the Scotbac and the Scotcert start a year earlier than the present courses for the Higher, and that work for the SCE Standard Grade be completed a year earlier, by the end of the third secondary year (pupils in Scotland transfer to secondary school at roughly 12 years of age).

In the consultation and public debate that followed the publication of these proposals, there was widespread endorsement of the Committee's analysis of weaknesses in the Scottish system. But there was also an equally widespread, indeed almost unanimous, rejection of the Committee's central proposal, that for a two-track system starting at 15 years. The most widely supported solution was a one-track system based on modules. There was less unanimity on the merits of a group award, as opposed to a single-subject award, and on the future of the SCE Standard Grade. Some argued for its retention as a two-year course leading to qualifications at 16 years. Others thought that an award at 16 years would decline in importance. Most conceded that there was some 'marking time' in the lower secondary school and that the work of the higher-attaining pupils in particular should progress faster at this stage.

As we write, the Government has yet to announce its response to the Howie proposals. However, the Howie report and attendant debate provides a useful touchstone for judging the relevance and acceptability in Scotland of our proposals for provision at the 14–16 stage and thereafter.

We are clear about several matters. First, we reject any two-track solution of a type advocated by the Howie Committee and we endorse a one-track solution, confident in the knowledge that this has widespread support in Scotland.

Secondly, we think it unfortunate that the remit of the Howie Committee was confined to post-compulsory schooling alone. We reiterate that the system of curriculum, assessment and qualifications at 16 years and thereafter should be comprehensive, covering not only schools but also learning at work, in part-time education, and in institutions other than schools. Again, we think that this principle will be widely endorsed in Scotland.

Thirdly, we are certain that the principle of entitlement should apply in Scotland. A person should have the right to receive education or training in all areas of the recommended curriculum, and up to the level embodied in the Advanced Diploma. That right is fundamental. Possibly of lesser importance is how that right should be secured. In England and Wales we plan to achieve this through the GED, which represents a return to awards on a group basis at 14–16 years and at 18 years. If Scotland were to follow this path, a variety of considerations would require attention. These include the timing and future of any award in Scotland before 17 or 18 years, and also the performance of the current national curriculum guidelines at 16 years. Under these, a majority of pupils cover a majority of the specified curricular areas, but receive certification on a single-subject basis. Nevertheless, this approach does not guarantee entitlement, whether at 16 years or thereafter. Nor does it guarantee breadth of study after 16 years, despite the emphasis on breadth incorporated in the curriculum guidelines for this stage.

Whatever approach is adopted in Scotland, it goes without saying that the status of Scottish awards must be at least as high as the Diploma we propose for England and Wales, and as awards elsewhere in Europe.

Finally, we recognise that in Scotland, no less than in England and Wales, a mix of factors will determine the form in which our principles are implemented and evolve. The work of the Howie Committee itself identified many of these factors and their interdependencies. In particular, we take seriously its view that a modular system runs the risk of burdening pupils and teachers alike with too frequent assessment, and that the alternative of lighter assessment may compromise the public standing of the final award. Somewhere between these alternatives, other issues must also be resolved: the balance between external and internal assessment; the harmonisation of norm-referenced and criterion-referenced assessment; and the rethinking of the academic and the vocational. In all these decisions, cost, too, will be a factor.

Nevertheless, we believe that these issues can be progressively resolved over time, and that our proposals for a broad, unified, comprehensive system based on the principles of individual entitlement and success will not only find favour in Scotland, but will themselves succeed.

Costs

Finally, we record that we believe that the proposals put forward in this chapter can be implemented without any significant increase in costs. In particular, whereas the modular system of learning which we wish to see introduced for 14–18-year-olds will of course generate costs, we estimate that these are likely to be wholly offset by the discontinuance of GCSE, 'A' levels and other examinations which are themselves costly to administer.

Notes

1 Phenix, P.H., 1964. *Realms of Meaning: A Philosophy of the Curriculum for General Education*. McGraw-Hill.
Hirst, P.H. and Peters, R., 1970. *The Logic of Education*. Routledge & Kegan Paul.
White, J., 1973. *Towards a Compulsory Curriculum*. Routledge & Kegan Paul.
Hirst, P.H., 1974. *Knowledge and the Curriculum*. Routledge & Kegan Paul.
Lawton, D., 1975. *Class, Culture and Curriculum*. Routledge & Kegan Paul.
Her Majesty's Inspectorate, 1983. Curriculum from 11 to 16: Towards a Statement of Entitlement. HMSO.
Her Majesty's Inspectorate, 1985. Curriculum Matters 2: The Curriculum from 5 to 16. HMSO.
2 Finegold, D. and others, 1990. A British 'Baccalauréat'. Institute for Public Policy Research, Education and Training Paper No 1.
3 Royal Society's Education Committee, 1991. Beyond GCSE. Royal Society.
4 Dearing, R., July 1993. The National Curriculum and its Assessment: An Interim Report. National Curriculum Council and School Examinations and Assessment Council.
5 Committee of Inquiry into the Quality of the Educational Experience Offered to 3- and 4-Year-Olds, chaired by Mrs Angela Rumbold CBE MP, 1990. Starting with Quality. HMSO.
6 Dearing, R., *op cit*, paragraph 3.14 viii.
7 *Ibid*, paragraph 5.28.
8 McPherson, A., 1992. Measuring Added Value in Schools. NCE Briefing No 1. National Commission on Education.
9 Dearing, R., *op cit*, Annex 5, paragraph 8.

5
Innovation in Learning

The Need for Innovation

Education is big business. There are 700,000 teachers employed in the United Kingdom and we spend £27 billion of public money on it annually. Training is big business too. Employers alone spend upwards of £35 billion a year on it. There are at least 14 million students and trainees in any one year, and probably many more.

Like all successful businesses, education and training must innovate and invest in the future. Moreover, these are knowledge-based businesses in which the needs of students (the customers) are constantly changing and developing, the surrounding circumstances (the challenge of foreign competition, the needs of society) are always on the move and where, above all, technology (the technology relevant to teaching and learning) is already in a state of continuing revolution.

It is of the first importance, then, that innovation in education and training should have a prominent place in the attention of decision-makers at all levels. It is constant innovation that will drive provision in the United Kingdom up to the highest levels of quality, while also opening it out to all who can and should in future benefit from it; and it is constant innovation that will enable the cost of education and training to be contained within bounds tolerable to tax-payers and employers alike.

Innovation involves discovering new ideas, developing methods of applying those ideas to particular problems or situations, and bringing them into use on a wide scale. In Britain we have always rated highly the ability to discover new ideas. We have attached less importance to their development, and all too often we have been poor at implementing them generally.

There is a particularly brilliant exception to this generalisation in British education, namely the development of the Open University. Even there, the question now arises whether, in spreading high-quality education to many more people, we are poised to take sufficient advantage of the unique experience and knowledge available in that institution.

Looking more generally at education and training, it is our conclusion that events are following a familiar British pattern. There is much excellent pioneering work going on both in trying out new approaches to learning and in applying new technology – which usually means information technology – but arrangements to bring new methods into general use are deficient. And yet that last step is crucial for the future and should be receiving high priority.

In this chapter we draw attention to examples of approaches to learning which hold out promise for the future. We examine the advances being made in improving educational technology – a broad term covering every kind of technology from blackboard and chalk to sophisticated uses of information technology (IT) – and conclude with recommendations designed to speed up and take much greater advantage of innovation in the future. Success will represent an important part of achieving a 'new deal' in the classroom.

Better Learning in Schools

Raising expectations

People learn in many ways. Some are more comfortable with the written word. Others find aural or visual material more accessible or learn best through practical examples. Most people learn in all these ways to some extent.

Teachers themselves are powerful 'role models' who may exercise a profound influence for good or ill on pupils' achievements. The enthusiasm and example of a good teacher is often the most important factor in motivating a pupil to learn – and to want to learn. But even with an experienced and competent teacher, effective learning is not guaranteed. Disaffected pupils can resist even the best teaching, just as effective learning can take place despite poor teaching. It is difficult to define effective teaching because successful teachers often adopt several teaching styles, using each as appropriate. Good communication between teacher and learner, particularly for older pupils, is crucial in selecting the right approach. Unfortunately, as a survey for the Commission showed, this is often lacking.[1]

Clearly the quality of learning can be improved for many more pupils by *raising expectations* about what they can achieve and by paying closer attention to their individual needs. Successful approaches involve greater flexibility about the means, time and place in which learning takes place. Helping pupils and students to play a greater part in their own learning and making full use of resources both within and outside the school are important. Evolving techniques for applying new technology also have great potential.

Thinking skills

Effective learning requires the development of thinking

skills. Teachers need to create situations and tasks which encourage pupils to think hard in order to make progress. A new approach to the teaching of science using activities designed to promote higher level thinking has been developed through the Cognitive Acceleration through Science Education (CASE) project.[2] This approach has since taken root in a small number of schools around the country. The research involved challenging children aged 11–13 to confront intellectual problems. They were encouraged to think consciously about problem-solving so that they could generalise from their own experiences. Both teachers and learners made conscious efforts to create bridges between newly learned principles and new contexts such as applying science learning to other subjects or to the world outside school. To teach in this way, teachers need to recognise the characteristics of higher level thinking in order to help pupils develop reasoning patterns for themselves.

This research suggests that the achievement of 'ordinary pupils ... in ordinary schools' can be raised 'through a well-timed, well-targeted, and well-delivered programme to develop the intellectual ability of pupils aged from 11–13 years'. The researchers noted: '. . . a profound and permanent effect on the children's ability to learn new material . . .' not only in science, the subject of the research, but also in mathematics and English. Table 5.1 shows that a substantially higher proportion of participating pupils obtained passes in the GCSE at grade C or above, compared with those in the control group.

Table 5.1 Percentage of pupils obtaining GCSE grade C or above, comparing a special teaching approach (CASE) with a control group.

Percentages

| Subject | Boys 1989 | | Girls 1990 | |
	CASE pupils	Control group	CASE pupils	Control group
Science	41.7	12.8	50.0	33.3
Mathematics	49.1	16.4	55.2	42.4
English	44.6	16.1	85.2	58.1

Source: Adey, P., and others, 1991.[2]

We are impressed by these results. There appears to be a strong case for the lessons derived from such work to be made more widely available. Evidently better thinking skills make an important contribution to raising expectations and thus to raising levels of achievement. Professor Nisbet has said: 'By the beginning of the twenty-first century, no curriculum will be regarded as acceptable unless it can be shown to make a contribution to the teaching of thinking.'[3]

Flexible learning
The process of learning is as important as its content, since it often determines how much information and understanding is retained and the extent to which it can be applied in practice. Changes in society and in the world of work are making it more important for people to be adaptable and ready to apply their knowledge and skills in many contexts. Having some choice in how they learn may offer secondary school pupils a better preparation for such demands than some traditional learning methods do.

'Flexible learning', an approach used to good effect in delivering the Technical and Vocational Education Initiative,[4] uses small group tutorials, individual action plans and study guides. Pupils can learn at their own pace with opportunities to go over material again or to move on as appropriate. By organising and using learning activities, environments and resources flexibly, teachers can stimulate the capacity, encouraged during primary schooling, to learn independently. This is probably becoming more important than whether a pupil has 'academic' or 'vocational' potential.

The approach enables teachers to draw on a range of teaching styles so as to meet a wider range of individual needs. This is important. HM Inspectorate (HMI) has often commented on teachers' failure to identify the needs of individual pupils, particularly the less able and also the very able pupils. Concentrating on fixed-pace, whole-class teaching can leave the learning requirements of many pupils unsatisfied. Relying on self-paced work can result in low productivity. Learning in groups can be more effective than either of these if members of the group have the right 'mix' of ideas and approaches.

A flexible learning project teaching geography to secondary school pupils found that: 'Brighter pupils are not held back as they are in whole-class situations; instead they are able to progress at a pace and to a depth more suited to their ability and consequently are fully stretched.'[5] But, as Figure 5.1 shows, the project also found that flexible learning helped a larger proportion of pupils to achieve higher grade GCSEs.

Figure 5.1 GCSE grades obtained by geography candidates in the period 1989–92, using traditional and flexible learning techniques.

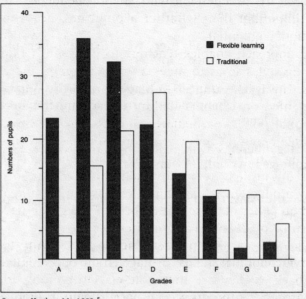

Source: Hughes, M., 1993.[5]

Furthermore, of those using flexible learning 68% achieved a higher grade in geography than their average grade in other 'traditionally' taught subjects, as compared with 43% of those taught geography in a traditional way.

But equally notable in this study was the teacher's observation that pupils of all ages and abilities reported an increase in motivation and that they worked harder and for longer on more effective learning activities. Assessment can also be integrated into teaching, and, in the longer term, teaching time can be better used as pupils become more self-reliant. Flexible learning can also provide organisational benefits, for example, by allowing schools and colleges to cater for a wider range of students, including adult returners.

Some potential benefits of flexible learning have been described vividly by pupils themselves:

> 'It gives us lots of responsibility and independence . . . I can push myself more . . .'

> 'We have all done loads more work than in other subjects . . . I have learned a lot . . .'

> 'I am always thinking about how the things I am doing in lessons are helping me to learn. I have much more self confidence . . .'

> 'The big difference with geography is that we are encouraged to think for ourselves.'

Pupils' enthusiasm and increased effort were also noticed by parents:

> 'It is with some envy that I watch her work in this way. I am grateful that she has been given the opportunity.'

Such evidence supports schools in adopting flexible learning so as to raise both expectations and the quality of learning in the classroom. However, it has been impressed upon the Commission that 'flexible learning done badly can be disastrous'[5] and pupils must be emotionally and intellectually ready to take some responsibility for their own learning. 'Self-directed learning does not work with non-self-motivated people.'[6]

We believe that, by the age of about 14, pupils should be equipped to work independently in a flexible learning environment. The foundations of independent learning can be laid even in the pre-school years. They can be encouraged throughout primary schooling, and the teaching of study skills can assume greater significance at the upper primary level. This should increase at the early secondary stage when thinking skills should also be developed. If these skills are to be relevant, they should be integrated into the curriculum rather than taught separately; the school should constantly reinforce them so that each child acquires and retains the learning 'habit'. By making such a continuing commitment to improving pupils' learning, schools can enable young people to acquire skills which will be of value throughout their lives.

Supporting independent learning

Confidence in studying independently provides the foundation for successful flexible learning and for learning throughout life. 'Supported self-study'[7] complements the use of flexible learning as well as helping institutions to respond to rising post-16 participation and the increasing diversity of students' interests. In supported self-study the teacher helps students to plan the best use of study time, offering guidance, setting targets, organising pair and group work, and assessing outcomes before planning the next stage. Better use of this 'non-contact' time enables teachers to make more effective use of contact time with students. This time can then be made more productive by using approaches which increase participation and motivation, such as presentations and group work.

Using the community

Schools and further education (FE) and sixth-form colleges can improve the quality of learning and the range of resources available by drawing on the skills and knowledge of others in the community, by involving families more explicitly and building links with employers and other local organisations. More learning can then take place outside schools. Schools can also become 'learning centres' welcoming the whole community. Opening up schools in this way offers children greater access to the 'real world' and makes it easier to treat older children in a way which will prepare them for their adult roles. Chapter 7 examines how schools and their communities can work together to enhance the quality of education provided. The use of 'outsiders' to support teachers in the classroom is considered in Chapter 8. Greater use of communications technology means that the size of 'communities' will grow, thus increasing opportunities still further.

Some institutions are experimenting with different patterns of working day, week or year. This is often at the behest of pupils who choose to come into school before and stay beyond the timetabled periods to complete a piece of work or to use the school's facilities. The longer working day is already a feature of City Technology Colleges, though whether it is appropriate for any particular school will depend very much upon the facilities which it is able to offer. We commend the development of an ethos in secondary schools which allows them to break free of the strait-jacket of set hours and set periods.

Innovation Beyond School

Much that applies to schools also applies to learning in colleges, universities and training centres. Adults who have not already developed thinking and study skills need to have opportunities to do so. Flexible approaches should be found to meet the needs of the increasing numbers seeking further and higher education.

As demand for further and higher education grows, institutions will be forced to move away from a dependence on contact hours as the prime means of teaching. Students' ability to work independently will become increasingly important. Sharing resources and knowledge between colleges and universities and vigorous research and development in innovative teaching will avoid duplication of effort and should be encouraged and supported.

These issues were recognised in relation to the higher education sector in the report 'Teaching and Learning in an Expanding Higher Education System'[8] which argued for:

- a significant improvement in the effectiveness and quality of teaching in higher education;

- a raising of the status of teaching in higher education;

- a greatly increased flexibility in the higher education sector, with wider access, better articulation with other sectors, and a much wider span of involvement with continuing professional education and other forms of in-work training;

- the formation of communities dedicated to the creation, development and use of innovative teaching systems and techniques;

- a vigorous programme of research and development in teaching methods and educational technology shared between many institutions.

The further education sector is already moving in this direction with professional development for teachers, growing use of educational technology and collaboration with other sectors. The impetus behind new ways of providing education and training comes from the need to improve access. For those who have finished their compulsory schooling and who have commitments which limit their opportunities for study, this is one of the main issues affecting learning. If more adults are to be brought into education and training, there must be more than one pathway through 'the system'.

The Open University has been a world leader for the past twenty years in developing open learning materials for those who are unable to attend conventional classes but who can study independently with the support of tutors and assessors. This approach creates high-quality learning by building on student commitment, high-quality tutoring, and summer schools to bring students together. By harnessing new technology and investing in research into how people learn, the Open University maintains its world-wide reputation for the quality of its courses.

Other providers use distance and open learning to reach students with a variety of needs and interests, and scope exists to increase their use further, for example, in further education. The National Vocational Qualification (NVQ) framework uses a flexible open and modular approach with individual programmes which help not only learners but also their tutors, mentors and assessors.

Employers, often in partnership with colleges, are in a strong position to find new ways to help employees to continue with their learning, as we describe in Chapter 12, not only through job-related training but also non-vocational courses and developmental opportunities.

'Learning shops' set up in the United States may offer a model for improving access to adult education and training in this country. Local learning centres could be set up by Education and Training Boards (see Chapter 13) in association with Training and Enterprise Councils, perhaps with private sponsorship. Based in schools, colleges or libraries, they could provide adults with access to learning materials and information about courses as well as a place to study.

We would like to see pump-priming investment to support developments like these. They have a potentially important part to play in ensuring that good quality education and training is made available to all, especially those who currently feel excluded.

Educational Technology: The Potential for Improving Learning

The great potential of educational technology lies in its capacity to provide flexible and supportive learning environments. The technological possibilities are rapidly becoming more sophisticated and potentially will have a profound effect on teaching and learning. The introduction of the photocopier demonstrated the degree to which teaching can be revolutionised by the use of new technology. In future IT can be expected to expand opportunities for teaching and learning much further.

No country claims to have made substantial progress so far in applying IT in schools, though there is agreement about its likely impact. It is impossible to know at present what form the technological 'revolution' will take or precisely when it will occur, but there is every likelihood that it will have effects going well beyond the organisation of teaching and will necessitate thinking out afresh the role and organisation of schools. Meanwhile schools and teachers must be able to make full use of advances in the technological 'toolkit' and to take advantage of the opportunities which IT in particular will be offering.

How IT is used

Where it is properly implemented within the curriculum, IT is already enriching the quality of learning.[9] The use of computers removes some of the laborious and unproductive work involved in collecting data. It aids concentration and allows learners to work independently at their own speed, and, where the work has been well planned by the teacher, to work for longer without needing support or prompting. Pupils can review their own progress without feeling threatened or fearing mistakes. It also encourages co-operation, collaboration and communication between pairs or groups of pupils and, by improving the presentation of work, builds confidence and motivation, not only in the use of IT but also in the subject in which IT is used. It also extends the range of work which can be offered, for example by simulating difficult, dangerous or costly experiments and investigations, such as the study of sources of pollution.

When attached to a computer, 'CD ROM' discs – specially programmed compact discs – provide access to large quantities of text, pictures and numerical data. This technology, which is being widely introduced in schools, is revolutionising access to libraries of material by making it possible to store and examine enormous amounts of information very cheaply. The application is still at an early stage, and teachers need training to use it effectively. Its potential lies in providing sufficient data storage to allow interactive learning software to be developed which combines text, graphics, sound and eventually television quality pictures in programs which enable pupils to participate more actively in their own learning.

Telecommunication networks, both within establishments and between them, are providing access to a growing variety of computational tools and learning materials, increasing the scope for collaboration between sites and institutions all over the world. Safeguards will be necessary to ensure compatibility and to maintain standards in educational software.

By the next century laptop computers, smaller and more powerful than those of today, are likely to become a major means of personal and mass communication and to take the place of the notebooks and papers which today's students carry with them.

An important advantage of computers is that they help teachers to address specific needs more precisely, particularly for those with learning difficulties and for the more gifted: in fact just those people who are often least well catered for by traditional methods. Pupils with learning difficulties, for example, use computer simulations in musical composition, drama, creative writing of many kinds and art work. The development of language and social skills is a major element in such work. Computer software offers practice in numerical manipulation or language skills to those with special needs, though discrimination in its use and teacher support are required. Specially adapted word processors can be used to help people who have difficulties in communicating. Almost all special schools now have access to suitable IT equipment, though there is still scope to make more use of IT in mainstream schooling for pupils with special needs, not only in the practice of literacy and numeracy skills but also in improving access to a broad curriculum.[10]

IT is playing an increasing role in the delivery of further, higher and adult education and training. It is making learning available to much larger numbers by giving students more choice over the time, location and pace of learning, and by securing a greater commitment to learning. At Wirral Metropolitan College, for example, the use of IT has increased study time by an average of five hours a week per student, without increasing staff resources. It is also making college facilities available to employers and others in the community.[11]

Higher education institutions are using new technology to develop course materials for providing computer-based learning, promoting computer literacy and IT skills and enhancing the presentation of teaching. At Heriot-Watt University, for example, the Computer-Aided Learning in

Mathematics project provides a good example of how IT can deliver 'drill and practice' in a subject traditionally taught by giving students large numbers of problems to solve. Examples like these illustrate the great potential for improving learning through the use of IT.[8]

Limitations in the use of IT
There are serious imbalances in the provision of IT in schools and colleges. Though the availability of micro-computers in schools has grown significantly since the mid-1980s a survey by the Department for Education in 1991[12] showed:

- variation in provision between schools – the pupil: micro ratio in primary schools ranged from 1:1 to 115:1;

- restricted access in secondary schools where, although provision is generally better, 45% of computers were permanently located in computer rooms;

- variations in spending on computers, and particularly the dependence of the primary sector on funding by parent associations (27% on average and 38% in prosperous areas).

Nor is the number of computers in schools a reliable indicator of how effectively IT is being used. The DFE survey reported that IT had made a substantial contribution to teaching in only just under a third of schools (about the same proportion in secondary and primary schools). And while 89% of mathematics departments in secondary schools used IT, no more than 9% felt that it made a substantial contribution. Such figures highlight the need to monitor the quality of IT applications as well as the scale of provision.

We have noted examples cited by the Office for

Standards in Education of indifferent use of IT.[13] Recent work at King's College, London, on the use of IT in schools[14] has also shown that its contribution is not consistent across subjects or ages. There are applications which occupy the time of students without challenging them; which display results which have called for little judgement or which have been derived by blind trial and error; which encourage plagiarism rather than inventiveness; or which fail to develop understanding or capability. Some failures are due to problems experienced by pupils, for example, difficulties in using a particular software package; others, however, are due to problems which teachers experience, for example, difficulty in understanding the philosophy underpinning a particular piece of software or the implications for its effective use in education.

IT in schools should be used '...both to enhance and extend learning, and to promote an understanding of IT itself.'[9] In fact most uses of IT are still limited to communicating information and handling data at a very basic level. Few schools are yet in a position to cover adequately the other aspects required by the national curriculum: simulation, measurement and control and the application and effects of IT. Nor is there much depth of analysis or development of problem-solving skills. As HM Inspectorate observed, too many pupils are experiencing a '. . . very limited diet of IT and to a relatively superficial level . . .'[9]

The way forward for IT
For pupils who have the ability and interest, intellectually demanding work with IT should be available which covers not only information systems and approaches to solving problems but also computer operations and software design. Teaching in this area requires expertise in computing and systems design and, preferably, a first-hand know-

ledge of how the world outside school makes use of IT.

Another factor drawn to our attention is the need to be aware of gender differences in pupils' progress in using new technology. Confidence in using computers is not evenly distributed between girls and boys; girls are more likely to assume less active roles if working in mixed groups. Greater use of separate computer sessions or groups of machines reserved for girls could help to over-come the reluctance of girls to break into a preserve for boys who may be confident but not necessarily expert.

The key difference between a good application and a poor application of IT appears to be well-trained, well-prepared and well-motivated staff supported by adequate investment. It is essential to recognise the educational purpose to be served and not just to make poor use of available but inadequate technology. The effective use of IT demands more than improvisation by teachers who are working things out as they go along. The in-service train-ing of all teachers to use and assess IT within their own subjects and to strengthen the number with more detailed IT knowledge and expertise is a continuing necessity. Adequate revenue funding is essential to allow schools to keep abreast of new developments and to replace ageing hardware. We place high priority on good quality IT pro-vision as part of a continuing commitment to improve-ment in learning.

The National Council for Educational Technology (NCET) acknowledges the difficulties which schools and colleges face in trying to make sensible investment deci-sions when both technology and educational require-ments are changing so rapidly.[15] It concludes that many have reached the third of five stages of growth in their use of IT. They have passed an initial stage typified by individual enthusiasts exploiting particular applications in their own areas and a second stage where IT is generally accepted as an important tool and cross-organisational policies and training programmes are often developed. They have reached the third stage, which involves more fundamental change, as senior management develops a strategy to make use of IT to further the aims of the organisation and make it more effective. Later, IT may redefine the way the organisation communicates to the outside world and finally IT may change the nature of the business itself. It is in this way that the revolution referred to at the beginning of this chapter is likely to come about.

Broadcasting
Some people are concerned about the influence upon children of television and therefore resist its use in education. But good quality, well-presented, television and radio broadcasts can be a valuable resource for schools. They can help to engage pupils' interest and provide a stimulus for teachers which can be used to support and enrich the curriculum. Broadcasting is widely used, with nine out of ten schools registered as users. A recent HMI report has found improvement in the quality of use; 80% of primary lessons which used broadcasts in their teaching were classed as satisfactory or better.[16]

Good use of broadcasting involves careful selection of programmes to serve the aims of the teacher and the school. Its use to support topic work gives pupils insights into other countries and cultures, past and present, in a way which would be difficult to improve upon other than through first-hand experience. Broadcast programmes also help to counter some teachers' limited expertise, for example, in primary music teaching.

Careful planning, together with high teacher expectations and good quality follow-up work, is important. Most teachers use pre-recorded programmes to give pupils opportunities to discuss and clarify ideas and to demonstrate and practise techniques. The technical quality of educational broadcasts is high, though there is a need for training to develop some teachers' skills in using them more effectively. Lessons are unlikely to be effective if the programmes have been poorly selected, or if they are not suitable for the age group or if the teacher has not previewed the material and integrated it into lesson planning. Practical issues, such as class size and the quality of acoustics and accommodation, also affect what can be achieved through such lessons.

In adult colleges by far the most successful use of broadcasting is in language learning: some 70% of colleges which teach languages use broadcast material. Satellite broadcasts, especially if they can be recorded and distributed centrally or regionally, will increase the volume of good educational material which is available.

One of the strengths of broadcasting is that it can be used by learners at home. The universal accessibility of broadcasts means that a greater range of opportunities is available for learners to learn what they want, when they want and where they want, so providing truly flexible learning for a wider population. It opens up access for adults for whom education and training provision is currently limited, including perhaps those who live in rural areas or those whose working hours or domestic commitments make it hard for them to take conventional courses.

Broadcasting is easy to use and good at awakening or rekindling interest. It has an important part to play not only in increasing access to specific courses of study but in reaching a mass audience, many of whom are not highly motivated to learn, helping to raise general educational levels within the population and promoting the importance of learning in our society. We refer in Chapter 12 to how broadcasting can encourage people to return to learning and we recognise it as having an important and expanding role in offering new opportunities for learning.

Fostering Creativity and Innovation

Recognising the part played by teachers
If we are to raise standards in teaching and learning, drawing whenever appropriate upon the lessons of research, we need a climate in which teachers are encouraged to reflect on their own practice and to experiment with different approaches to teaching, always with the aim of achieving the most effective learning for their pupils and students. The OECD[17] recommends that a great deal of research and development activity should in future become part of normal educational practice, much of it being undertaken at local level. Teachers must be encouraged to be well-informed and creative partners in the drive to improve the quality of teaching and learning.

Good lesson planning and preparation is the key to all good teaching and learning. Approaches like those described in this chapter have significant implications for the role of teachers in the classroom. Many of them will already be familiar to some teachers. Primary teachers are already trained to draw upon a variety of teaching styles and techniques. But most school teachers will have had little experience of academic tutoring, for instance, and many will need training in the effective use of group work, in integrating continuous assessment into teaching and in teaching study skills.

We are not satisfied that the quality or extent of provision of initial teacher training in IT meets current needs. All teachers must be properly prepared during their initial training to be confident in the use of IT in teaching their subject, including basic computer literacy. Since

June 1992 secondary teacher training has required only that teachers should be able by the end of their training to 'demonstrate ability to select and use appropriate resources, including IT.'[18] Given the need to prepare pupils for a world in which the use of IT is commonplace, this requirement is insufficient. We consider that the recommendations of the Trotter Report of 1989 provide a better basis for the teaching of IT.[19] These require new teachers to be able:

- to make confident personal use of a range of software and IT appropriate to their subjects;

- to review critically the relevance of software and IT devices to their chosen studies, and judge potential value for use in the classroom;

- to make constructive use of IT in teaching, and prepare to put into effect schemes of work which incorporate appropriate uses of IT;

- to evaluate the ways in which use of IT changes the nature of teaching and learning.

Higher education institutions and schools which provide initial teacher training should have higher levels of expertise, equipment and technical support so that they can train teachers effectively. In-service courses which use IT should be long enough to enable teachers to become immersed in the technology and gain confidence in its use in teaching their subject. IT considerations should be integrated into all general in-service training.

We make recommendations in Chapter 14 about increased funding for teacher training; in part this should be used for improving training in IT. Teachers also need training and support to adapt successfully to flexible learning, managing independent learning, involving peo-

ple in the community and making full use of advanced
educational technology.

Supporting innovation by schools and other institutions
There has always been a need for regular revenue funding
to allow schools, colleges and universities to maintain a
wide variety of interesting, relevant and up-to-date
resource materials. New opportunities in the use of IT add
to the need, and necessitate annual assessment and
updating of hardware and software requirements. An
overall rationale built into the school development plan,
based on a continuing commitment to improvement, is
needed to determine the funding of all learning resource
equipment and materials, including books, so that their
use can be planned in a coherent way.

To encourage schools to innovate, we recommend that
'innovation' funds should be made available through our
proposed Education and Training Boards (see Chapter 13)
for schools which have well-thought-out proposals for
improving their teaching and learning methods and the
resources they use.

We agree with the OECD when it argues that research
and development in education must be greatly increased
if teachers are 'to perform as high-level professionals,
well-informed and able to co-operate in solving complex
problems of learning and management'. Around £16 million was spent on research into education in the UK during 1988–89, less than 0.1% of total spending on education. Given the importance of education to society and the
economy, the amount appears to us to be quite inadequate and needs to be greatly increased. To ensure that it
is well spent, however, requires a further step to which
we devote the last section of this chapter.

A Lasting Commitment to Innovation

To plan, implement and manage major changes in the educational system requires:

- a sound and extensive body of knowledge and proven experience on which to base decisions;

- the development and, where appropriate, standardisation of new methods, techniques, approaches and systems across the whole of education;

- the continuing training of the teaching profession in the use of new methods and technologies;

- the careful evaluation and field testing of new methods and technologies;

- the development of a broad consensus in the teaching profession about the management of change;

- a research programme to develop and assess new methods and new technologies;

- the creation of a community within the teaching profession dedicated to innovative learning, the development of new methods and the imaginative use of advanced technology.

Knowledge must be made more productive. The country must not fail to take full advantage of the valuable research and experimentation which is already carried out. Mechanisms for evaluation, development and implementation are weak. Local innovation and creativity provide illustrations and examples of what might be achieved, and that is good as far as it goes. What is needed is a thoroughgoing national commitment to high-quality implementation of proven advances.

At the same time, we are concerned at gaps in knowledge about teaching and learning which have been drawn to our attention, for instance, concerning the effect of class size on learning or the relative merits of different reading recovery schemes.

We believe that a body should be established responsible, not only for initiating and stimulating research, but for ensuring that findings are evaluated in a range of contexts and that means are found for disseminating and implementing that research which is clearly of benefit. It would have an important role in encouraging collaboration and the development of new learning materials, including those using advanced technology. The case for such a body has already been made with respect to the higher education sector (a 'Teaching and Learning Board')[8] and it has been argued elsewhere that there is an urgent need for 'an organisational infrastructure capable of ensuring a continual improvement in student learning'[20]: an infrastructure designed to support research and development and its transfer into practice.

We recommend the establishment of a Council for Innovation in Teaching and Learning. Its terms of reference should include:

- working with curriculum and research bodies, including for example the National Foundation for Educational Research, to identify areas where new research could be beneficial;

- commissioning theoretical and practice-linked research and development, taking account of the need to ensure that research funds are well used, that timescales are appropriate and that programmes incorporate longer-term strategic research as well as short-term projects and reviews;

- promoting the evaluation of new teaching and learning methods and materials, including the assessment of their suitability for different learning stages and situations and the assessment of contextual and organisational factors which influence learning, including the structure of assessment and qualifications;

- ensuring the effective dissemination of research to teacher training institutions, education and training providers and professional organisations through publications, bibliographies, conferences, and teacher training materials;

- advising Secretaries of State on innovation policy;

- producing for wider circulation (for example to parents and employers) a brief annual report on research and development in teaching and learning in the UK and its implementation in practice.

The new Council might take over and expand the remit of an existing organisation such as the National Council for Educational Technology, which was established by the Government to be the national focus of expertise for technology in learning. The body which we envisage would, however, be concerned with innovation in teaching and learning across all sectors of education and training. It would provide a focus for all research investment and an infrastructure to encourage greater productivity. It could work through regionally-based teaching and learning centres, perhaps based in university schools of education, providing high-quality resources and expertise for schools, colleges and universities in their areas and working in partnership with them. It would concern itself particularly with practical implementation.

We emphasise strongly that the country needs full-blooded commitment to innovation in education and training which is supported by good quality research and by that element which is most conspicuous by its absence at present, the determination to implement new advances in teaching and learning and applications of new technology systematically and on a large scale.

We consider that the most important task facing the new Council will be to develop a national policy for the implementation of new approaches to teaching and learning of all kinds and to secure the commitment of Governments to give that policy unreserved backing and support.

Notes

1   Keys, W. and Fernandes, C., 1993. What **Do** Students Think About School? A Report for the National Commission on Education. National Foundation for Educational Research.

2   Adey, P., and others, 1991. Better Learning: A Report from the Cognitive Acceleration through Science Education (CASE) Project. Centre for Educational Studies, King's College, University of London.

3   Nisbet, J., 1991. In: Coles, M.J. and Robinson, W.D. (eds.). *Teaching Thinking: A Survey of Progress in Education.* Duckworth.

4   Eraut, M. and others, 1991? Flexible Learning in Schools. A Handbook Developed from the Research Project 'The Effective Management of Flexible Learning in Schools'. Employment Department.

5   Hughes, M., 1993. *Flexible Learning: Evidence Examined.* Network Educational Press Ltd.

6   Anderson, E., Headteacher, Eton College, 1993. Evidence to the Commission.

7   Boothroyd, C., 1993. Evidence to the Commission. Northumberland County Council, Education Department.

8   Committee of Scottish University Principals, 1993. Teaching and Learning in an Expanding Higher Education System. Report of a Working Party.

9   Department for Education, 1992. Information Technology in Secondary Schools. A Report by HMI. HMSO.

10 DFE, 1990. Information Technology and Special Educational Needs in Schools. A Report by HMI. HMSO.

11 Wirral Metropolitan College, 1993. Evidence to the Commission.

12 DFE, 1993. Survey of Information Technology in Schools. *Statistical Bulletin 6/93.*

13 Office for Standards in Education, 1993. Evidence to the Commission.

14 Watson, D. and others, 1993. The Impact Report. An Evaluation of

the Impact of Information Technology on Children's Achievements in Primary and Secondary Schools. King's College, London.

15 National Council for Educational Technology, 1993. Investing in IT. Guidelines for Headteachers on the Purchase of IT Equipment. NCET.

16 OFSTED, 1993. The Use of Educational Broadcasts in Primary Schools. Department for Education.

17 Organisation for Economic Co-operation and Development, 1992. High Quality Education and Training for All. OECD.

18 DFE, June 1992. Initial Teacher Training (Secondary Phase). Circular No. 9/92.

19 Information Technology in Initial Teacher Training Expert Group, chaired by Miss J. Trotter, 1989. Information Technology in Initial Teacher Training. HMSO.

20 Laurillard, D., 1993. *Rethinking University Teaching: A Framework for the Effective Use of Educational Technology*. Routledge.

6
A Good Start in Education

Introduction

Throughout the United Kingdom there are wide variations in provision for children below compulsory school age. Some pre-school services have explicit educational aims, while others are concerned mainly with day care, and some offer a combination of day care and education. Some children are taught free of charge by trained teachers in nursery schools or classes. Others attend playgroups or nurseries for which their parents pay, and many are in the care of paid childminders. Children needing specialist help may be in day nurseries run by social services departments. A minority has no experience of pre-school groups of any kind outside the home. This diversity does not mean effective choice for parents, still less the guarantee of high quality educational experience for young children.

How important is it for children to receive education before they reach compulsory school age? It may be argued that, when resources are in short supply, we should concentrate public funds on compulsory schooling and on education and training to equip young people for work. Indeed, the view of the Department for Education is that school-age children should have priority, and that the extent and nature of provision for younger children is a matter for local authorities and schools to decide.[1]

That view ignores the significance of the first five years of a child's life in preparing 'the foundation for all skills and later learning'.[2] In these early years a high percentage of children's learning takes place. They grow in their physical competence, in their knowledge of how the world works, and in their skills for getting on with others. It is a time when children establish attitudes and behaviour patterns which are vital for future learning progress and social development. They also begin to develop a sense of self, and of self-esteem, which helps educational achievement later.[3] Thus, by confining attention solely to compulsory education, opportunities to increase attainment are neglected.

Children do not begin school with equal chances of benefiting from it. It is estimated that just under a third of under-5s – a higher proportion than of all children – live in households with less than 50% of the national average income.[4] Poverty and the associated problems of poor housing, inadequate nutrition and ill-health create stressful conditions for parents raising families and can jeopardise children's success in school. Over 20% of young people in some poor urban areas in England leave school without qualifications, compared with about 9% in the country as a whole.

Educational achievement is strongly associated with family background. Parental education, particularly the level of education achieved by the mother, has a powerful influence on children's educational progress. When the mother herself has not had the benefit of a good education or learned to recognise its value, there is a risk that her child's early learning experience will be impoverished unless there is outside help.

Our society is becoming increasingly multicultural. For

many schoolchildren English is not the language spoken at home. This is true of more than a quarter of 7-year-olds in Bradford, for example. Results from the national tests of 7-year-olds revealed, not surprisingly, that such children tended to perform less well than those whose mother tongue was English. Pre-school education which helps ethnic minority children to develop their English language skills will therefore have positive benefits.

Even at the beginning of the infant school stage, differences in children's skills are apparent and these differences tend to persist throughout primary schooling and beyond. Indeed, studies show that pupils' early attainment at school is a good indicator of later educational success, and perhaps a more reliable indicator than family background.[5] This underlines the importance of encouraging success from the earliest possible moment.

It is essential that when children start school they are ready to take advantage of what school has to offer. Pre-school education alone cannot ensure that, but it can make a significant difference. If we are determined to seek every worthwhile opportunity to improve children's chances of learning to succeed, the potential offered by good early childhood education must be seized.

This chapter examines the case for greater investment in high-quality provision for under-5s. We consider the evidence on the effects of pre-school provision, and go on to discuss the demand created by changes in the family, in employment patterns and in social conditions. Next we review the extent and quality of present arrangements. We conclude with recommendations for expansion and improvement. Our main concern is with educational services rather than day care, though we argue that the two cannot be separated.

Effects of Early Childhood Education

Those who wish to expand and improve pre-school education are under pressure to justify any claims for increased resources by demonstrating that better services will result in measurable long-term benefits. This is a difficult proposition since any benefits which a child experiences as a result of attending a nursery class or playgroup will clearly be affected by subsequent experience in school. For example, nursery provision may advance children's language development, but the extent to which this progress is sustained will be influenced by the quality of language teaching at primary school. A specially-designed and well-controlled longitudinal research project would be required in order to provide reliable evidence, and such a study has not yet been carried out in this country.

The research which has already been undertaken, supported by informed opinion, does provide convincing evidence of the beneficial impact which good pre-school services can have on young children's learning and social behaviour. Studies in the USA and in the UK have amply demonstrated this potential. A summary of some important indicators is offered here.

A large-scale study which examined the relationship between children's pre-school experiences and their attainment at 5 and 10 years of age reported marked differences in ability, attainment and behaviour at age 10 between those who had attended pre-school groups and those who had not.[6] The authors concluded that children from small home-based playgroups (in predominantly middle-class areas) and children from nursery schools did particularly well.

A small study of working-class children during their first year in primary school reported that 'graduates' of well-resourced local authority nursery education showed certain advantages in their ability to settle into school, compared with children who had attended poorly resourced playgroups.[7] Children from nursery classes were more likely to play in a purposeful and creative way, to persevere when they encountered difficulties in their school work, to engage in connected conversation, and to show greater motivation for school, spending more time on 'academic' tasks.

One researcher in Britain has pioneered highly structured enrichment programmes for pre-school children, demonstrating that it is possible to reduce the gap between the academic performance of disadvantaged and advantaged pupils.[8] This study also suggests that parental involvement in pre-school education can have beneficial effects on the younger siblings of the child receiving education.

In the United States, a review of a wide range of pre-school programmes concluded that early intervention to provide for the children of low income families can have measured effects throughout childhood and into adolescence.[9] Children who had participated in pre-school programmes were more likely to succeed in school, showed better self-esteem, had more realistic vocational expectations and were prouder of their achievements. Important features of these projects were that they were all carefully designed and well-supported, with high ratios of adults to children and active parental involvement.

An American programme known as the High/Scope Perry Preschool Project has attracted considerable attention in the UK, due in part to the striking cost/benefit claims which have been made.[10] High/Scope was a high-quality, active learning pre-school programme which concentrated on guided play. Adults encouraged and supported children in planning and reviewing their own activities, helping them to develop persistence and to believe in their talents.

The project has followed the lives of 123 children from disadvantaged African American families, comparing those who took part in the pre-school programme with a control group of children who stayed at home. The participants were regularly assessed during childhood and into adulthood, most recently at age 27.

Throughout their school years, the High/Scope children did better than their peers who had not attended the nursery programme, spent less time in remedial classes and were more likely to have completed school or training. As adults, they were more likely to have jobs, to own homes, and to be higher paid, and were less likely to have received social services assistance or to have been involved in crime. It has been calculated that for every dollar invested in the children who attended the programme, $7.16 (after controlling for inflation) is returned to the tax-payer by way of savings on the costs of juvenile delinquency, remedial education, income support and joblessness.

The case for investment in early education rather than reliance on remedial programmes has been made in England by the Family Policy Studies Centre.[11] It argues in a recent report that pre-school provision, by giving children an educational 'head start', encourages school success and thereby makes an important contribution to reducing the danger that children will be attracted to delinquent peer groups and criminal activities.

Effects of Day Care

Many under-5s in the UK are placed in centres or nurseries which are predominantly concerned with day care rather than education, and children of working parents often experience a mixture of both.

Where there are above average levels of day care, where the quality of the care is high, or where the children come from a mixed social background, there have been positive results.[12] In Sweden for instance, where local authority nurseries are available to families from all walks of life, it has emerged that day care experience can give children a better start in school. In the USA, it has been found that children who attend high-quality nurseries subsequently perform well in educational and social assessments at school. Encouraging evidence also comes from a study in Manchester.[13] There, levels of day care are above average, and day care children are reported to be socially and intellectually ahead of children who do not have this experience.

In one UK study day care children performed less well towards the end of primary school compared with other children. This result must be qualified by the observation that publicly-funded day care in the UK is usually highly selective, concentrating on children from families known to be in need, who require a high degree of support which day care staff may not always be well-qualified to give. We should also ask whether the quality of the curriculum offered in day care centres and nurseries is high enough. A recent study found that staff in nurseries run by social services were less well-equipped to provide a high-quality nursery curriculum than teachers in the education sector.[14]

Changing Employment Patterns and Social Conditions

The potential advantages to later learning form an important aspect of the case for good early years provision. Many parents, however, would see the issue in far more immediate terms. For them, financial need, the demands of work and the daily stresses of family life loom large.

Social and employment conditions have changed, creating new needs and expectations.

The growth of two-earner households, the rise in the proportion of children living in single-parent families, and the increase in family breakdown and divorce all have a bearing on the quality of children's lives. Children in remote rural areas as well as those living in high-rise flats in urban areas suffer from isolation, lacking social contact and safe places to play. This led a parliamentary committee in 1988 to say that the case for under-5s provision should not be put solely in terms of longer-term benefits.[15] Pre-school education 'is not merely a preparation for something else, but caters for the child's needs at that time and may be justified in those terms'.

Women's participation in the labour market is growing. In future, women's employment patterns will resemble those of men far more closely than in the past. Already, women account for 49% of employees in the UK. Employment rates for women with a child under 5 are rising: 43% in Great Britain were in full- or part-time work in 1991 compared with 35% in 1987 and 30% in 1985. It is estimated that 48% of women in Great Britain with children under 5 will be in employment by 2001.[16] With improvements in day care provision and greater flexibility of working hours, and assuming an expansion in the national economy to allow more women to work, this rate could increase to 65%.[17]

For lone mothers, employment rates are lower, though the need for paid work is arguably greater. The rate of full-time employment among lone mothers with a child under 5 in the UK is the lowest in the EC. Surveys suggest that many non-working mothers would like to take up employment if suitable, affordable child care could be found.

Child poverty is associated with mothers not working. In 1988–9, dependent children in single-parent families without work were over-represented among those in the bottom 20% of the income distribution, accounting for 29%. In the child population as a whole, approximately 18% were estimated to live in single-parent families in 1991, compared with 11.4% in 1981.

It is claimed in a recent study that analysis of the costs and benefits of expanded public child care shows that there would be economic benefits to the Exchequer resulting from tax paid by women working, and from a reduction in the dependence of families on state benefits.[18] There would be potential to generate new income (with tax flowbacks) from extra jobs in child care. In addition, it is suggested that women's pay and career opportunities would be enhanced: their loss of earnings from time spent caring for children would be smaller, and increased work experience would give them access to higher incomes.

Major employers are now calling for 'a national strategy for accessible, available, affordable, quality child care' on the grounds that this would help companies to be competitive in world markets and prevent wastage of resources invested in the training of female employees who are unable to continue their careers after the birth of their children.[19]

What the Evidence Tells Us

The Commission draws the following conclusions from its review of research and other evidence:

1 To make an effective contribution to children's later learning and behaviour, and reduce the need for remedial work, early childhood education and care services must be of high quality: well-resourced, with appropriately trained staff and suitable adult to child ratios.

2 A high-quality nursery curriculum is one which enables children to enter school with a positive outlook, by developing self-esteem, commitment to

learning, and a belief that if they try, they can succeed. The curriculum should value and give expression to children's different cultural backgrounds. It should encourage all children's language development, paying particular attention to the needs of those whose mother tongue is not English.

3 Early childhood programmes are more likely to succeed where there is effective parental involvement. This does not mean that involving parents can be an alternative to employing sufficient numbers of highly qualified professionals. Nor does it imply that all parents will be willing or able to accept the same degree of involvement. The message we wish to convey is that pre-school programmes create opportunities for professionals to support parents in their role as 'first educators' of their children, and to establish from a very early stage the idea of parent-professional partnership based on mutual respect and a shared purpose.

4 Good pre-school programmes can be particularly beneficial for children from disadvantaged backgrounds and for those over the age of 3.

5 There is value in developing services which cater for all children, rather than segregating and hence stigmatising children from the neediest families.

6 Good pre-school services will help to reduce the stress on families and children, particularly those living on low incomes, and contribute to lifting children out of poverty by enabling mothers to work.

7 As part of wider employment and social policies, good pre-school education and affordable child care will help parents to reconcile the demands of responsible parenting and work outside the home.

8 Better provision for under-5s will yield benefits for the economy.

Under-5s Provision in the UK

We illustrate five aspects of provision for under-5s, concentrating mainly on educational provision in maintained nursery and primary schools:

- growth in participation;
- the uneven spread of provision;
- the different treatment of 3- and 4-year-olds;
- 4-year-olds in infant classes;
- the diversity of providers.

Growth in participation
There has been a substantial increase since 1980–81 in the number of pupils under 5 attending all types of school (both maintained and independent) in the UK, as Table 6.1 shows.[20] Overall, the numbers have increased by 39%. This represents a growth in participation of 8.5 percentage points, mostly attributable to part-time attendance. About 50% of 3- and 4-year-olds attended school in 1990–91.

Table 6.1 Pupils aged under 5 attending all types of school, 1980–81 and 1990–91, United Kingdom.

	All pupils aged under 5		
	1980–81 (Thous)	*1990–91 (Thous)*	*Increase*
Mode of attendance			
Full-time	326	406	+25%
Part-time	247	394	+60%
All pupils	573	799	+39%
Participation rate	44.3%	52.8%	+8.5

Source: Government Statistical Service.[20]

Uneven spread of provision

It is important to note that Northern Ireland differs from the rest of the United Kingdom in having a compulsory school age of 4 rather than 5. Children who reach the age of 4 by 1 July start school in the following September, a policy which was introduced from 1990–91. In Scotland, children who reach the age of 5 by the last day of February are required to start school in the previous August. Elsewhere in the UK, children are not legally required to attend school until the term following their fifth birthday.

Publicly-funded provision for under-5s is unevenly spread in the United Kingdom, as Table 6.2 illustrates. In Wales, 68% of under-5s were receiving education in 1992, compared with 49% in England. More than a third of under-5s in Wales and Scotland were in nursery schools and classes, compared with a quarter in England. The percentage of under-5s taught in infant classes ranged from 32% in Wales and Northern Ireland to 7% in Scotland.

Table 6.2 All pupils under 5 in public sector schools, 1991–2.

| | | *Percentage of 3- and 4-year-olds* | |
	Nursery schools and nursery classes	*Infant classes*	*Total*
England	26	23	49
Wales	36	32	68
Scotland	34	7	41
N. Ireland	15	32	47

Sources: See note.[21]

There are also variations within countries.[22] For example, in all but one Welsh authority over 50% of 3- and 4-year-olds received education, while in England the percentage of under-5s in nursery and primary schools ranged from under 20% in three authorities (Bromley, West Sussex and Wiltshire) to over 80% in six authorities, including five metropolitan areas. In two English authorities – Cleveland and Walsall – over 90% of under-5s received education.

Different treatment of 3- and 4-year-olds
Of particular interest is the differing nature of provision made for 3- and 4-year-olds, shown in Table 6.3. Here, Northern Ireland's compulsory school age of 4 rather than 5 must be borne in mind.

Table 6.3 Three- and four-year-olds in public sector schools, 1992.

	Population		Pupils in nursery schools & nursery classes and participation rate				Pupils in infant classes in primary schools and participation rate			
	Aged 3	Aged 4	Aged 3		Aged 4		Aged 3		Aged 4	
	Thous	*Thous*	*Thous*	*%*	*Thous*	*%*	*Thous*	*%*	*Thous*	*%*
England	655	632	247	37.7	55	8.7	1	0.2	299	47.3
Wales	39	39	16	41.6	10	25.3	1	3.7	24	62.1
Scotland	67	65	12	18.6	32	49.2	0	0	9	14.5
N. Ireland	26	26	4	15.0	4	14.8	0	0	17	63.1

Sources: See note.[23]

In England, more than a third (38%) of 3-year-olds were receiving education, the vast majority in nursery rather than in primary provision. Over 50% of 4-year-olds were receiving education, but most of these were placed in infant classes in primary schools, normally on a full-time basis. This type of provision may not always be suitable for such young children, as we indicate in the next section of the chapter. Scotland presented a different pattern, with 49% of 4-year-olds in nursery schools and classes, and under 15% in infant classes. In Scotland and Northern

Ireland, under 20% of 3-year-olds received education.

In the case of England, there were marked contrasts in the patterns of provision adopted by local authorities.[24] For example, Gloucestershire had no nursery schools or nursery classes, but admitted 94% of rising 5s and younger 4-year-olds to infant classes in primary schools. Birmingham admitted 97% of 4-year-olds to infant classes, but also catered for substantial numbers of 3-year-olds in nursery schools and classes. In Hillingdon only 5% of 4-year-olds entered infant classes; overall, 50% of under-5s were in pre-school provision, the majority in nursery classes.

Four-year-olds in infant classes

Growing parental demand for under-5s provision, combined with a shortage of nursery education places, and the availability of spare capacity in primary schools, has led to many children being admitted early to primary school, sometimes a year before they reach statutory school age. Early admission has become widespread in England and Wales, with only a minority of the age group attending nursery schools and classes.

Compulsory schooling in the UK starts earlier than in many other European countries. In France, Italy and Belgium, children start at age 6, in Germany between 6 and 7, and in Denmark at 7. One researcher warned in 1989 that in this country: 'if present trends continue, it will not be many years before virtually all children enter primary school before they are 5. The age of starting school will have become 4, in practice if not in statute.'[25] As we have noted, it is now statutory in Northern Ireland for children to start school at age 4.

It has been recognised that provision in infant classes can have serious drawbacks for 4-year-olds. The worry is that 'classroom organisation, curriculum objectives and teaching styles designed with one age group in mind are being applied to children up to a year younger'.[26] To this might be added unsuitable class sizes, inappropriate ratios of adults to children in the classroom, and an over-long school day. Indeed, local authority inspectors and advisers in England argued in evidence to a Parliamentary Select Committee in 1988 that it could be harmful to impose on 4-year-olds a curriculum designed for 5- and 6-year-olds.

The situation is different in Northern Ireland. Given the earlier compulsory school age, the national curriculum for the first year of primary school is designed to meet the developmental needs of 4-year-olds, concentrating on learning through experience and emphasising play. There are, however, concerns about the appropriateness of the provision made in primary classes for 4-year-olds who have not yet reached compulsory school age in September but join a class of more experienced pupils later in the year.

When HM Inspectors surveyed nursery and primary schools in England in the mid-1980s, they concluded that nursery schools and classes generally offered a broader, better balanced education for under-5s than infant classes.[27] Only a small number of the infant classes in their survey demonstrated work that was well-suited to under-5s; in most, the curriculum was not sufficiently matched to their educational needs.

The initial training of teachers in reception classes in England is a cause for concern. No up-to-date national information is published, but we note that a survey released in 1990 showed that only 12% of a sample of these teachers had initial training relating to under-5s.[28] Forty per cent were trained for age groups over the age of 7.

Some improvements are becoming apparent as a result of efforts by LEA early years advisers and teachers to adapt the curriculum and teaching methods to the needs of 4-year-olds. In a report on standards in education in 1990–91, HMI stated that in primary school reception and mixed-age classes, 'the standards of work and the curriculum for 4-year-olds ranged from good to poor but in general were better matched to pupils' needs than in previous years.'[29] Fears that the introduction of the national curriculum would result in 'the force-feeding of under-5s with inappropriate work' have proved unfounded, according to the inspectors. They believe that the national curriculum is exerting a beneficial effect: as early years teachers now have more certain knowledge of what will be taught in the first stage of the national curriculum, they are better able to plan a balanced programme for under-5s.

The ratio of adults to children is improving in some schools, where, for example, schools have used the freedom offered by local management to recruit non-teaching assistants and are deploying them to work with the youngest children.

It is vital that when children begin schooling it should not be a distressing and alienating experience. Even for those who have had the benefit of pre-school provision, starting school can prove daunting, and studies have found that between 13% and 15% of children have difficulties in adjusting.[30] More provision for under-5s does not necessarily mean better provision; improvements in quantity need to be combined with greater quality. Attention must be given to ensuring that, when they enter school, children are ready to benefit from the more formal structure it offers.

Information was not available to enable the Commission to reach a comprehensive and accurate judgement about the quality of provision for 4-year-olds in infant classes. A new survey by HMI on standards in reception classes (which some schools provide for children admitted before the age of 5) was awaited when we completed our report.

A diversity of providers

We have so far concentrated chiefly on provision for under-5s in maintained nursery and primary schools. However, a key feature of present arrangements is the great diversity of agencies in the maintained, private and voluntary sectors offering different kinds of services, some educational, some primarily concerned with day care, and some combining the two. Briefing No. 8 for the Commission outlines the five major categories: nursery education (including nursery schools and nursery classes in primary schools); reception classes which admit children under compulsory school age; day nurseries; playgroups; and childminders.[31] Within the range there is a mixture of public and private provision.

The huge increase in private services – private nurseries, playgroups and childminders – is evident from Table 6.4. The largest category, in terms of the number of places, is that of playgroups. Parents' ability to pay is clearly a strong determining factor in the kind of early education and care which children receive. It is important to note that most playgroups offer approximately two sessions (a total of five hours) per week, whereas most nursery education takes up two and a half hours per day. With regard not only to the balance of public and private provision, but also to the number of hours offered, the UK may be thought to compare unfavourably with other EC countries, offering publicly-funded provision for less than 50% of children between the age of 3 and the start of compulsory schooling. This contrasts sharply with over 95% in France and Belgium; 85% in Denmark and Italy; and 77% in Germany.

Table 6.4 Number of places in early childhood care and education provision, 1980, 1991, England.

| | | | Number and percentages |
Type of provision	1980	1991	% change 1980–1991
Nursery education	130,997	177,863	+36
Reception class	205,673	272,178	+32
Local authority day nurseries	28,437	27,039	–5
Private nurseries	22,017	79,029	+259
Playgroups	367,868	428,420	+16
Childminders	98,495	233,258	+137

Source: Sylva, K. and Moss, P., November 1992.[32]

We recognise that the picture of educational provision for under-5s is not static. For example, following the May 1993 county council elections some new councils are adopting policies to extend or improve their nursery education provision. Our review of the available data indicates, however, that there are insufficient high-quality nursery education places for 3- and 4-year-olds to meet the demands of the next century. Though there is diversity, there is unequal access and limited effective choice for parents. While we acknowledge that the quality of what is offered to 4-year-olds in primary schools in England is improving, it is important to register the weight of concern expressed in evidence to the Commission that much provision for this age group remains inappropriate.

How Much Does Present Provision Need to Improve?

Several reports have attempted to gauge the shortfall in provision of education and care services. There are many difficulties in assessing the volume of unmet demand for different types of service and it is unlikely that this can be predicted accurately. Research for the National Children's Bureau has concluded that a mixture of provision will continue to be required: a choice of educational provision as between nursery schools/classes and playgroups, and also a mix of care and education.[33] For example, by concentrating solely on nursery education, we would risk neglecting the most disadvantaged children, whose parents need ready access to a combination of day care and education facilities.

In 1972, a Government White Paper (Education: A Framework for Expansion) recommended that educational provision should be sufficient to cater for 50% of 3-year-olds and 90% of 4-year-olds. Given the increase in demand for under-5s provision since that date, these figures might need to be revised upwards: the National Children's Bureau study suggests targets of 85% of 3-year-olds and 95% of 4-year-olds.

How do these targets compare with present levels of provision? As shown in Table 6.3, 38% of 3-year-olds and 56% of 4-year-olds in England were in maintained nursery and primary schools in 1992. A small percentage (around 4%) was in independent and special schools. Assuming no increase in this proportion, we would need to see provision for 3-year-olds in nursery and primary schools more than doubled, and that for 4-year-olds increased by two-thirds, if these targets are to be reached solely on the basis of the maintained sector.

There are indications that parents prefer pre-school settings with educational objectives. This does not imply an exclusive preference for nursery education in the form of nursery schools and classes: some diversity of provision seems more likely to meet parents' wishes. Playgroups represent a major proportion of all under-5s provision. Many are excellent, but quality within this sector is known to be highly variable, and concern has been expressed about under-resourcing, inadequate premises, lack of suitable equipment, insufficient training, and high staff turnover. If playgroups are improved – by employing more staff with suitable qualifications, offering greater local authority support, increasing the number of sessions for each child and making more places available free of charge – they are likely to meet part of the demand for nursery education.

We have noted that it is difficult to judge the amount of improvement needed in primary school provision for 4-year-old children who are below the compulsory age for starting school. A Parliamentary Committee recommended in 1988 that: 'no further steps be taken by LEAs towards introducing 3- and 4-year-olds into inappropriate primary school settings.'[34] The National Children's Bureau's study assumed limited expansion in primary school provision for under-5s to keep up with the expected increase in the number of children aged 3 and 4; the main expansion to meet demand would come from nursery schools and classes.[35] That report, like the Parliamentary report and that of the Committee of Inquiry which advised the DES in 1990,[36] called for current primary provision for 4-year-olds to be brought up to the standard of good nursery education.

Recommendations

High-quality publicly-funded education provision should be available for all 3- and 4-year-olds. The opportunity for every child to learn to succeed right from the start should not rest on such factors as:

> where a child lives, when his or her birthday is, whether the parents have access to information about services and whether they can afford fees where there is no public provision.[37]

There is both demand and need for a diversity of early childhood services in the UK, with an emphasis on provision which offers a high-quality educational component specifically designed to meet the learning needs of children under compulsory school age, and with educational facilities well co-ordinated with day care. Over a number of years, a consensus about the value of good pre-school provision has grown: action should now be taken to ensure that well rehearsed and desirable aims are put into practice as soon as possible.

Although we have concentrated on the needs of 3- and 4-year-olds as a matter of priority, we are aware that increasing numbers of children under the age of 3 are cared for away from home. Educational policies should also address their needs. Many special educational needs, for example, can be identified before the child is 3 years old. There is a case for regarding 0–5 as the first stage in our education system.

As to the type of educational provision we would advocate, the ideal would seem to be an expansion of nursery education based on nursery schools and nursery classes in primary schools. However, because of the wide variety and levels of provision existing in different parts of the UK, we favour a more pragmatic approach at this stage, taking account of the current state of provision in each local authority, whilst not compromising on quality. A range of providers could contribute to an expansion of nursery education, provided that they offer learning programmes of good quality which match the developmental needs of the children they serve.

A statutory nursery education service

This leads us to recommend a national strategy for improving early childhood education and care. A major component should be a statutory requirement on local authorities to ensure that sufficient high-quality, publicly-funded nursery education places are available for all 3- and 4-year-olds whose parents wish it. Places should be offered on a half-time basis for 3-year-olds and on a full-time basis for 4-year-olds, though with reasonable flexibility to cater for children requiring shorter or less frequent periods of attendance. This goal can be achieved by developing a range of facilities in accordance with local circumstances, children's needs and parental preferences.

National standards
As a first step, national criteria should be devised to ensure that all facilities meet the educational standards of good nursery schools and classes. These should cover:

1 A curriculum for 3- and 4-year-olds, which we believe should be broadly defined and not unduly prescriptive.

2 The training and continuing professional development of education and care workers.

3 Teacher to pupil and adult to child ratios in all types of settings for the education and care of under-5s.

By 'curriculum' we do not imply an excessively formal school-based programme, but one which is geared to the needs of young children and emphasises first-hand experience and the central role of play and talk in learning and development.

We place particular emphasis on appropriate training. Whether in day care facilities, playgroups, nursery schools and classes or in primary school infant classes, the education of children under compulsory school age should be the responsibility of staff with an appropriate early years education qualification. Teaching very young children is a complex task demanding a high level of skill and understanding. The Commission supports graduate-level training. We welcome the efforts now being made to establish a variety of routes to qualification, including higher level NVQs, and modular degrees specialising in early childhood study, which might be combined with teacher training. Consideration should also be given to incorporating a multiprofessional dimension in training, so that both child care and education are covered.

Developing these standards and preparing advice on implementation for local managers and practitioners should be a task for the national authorities concerned with the curriculum and with teacher management, drawing on the guidelines already proposed by the Government's Committee of Inquiry into the quality of education for 3- and 4-year-olds.[38] Implementing and monitoring the standards should be a matter for local Education and Training Boards – the organisations which the Commission suggests establishing in the place of Local Education Authorities, and which we describe in Chapter 13.

Targets for improvement
National standards should be accompanied by targets for improvement. The Commission recommends the following:

- within 5 years at most, nursery education places, meeting nationally agreed standards, for children in deprived areas within each local authority. We emphasise that this target should be seen as part of a wider plan to provide places for all children in the longer term, to avoid attaching social stigma to provision for the neediest children;

- within the present decade, nursery education places,

meeting nationally agreed standards, in every local authority area to cater for a minimum of 60% of all 3- and 4-year-olds;

- within 5 years thereafter, sufficient nursery education places, meeting nationally agreed standards, in every local authority area to cater for 95% of 4-year-olds and 85% of 3-year-olds.

Local reviews of nursery education

We recommend that Education and Training Boards develop and publish plans, no later than 1995, for improving under-5s provision. To identify the amount of improvement needed to meet the targets, the Boards should mount reviews of the availability and quality of services. Wide consultation with providers, including private and voluntary agencies, as well as with members of the public, should be a feature of the reviews.

Under the Children Act 1989, local authorities are already required to carry out three-yearly reviews of their services for young children, taking into account the educational input into any child care setting. The local reviews which we recommend would build on these arrangements. Co-operation between different departments within local authorities, particularly education, social services and health, will be essential in overcoming fragmented policies and provision. Encouraging progress in this direction is already happening as a result of the Children Act.

Following publication of plans for under-5s provision, it should be the responsibility of Education and Training Boards to secure suitable nursery education places in sufficient numbers and to monitor progress towards local and national targets. Continuing high standards should be promoted through the local and national inspection system which we describe in Chapter 13.

Several issues should receive particular attention in the local reviews:

1 The quality of education offered to under-5s in infant classes in primary schools. For example, what proportion of teachers are trained early years specialists? What is the ratio of adults to children in infant classes? How big are the teaching groups to which children are allocated? Are the needs of 4-year-olds well met by the curriculum, the teaching methods used and the length of the sessions?

2 Priorities which demand targeted resources in the short term. Education and Training Boards should concentrate funding for immediate expansion and improvement on deprived areas, in order to help children living in areas of urban disadvantage or rural isolation. Other needs which might give rise to targeted pre-school provision would include children with special educational needs and children whose mother tongue is not English. The Boards' overall plans for nursery education should take account of their duty under the Children Act 1989 to make provision for individual children identified as being 'in need'.

3 The availability of suitable, affordable day care and out of school care linked with education. Parental choice of under-5s provision is influenced by ease of access. Some may want a combination of education and care services. Many may, of necessity, opt for whole-day care arrangements of poor quality because nursery education is part-time. From the point of view of the individual child who may experience both kinds of services in the course of a day or week, a certain continuity of aims and standards between different types of provision is desirable. The extent of co-ordination between care and education services is therefore an important matter, and we note with approval that in several local authorities, all pre-school services are now under the responsibility of the education department. For all these reasons, the

availability and quality of day care facilities, and the
identification of requirements for additional public
funding, should form part of local reviews.

Some authorities have recognised the value of an
integrated approach by setting up combined nursery
centres, jointly funded by education and social services departments, offering both day care and nursery
education, often in conjunction with other family
support services. By 1990, no more than about 50
such centres existed. Local reviews should consider
the benefits of this model in responding to the needs
of disadvantaged areas.

Funding

Finally, the issue of funding for improvement must be
addressed. Central government funds directed to
Education and Training Boards for nursery education
should be based on an assessment of the number of 3-
and 4-year-olds in the population, the amount of local
provision already in existence, and additional needs created by local targets for expansion and improvement. It will
not be sufficient to consider the cost of expanding nursery
schools and classes: government funding will also be
needed to enhance the quality of the educational experience offered in playgroups, nurseries, and for children
below compulsory school age in infant classes. The
Commission believes that, where insufficient places are
available in maintained nursery education, the educational element of playgroup and day care provision should be
free of charge.

The great diversity and unevenness of present provision
make it difficult to calculate with any precision how much
additional expenditure will be required to achieve the
Commission's aims for nursery education. We estimate
that to provide nursery education of good quality
(whether in nursery schools and classes or in playgroups

and day care settings) to meet our long-term target of provision for 85% of 3-year-olds and 95% of 4-year-olds will eventually require additional annual expenditure of approximately £860 million, excluding capital expenditure. Possible mechanisms for raising education funding for this and other purposes are illustrated in Chapter 14.

To set against expenditure on developing a high-quality education service for under-5s, the Commission stresses the hidden cost of taking no action. We are persuaded that the gains made by children who receive high-quality pre-school education will reduce the need for remedial education at a later stage, help to ensure that we do not waste talent, and perhaps also reduce the social costs which arise from youth unemployment and juvenile crime.

To ensure that Education and Training Boards are locally accountable for their decisions, information about the amount of central government funds passed to the Boards for nursery education purposes should be made public.

The issue of day care funding is not part of the Commission's remit, except in respect of improving the quality of the educational component of care. We recognise that there is considerable unmet demand for day care and out-of-school care for young children. We note that, in 1991, the National Children's Bureau claimed that a fourfold expansion in day care places was required. The Commission's view is that high-quality day care should receive public subsidy, and that parents should pay for it according to their means.

Through national and local commitment to improved standards, coupled with short- and long-term targets for expansion in provision, we can begin to make progress towards three goals: giving every child the opportunity of a good foundation for learning; removing inequalities in provision across the country; and bringing the UK into line with the levels of pre-school services offered in many other parts of the European Community.

Notes

1   Department for Education, March 1993. Questions Addressed to the Department for Education by the NCE. A Note by DFE.
2   Pugh, G., November 1992. An Equal Start for All Our Children? The Second *Times Educational Supplement*/Greenwich Lecture.
3   Keys, W. and Fernandes, C., 1993. What **Do** Students Think About School? A Report for the National Commission on Education. National Foundation for Educational Research, Part II, p. 12.
4   Cohen, B. and Fraser, N., 1991. Childcare in a Modern Welfare System. Towards a New National Policy. Institute for Public Policy Research.
5   Mortimore, P. and others, 1988. *School Matters*. Open Books.
6   Osborn, A. F. and Milbank, J.E., 1987. *The Effects of Early Education. A Report from the Child Health and Education Study*. Oxford University Press.
7   Jowett, S. and Sylva, K., 1986. 'Does Kind of Pre-School Matter?' *Educational Research*, 28 (1), 21–31.
8   Athey, C., 1990. *Extending Thought in Young Children*. Paul Chapman Publishing.
9   Consortium of Longitudinal Studies, 1983. *As the Twig is Bent: Lasting Effects of Pre-School Programmes*. Lawrence Erlbaum Associates.
10 Schweinhart, L. J. and Weikart, D. P., 1993. A Summary of 'Significant Benefits: the High/Scope Perry Preschool Study through Age 27'. High/Scope UK.
11 Utting, D. and others, June 1993. Crime and the Family. Improving Child-Rearing and Preventing Delinquency. Family Policy Studies Centre Occasional Paper 16.
12 Pugh, G., *op cit*.
13 Howes, C., 1990. 'Can the Age of Entry into Child Care and the Quality of Child Care Predict Adjustment in Kindergarten?' *Developmental Psychology*, 26 (2), pp. 292–303.
14 Sylva, K. and others, 1992. 'The Impact of the UK National Curriculum on Pre-School Practice: Some 'Top-Down' Processes at Work.' *International Journal of Early Education*, 24, pp. 40–53.
15 House of Commons Education, Science and Arts Committee, January 1989. Educational Provision for the Under Fives. HMSO.
16 Holtermann, S., 1992. Investing in Young Children. Costing an Education and Day Care Service. National Children's Bureau Early Childhood Unit.
17 *Ibid*.
18 Cohen, B. and Fraser, N., 1991, *op cit*
19 Employers for Childcare, May 1993. Good Childcare, Good Business.
20 Government Statistical Service, 1993. Education Statistics for the

United Kingdom. 1992 Edition, Table B page 4 and notes.

21 Sources:
England: Department for Education. *Statistical Bulletin* 11/93, May 1993.
Wales: Welsh Office. Pupil count as at January 1992. Ages as at 31 December 1991.
Scotland: Scottish Office Education Department. School Census September 1991.
Northern Ireland: Department of Education. Pupil count as at January 1992. Ages as at December 1991.
Note variation in pupil count between countries.

22 See:
(i)　Statistics of Education and Training in Wales: Schools. No. 1 1993. Table 2.04.
(ii)　Department for Education, *Statistical Bulletin* 11/93. Pupils Under Five Years of Age in Schools in England – January 1992.

23 Sources:
(i)　England: Based on: Department for Education. *Statistical Bulletin* 11/93. May 1993.
(ii)　Wales: Welsh Office. Pupil count as at January 1992. Ages as at 31 December 1991. Population figures are provisional mid-year estimates for June 1991.
(iii)　Scotland: Scottish Office Education Department. School Census September 1991. General Register for Scotland mid-1991 population estimates.
(iv)　Northern Ireland: Department of Education. Pupil count as at January 1992. Ages as at December 1991. Age breakdown of pupils in nursery classes estimated according to the split in nursery schools. Government Actuary Department mid-1991 population estimates.
Note variation in pupil count, age details and population estimates between countries.

24 See 2(ii).

25 Woodhead, M., 1989. 'School Starts at Five ... or Four Years Old? The Rationale for Changing Admission Policies in England and Wales.' *Journal of Education Policy*, 4 (1), pp. 1–21.

26 *Ibid*.

27 Her Majesty's Inspectorate, 1989. Aspects of Primary Education. The Education of Children Under Five. HMSO.

28 Pascal, C., 1990. *Under Fives in the Infant Classroom*. Trentham Books.

29 HMI, 1992. Education in England 1990–91. The Annual Report of HM Senior Chief Inspector of Schools. Department of Education and Science.

30 Woodhead, M., 1989, *op cit*.

31 Sylva, K. and Moss, P., November 1992. Learning before School. NCE Briefing No. 8. National Commission on Education.

32 *Ibid*, Table 1.

33 Holtermann, S., 1992, *op cit*.

34 House of Commons Education, Science and Arts Committee, 1989, *op cit.*
35 Holtermann, S., 1992, *op cit.*
36 Committee of Inquiry into the Quality of the Educational Experience Offered to 3- and 4-Year-Olds, chaired by Mrs Angela Rumbold CBE MP, 1990. Starting with Quality. HMSO.
37 *Ibid.*
38 *Ibid.*

7
Successful Schools for All

Introduction

Good schools are at the heart of good education. Raising educational achievement to much higher levels in the coming decades demands an all-round improvement in quality. Every school can increase its success, and many examples of excellent practice already offer inspiration. Outstanding leadership and commitment to good teaching are key factors. Our goal is 'a new deal in the classroom': a school environment in which every child can thrive.

We open this chapter by highlighting features of successful schools. We then focus on basic skills and ways of improving achievement in this vital area. We make recommendations on reducing class sizes to create an environment conducive to learning in the crucial early stages of schooling. Next, we take a more general look at pupils' motivation to learn and at ways of ensuring steady progress for all. Here we emphasise the importance of a positive school ethos, and make recommendations on guidance and learning support for pupils.

We respond to concerns about the education of children with special learning needs, before turning to the role of the school within its community. Then, we consider how schools can initiate improvements from within as well as working in partnership with others to bring about change. We draw attention to the urgent need to improve the achievement of some schools working in extremely difficult circumstances in deprived areas.

Finally, we look at the pattern of schools which exists in this country, and consider how this may affect the drive to promote learning for all in the twenty-first century.

Features of Success

The features which have been found most commonly to characterise successful schools may be summarised as follows:[1]

1 Strong, positive leadership by the head and senior staff.

2 A good atmosphere or spirit, generated both by shared aims and values and by a physical environment that is as attractive and stimulating as possible.

3 High and consistent expectations of all pupils.

4 A clear and continuing focus on teaching and learning.

5 Well-developed procedures for assessing how pupils are progressing.

6 Responsibility for learning shared by the pupils themselves.

7 Participation by pupils in the life of the school.

8 Rewards and incentives to encourage pupils to succeed.

9 Parental involvement in children's education and in supporting the aims of the school.

To these the Commission adds:

10 Extra-curricular activities which broaden pupils' interests and experiences, expand their opportunities to succeed, and help to build good relationships within the school.

These ten points provide a firm base for our proposals for raising achievement.

A Strong Foundation of Basic Skills

The spectrum of understanding and skills which young people need in preparation for full and active adult and working lives is becoming broader. It ranges from citizenship to familiarity with information technology, self-presentation and the ability to work well in a team. In our view the most essential life skills are literacy and numeracy, defined by ALBSU (the Adult Literacy and Basic Skills Unit) as 'the ability to read, write and speak English, and use mathematics at a level necessary to function at work and in society in general'. Sound achievement in these gives a foundation for all other learning.

Trends in literacy and numeracy standards
Literacy and numeracy, and reading skills in particular, have been at the centre of public concern about standards. Briefing No. 10 for the Commission examined the trends in performance from the late 1970s to the late 1980s.[2] It drew attention to a slight fall in reading standards among 7- to 8-year-olds in the late 1980s, but otherwise indicated little change in reading or in writing standards. In mathematics, the Briefing highlighted an improvement in performance in geometry, statistics and measures among 11- and 15-year-olds between 1982 and

1987, accompanied by a deterioration in their number skills.

The trends in mathematics are confirmed by international surveys in which English pupils are above average in geometry and statistics but below average in number work. While England's top-ability pupils at age 17-plus are among the highest scorers in mathematics, this country's below-average younger pupils do less well than those in many other developed countries. Surveys by the Assessment of Performance Unit (APU), among others, have revealed that by the age of 11 there is a very wide range of performance, and that 'the bottom 20 per cent of 15-year-olds still have a very limited grasp of even the most basic mathematical ideas'.[2]

Rising expectations

While the evidence does not demonstrate a substantial overall decline in basic skills, we believe that the expectations of employers and society are rising and will continue to do so. A minimal level of literacy is no longer adequate for 'responsible involvement in the social, economic and political life of the present day, nor to meet the specialised demands of many occupations'.[2] Culturally it has always been more acceptable to be innumerate than illiterate, but now the need for competence in mathematics is affecting more areas of daily life and work. Workplace changes are causing employers to place increasing emphasis on basic skills, and fewer jobs can now be done without these skills, particularly in reading and oral communication. Thus, young people with poor literacy and numeracy are likely to be much more vulnerable in the job market.

Attainment in basic skills at school

We lack measures of performance which directly relate literacy and numeracy attainment in school to the requirements of adult and working life. School-based literacy may not be sufficiently well connected with job-literacy. Attainment in school is measured by national curriculum assessments and by the results of GCSE examinations in English and mathematics. National curriculum assessments of 11- and 14-year-olds are not yet available.

England's GCSE results for 1991–2 show that 48% of 16-year-olds achieved grades A–C in English.[3] Seventy-nine per cent achieved grades A–E.[4] In mathematics, 37% of 16-year-olds achieved grades A–C, while 64% achieved grades A–E. Thus, a substantial minority of 21% achieved below A–E in English and a much larger minority of 36% was below this level in mathematics.

We conclude from these results that too many school leavers lack a solid foundation in literacy and numeracy. Our concern is reinforced by recent ALBSU surveys which reveal that a substantial minority of FE college students and 21-year-olds has serious problems in reading, writing, spelling or basic maths.[5] A much larger number 'seem to perform at a lower level than is required by the demands of everyday life and work in a developed, industrialised country'.

Raising achievement in basic skills
We consider that there must be a determined drive to raise performance in literacy and numeracy. It should include the following measures:

1 Early intervention. Chapter 6 advocates high-quality nursery education for all 3- and 4-year-olds which pays particular attention to the English language skills of children whose mother tongue is not English.

2 A strong emphasis on basic skills in primary school. We note the assessment made by HMI that, in primary

schools in 1990–91, 20% of work in reading and 30% of mathematics work was poor. Our primary curriculum framework, described in Chapter 4, increases the prominence given to basic skills. Later in this chapter we propose reductions in class sizes in primary schools. This should enable teachers to devote more attention to the progress of each child in acquiring basic skills.

3 Incentives and support for all pupils to improve their literacy and numeracy skills throughout schooling. Every school should make provision for pupils who need additional help or are ready to extend their skills. Such support should be easily accessible. It could, for example, include small group workshops to deal with common problems in spelling, hand-writing, reading and mathematics, or to teach advanced information handling skills. We note the dramatic improvements which can be made with appropriate use of information technology.[6]

4 Reading Recovery schemes, based on practice in New Zealand. Reading Recovery consists of intensive individual tuition, carried out by specially trained teachers, for pupils who are falling behind in their reading despite the best endeavours of their teachers and schools. It is of interest that in New Zealand around 20% of 6-year-olds were referred to the scheme in 1989 in spite of – or perhaps because of – the fact that primary schools in that country place great emphasis on reading. The cost of the New Zealand model of Reading Recovery has been esti-mated very approximately at £735 per child.[7]

5 Teacher training. We support the recommendations of the Council for the Accreditation of Teacher Education in 1992. These state that all courses of pri-mary teacher training should cover the teaching of reading, and that trainee secondary teachers should be made aware of the demands that may be made upon them to help students with reading problems

and to develop pupils' advanced reading skills.[8] It should be a requirement for all teachers – at secondary as well as primary level – to have a basic level of training in the teaching of reading and the identification of reading difficulties, and to accept responsibility for developing good reading standards among their pupils. We note that in New Zealand the time allocation for initial reading and language instruction in teacher training colleges is approximately double the minimum requirement for English in primary phase training courses in England.

6   Parental participation. The recent ALBSU survey of 21-year-olds[5] shows that there is a strong association between poor literacy and numeracy and families in which the parents are unskilled and have not gained any educational qualifications. There may be a background of low parental interest in schooling. This suggests that schools should make particular efforts to gain family co-operation in schemes to improve basic skills, for example, working alongside the parents of young children. The Commission welcomes the Government's recent decision to provide funding for ALBSU to stimulate the development of family literacy programmes and hopes that successful models will be widely implemented.

7   Well-defined standards. Work should be carried out to define appropriate standards of performance in school which reflect the changing requirements of adult and working life, and these should be kept under continuing review.

8   Opportunities beyond school. Schools alone cannot be expected to ensure that young people become literate for life: in Chapter 12 we make recommendations on ways of encouraging continual improvement in literacy and numeracy skills among adults.

Younger Children, Smaller Classes?

Can learning be improved by reducing class size in the early stages of schooling? Parents who choose to send their children to independent schools often do so because they believe that the smaller classes in these schools provide better conditions for learning. Common sense supports this: it is logical to assume that small classes allow teachers to give pupils more individual attention, which in turn leads to greater progress. Conversely, large classes in cramped accommodation can result in stressful conditions for teachers and pupils alike.

Evidence on class size

The Commission's Briefing No. 12 examines the issue of class size.[9] Although the evidence is not entirely clear-cut, research from the United States strongly indicates the advantages of small classes in the early years of schooling, particularly for the youngest pupils in a year group, for lower achievers and for pupils from deprived backgrounds. The theory that smaller classes benefit young pupils is supported by results from an evaluation of tests for 7-year-olds in England.

Younger pupils are clearly much more dependent on teachers than older pupils. This reinforces the argument for smaller classes for the youngest age range. However, as Table 7.1 demonstrates, our schools are organised on the basis that the older the pupil is, the smaller the class should be. Pupils over the age of 16 are taught in the smallest classes. The table also indicates the variation in class sizes within the UK. In Scotland, where teachers' conditions of service specify a 'normal maximum' and an 'upper limit', the average secondary school class has two or three fewer pupils than an English or Welsh class. Scotland also has the smallest primary classes.

Table 7.1 Average class size by country and phase, 1992.

| | | | *Average number of pupils* |
Phase	England	Wales	Scotland
Primary	26.8	25.4	24.7
Secondary	21.2	21.5	18.9

Source: Central Statistical Office, 1993.[10]

The primary/secondary imbalance can be illustrated further with statistics on English class sizes.[11] The average class size in primary schools has increased over the period 1983–92 by 1.6 pupils. In secondary schools, there has been little change, with the average size in 1992 roughly at the 1983 level. Over 20% of one-teacher classes in English primary schools had more than 30 pupils in 1992 compared with 4.4% in secondary schools. Only 11% of primary classes in 1992 had 20 or fewer pupils, the class size which is potentially the most effective, while the comparable figure for secondary schools was 43%.

Reducing primary class size
The Commission finds that there is a convincing case for substantial reductions in primary school class sizes. Our concern is to improve the standard of attainment as early in a pupil's career as possible. We therefore recommend the following:

- within five years it should be mandatory that no primary school pupil should be taught in classes of over 30;

- within five years classes in deprived urban areas and in schools which have high proportions of children whose mother tongue is not English should be reduced to a maximum of 20 in the first two years of primary school.

A target for maximum class size for *all* primary school classes should be set immediately and plans put in train to achieve this. We suggest a provisional target of 20, recognising that the amount of teaching and non-teaching support available to teachers will influence the manageability of classes. Criteria should be established for the amount of this support which class teachers require.

Many factors interact to produce teaching and learning of high quality. For example, the authors of Briefing No. 12 stress that 'the potential benefits of reducing class size will only occur if teachers alter their behaviour and classroom organisation'. Research should therefore be commissioned to assess the impact of different sized classes on teachers and pupils in primary and secondary schools in terms of the quality of teaching and learning and pupils' attitudes and behaviour.

It will be important to ensure that class sizes are not reduced simply by means of cuts in teachers' essential non-contact time. In Chapter 8 we note that the School Teachers' Review Body has indicated a willingness to consider a statutory minimum for primary teachers' non-contact time. The Commission regards it as a matter of priority to establish such a statutory minimum at a level of about 10 per cent of school hours, as indicated by HMI.

Our proposals for improving the balance between primary and secondary class sizes can be supported by reference to other OECD countries. The number of pupils per teacher in UK primary schools is higher than the OECD average and the differential between the two sectors is larger than in most other countries.[12] Three countries – the Netherlands, New Zealand and Sweden – depart from the general practice of allocating more teachers to secondary pupils than to primary pupils, demonstrating that it is not an immutable pattern.

Additional funding will be required to meet these

recommendations. This issue is addressed in Chapter 14.

Better Attitudes Towards School

Disenchanted pupils?
Self-esteem, attitudes towards school work, and educational aspirations are all connected with achievement. Poor achievement is naturally linked with pupils' overall attitudes towards school and learning. But the extent of poor achievement and negative attitudes is commonly misrepresented in public discussion. Sometimes the media give the impression that secondary schools are heavily populated with discontented pupils who find schooling irrelevant, and who show their disenchantment by disruptive behaviour, poor attendance and by leaving school as soon as the law permits.

The Commission's own survey of a representative sample of over 2,000 11- and 13-year-olds, carried out by the National Foundation for Educational Research (NFER), tells a different story.[13] The majority of these pupils demonstrated high expectations of learning and strong support for the value of schools. The vast majority believed that school should help them to do as well as possible in their exams and teach them things that would be useful when they entered jobs. Over 90% thought that school work was worth doing and more than 75% said that on the whole they liked being at school.

Along with this encouraging evidence there were signs of disaffection with certain aspects of school life and school work. Between the first and third years of secondary school, positive attitudes tended to deteriorate. While this may be due to a more discerning attitude on the part of the older pupils and to an unwillingness to express great enthusiasm, we are concerned that it also seems to indicate declining motivation as pupils progress through secondary school.

There is also a clear indication that a significant minority of pupils are hostile to school by the end of the first year in secondary school. Eight per cent of 11-year-olds in the survey found all or most of their lessons boring and 12% said that they did not like being at school.

Truancy

School attendance figures are an indicator of motivation. There is an identifiable pattern of truancy in secondary schools:

- less academically able pupils attend less regularly than the more able;

- attendance levels decline as the school year progresses;

- older pupils attend less regularly than younger pupils;

- attendance is lower in disadvantaged areas than in prosperous ones.

In a recent study of truancy in English secondary schools, just under a third of 14- and 15-year-olds reported that they had played truant at least once in the previous half term.[14] Eighteen per cent admitted playing truant at least once a month and over 8% at least once a week. The most common reason given was a wish to avoid particular lessons. Dissatisfaction arose from a lack of enjoyment, the irrelevance or excessive difficulty of the work, or a dislike for certain teachers. In our own survey, nearly a quarter of 13-year-olds reported that they had played truant in the past year. Most of the absence was attributable to casual truancy: a day or a lesson here and there.

Though these findings need cautious interpretation in view of the possibility that pupils exaggerated the extent of their truancy, they add support to other evidence showing that commitment to education declines through the secondary years. They also suggest a tendency for pupils to avoid those lessons which they find boring or difficult.

A positive school ethos

The NFER researchers found that pupils' positive attitudes towards school and education were associated with a 'positive school ethos'.[13] A school's ethos – its atmosphere or spirit – has a powerful impact on the effectiveness of teaching and learning. It is composed of many ingredients. In the NFER study, schools with a positive ethos were those which pupils thought had good teaching practices, such as frequent praise, high expectations and regular marking of work. Pupils also regarded such schools as having a good reputation, well-maintained premises, and clear, firm discipline.

An ethos which is conducive to good morale and high expectations among teachers as well as pupils is not a matter of accident, but a product of good management at every level. Better outcomes are likely if there are 'agreed ways of doing things which are consistent throughout the school and which have the general support of all staff'.[15] School leaders – headteachers, their senior staff and governing bodies – have a crucial role in developing and communicating the values which will encourage a sense of cohesion, shared purpose, and commitment throughout the school.

School ethos is such an important aspect of the quality of a school that it merits evaluation alongside more easily measurable outcomes, such as examination results. We therefore note with particular interest the 'ethos indicators' which the Scottish Inspectorate has developed.[16]

These help schools to examine their success by questioning parents, pupils and teachers on matters such as pupil and teacher morale, relationships within the school, leadership, discipline, communication with parents, and the physical environment.

School values
For pupils to be committed to learning, they need to feel valued at school and to feel that the curriculum is relevant to their lives and their futures. Unfortunately pupils often feel excluded from the dominant culture of their school, because of the different values which they bring from their home and community. This may be particularly so in the case of ethnic minority pupils. We recognise that it may not always be easy for teachers to respond to the different cultural identities present in a multi-ethnic school. Nevertheless, it is crucial that they strive to achieve a balance: on the one hand, celebrating diversity; on the other, helping pupils to recognise the values they all share.

Schools choose what kind of values they will emphasise. They may see their primary objective as ensuring that pupils achieve good results in examinations and that a high proportion goes on to higher education. They may take a wider view, aiming to foster not only enthusiasm for learning, but also confidence and the ability to adapt to change, to develop good relationships with others, or to take responsibility. In our view the important point is that the values which a school promotes should enable all pupils to identify with them and feel a sense of belonging.

Guiding Pupils' Progress

All pupils need to be advised about the choices available to them as they grow up: choices about different options for study and about their future careers in work, training or further education. Their progress needs to be recorded in a way that enables achievements to be assessed and further work planned.

There is an important role for guidance here. It can draw together the supervision of academic progress with the pastoral and caring aspects of schools' work and thus have a key influence on pupils' well-being and progress.

Guidance in Scotland

In Scottish schools, guidance has a statutory basis dating back to 1971. The structure adopted centres on the notion of a guidance team, led by senior staff with designated responsibility for guidance who are allocated additional non-contact time for this purpose. The key aim is that: 'each pupil knows and is known personally and in some depth by at least one member of staff.'[17] Designated guidance staff provide contact with other professionals within or outside the school (for example, school counsellors, careers officers, social workers and educational psychologists) when pupils have needs which demand a different kind of expertise. All teachers are regarded as 'first-line guidance staff', with a responsibility for pupils' personal and social development.

Guidance in England and Wales

Evidence to the Commission suggests that the workload currently associated with the national curriculum and assessment arrangements in England and Wales makes it difficult for schools to give sufficient time to guidance work. We note inspectors' calls for teachers to treat assessment and feedback to pupils as an integral part of the learning process. They point out that although the monitoring of pupils' progress may be satisfactory, teachers do not always act on the information so gained in ways that help pupils to improve their performance. In the

Commission's own survey, over 40% of 11- and 13-year-olds reported that they had not talked individually to their teachers about their work.[13] This is a disconcerting finding.

Careers guidance

Guidance about careers should, according to the author of the Commission's Briefing No. 15, occupy a pivotal position in schools.[18] It should link the school with the economic system and the needs of wider society. We are therefore concerned that many schools may lack appropriate expertise for this vital function. In Chapter 13, we propose the establishment of Community Education and Training Advice Centres (CETACs) whose role will include providing high-quality independent careers advice to assist careers work in schools and colleges as well as advice for individual pupils and parents.

An entitlement to guidance

The Commission is convinced that a well-structured system of guidance has potential for helping pupils to make progress; for promoting independent learning by pupils and developing their awareness of the directions they might take in future; and for encouraging the idea of a continuum of learning throughout schooling and beyond. Such support should be an entitlement for all children, from primary school onwards.

We recommend that the Department for Education and Training (a new Department which we propose in Chapter 13) – and until its establishment the Department for Education – should initiate a programme, the purpose of which will be to ensure that all school pupils receive the continuing guidance which they need throughout schooling. A good start will be to examine and capitalise on best practice both in Scotland and elsewhere in the

United Kingdom, paying particular attention to the amount of teaching time and the quality of expertise required.

Learning Support

Pupils who fall behind in their learning, or begin to find that lessons are either too difficult or insufficiently challenging, soon become bored and disillusioned. If this is allowed to continue, the consequences for their future progress are serious. Part of the answer lies in every school having a well-organised system of 'learning support' provided by trained teachers.

We have adopted this term from Scottish practice to describe the arrangements which ordinary schools make to address the needs and difficulties experienced by individual pupils at any stage in their learning. Some may have a learning difficulty which is temporary or prolonged; others may need intensive help following absence due to illness; some may demonstrate exceptional talent in academic, creative or sporting fields. Any of these circumstances could imply a need for extra support which might be short-term or substantial and continuing.

HMI have repeatedly drawn attention to teachers' failure to challenge pupils sufficiently and to respond adequately to the needs of the less able and the very able. In Scotland, where secondary schools employ specialist teachers termed 'learning support specialists' to work with classroom teachers, there may, nevertheless, be problems due to such things as poor management, shortages of resources and insufficient staff training.[19]

There may be a number of reasons why individual pupils' needs are not met. Very large classes in primary schools may be one. Others may be an overloaded curriculum and excessive or conflicting demands on teachers.

There is also a perception that more children who need extra support, for example with English language learning, are being integrated into mainstream schools without an accompanying increase in resources.

Each school should have a clear approach to learning support. In every school all teaching staff should regard a role in learning support as part of their normal work. Pupils should be aware that they can request additional help or take part in extra classes when they need or want to, and should be encouraged to do so as they take increasing responsibility for their own learning.

Aspects of good learning support practice which have been brought to our attention and which should, in our view, become more widespread include:

1 The deployment of trained teachers as learning support specialists who can assist in a variety of ways, such as:

   • teaching small group workshops or intensive short courses designed to tackle learning problems, or to extend pupils who excel in a particular subject or skill;

   • supporting particular classes or particular pupils;

   • redesigning parts of the curriculum in response to recognised needs;

   • demonstrating new teaching approaches.

2 The integration of learning support into the mainstream of the school's work.

3 The provision of staffing resources to enable regular staff development and co-operative teaching.

The examination and wide dissemination of good learning

support practice should be included as part of the programme which we recommend for the Department for
Education and Training in the previous section.

Meeting Special Needs

Schools and LEAs in England and Wales provide for an
estimated 1.2 million pupils with special educational
needs (SENs).[20] Our understanding of special needs and
the way we respond to them have advanced greatly in
recent years. The 1980s witnessed 'a sea change for the
better in the development of more positive attitudes to
the education of children with SENs in both ordinary and
special schools'.[21] Briefing No. 14 for the Commission
reviews the progress made and the challenges for future
provision.[22]

Progress since the 1981 Education Act
The 1981 Education Act recognised a continuum of special educational need, from children with severe and
complex problems, thought to constitute about 2% of the
school population, to a much larger group of about 18%
who at some time in their school career may experience
difficulty with learning for a variety of reasons. This continuum embraces a very wide range of need, from minor
and sometimes temporary learning difficulties, to physical or sensory impairment, emotional and behavioural
disorders, and profound and multiple problems. The
Commission would also argue for including as special
needs the needs of children who are exceptionally able
and talented.

The Act emphasised the right of children with special
needs to be educated with their peers in ordinary schools.
Importantly, it also recognised that special need should
not necessarily be seen as a deficit in the child, but instead

as an interaction between the needs of the child and conditions in the school, such as problems of access to buildings, a curriculum which is pitched at the wrong level, or inflexible teaching methods.

For children in considerable need who require additional or different provision from that which is generally made (the 2% group), the Act introduced a formal process of assessment culminating in the issuing of a statement describing a child's needs and the provision which should be made.

There has been a gradual trend towards greater integration of children with special needs into ordinary schools, instead of segregating them in special schools. In 1991, 1.47% of the school population aged 5–15 in England went to special schools, compared with 1.65% in 1987 and 1.72% in 1982.[23] Links have been established between special schools and ordinary schools, enabling joint lessons and other activities for children and teachers to take place. LEAs have developed SEN support services for ordinary schools. The national curriculum now offers the basis for a common entitlement for all pupils, including those with SENs, and teachers strongly defend the right of *all* pupils to experience the full range of the curriculum.

The overall trend towards integration conceals variations between LEAs. In 1991, 12 LEAs had less than 1% of pupils in special schools, while 14 segregated 2% or more. Such differences have led to a claim that 'children's and parents' experience of special education depends in part on where they live.'[23]

Current concerns
There is a fear that the climate created by more recent legislation could undermine previous achievements. Schools' funding is dependent predominantly on the number of

their pupils. This creates potential disincentives for a school to accept or to retain pupils who are difficult or expensive to teach and whose results or behaviour are unlikely to enhance the school's image. At the same time, LEAs have been required to delegate an increasing proportion of their funds to schools and consequently may have fewer resources at their disposal to support special needs. While no clear evidence has been found either in LEA schools or in grant-maintained schools of a trend away from taking children with special needs, two developments cause concern. First, there is reportedly increasing pressure to provide statements of children's special educational needs as a way of obtaining additional resources.[24] Between 1990 and 1992, the average percentage of 'statemented' pupils rose from 2% to 2.4%. In a sample of 46 LEAs in 1991, over 80% reported an increase both in the number and the percentage of pupils with statements.[24]

The second concern relates to the increasing rate of exclusion (suspension or expulsion) of pupils from school. One study reports an increase in all types of exclusion (fixed term, indefinite and permanent) for all age groups, including primary pupils.[25] Disproportionate numbers of children of Afro-Caribbean origin, particularly boys, are excluded. A recent report revealed that over 12% of excluded children had statements of special need, suggesting that, even with the aid of additional resources, schools are unable or unwilling to keep them.[26] HMI state that: 'it is evident that some schools are reaching too readily for this sanction and the criteria for excluding pupils are indefensibly wide.'[27] Once a child has been excluded from school, the amount of home tuition offered may be very inadequate. The curriculum in special units for excluded pupils is often 'narrow, irrelevant and inappropriate to their needs'.[27]

These are genuine worries which need to be addressed. They are reinforced by our knowledge of changes in society. We note that some excluded children have SENs as a result of emotional or behavioural difficulties. The incidence of these difficulties may increase in future, as a result of changing family patterns, the decline in stable family and community networks, and the great burdens facing many families – particularly single-parent families living in poverty – in rearing their children.

The way forward
The way in which schools develop the potential of pupils with special needs is a measure of their effectiveness. We have progressed beyond the stage when children could be categorised as ineducable. It has been demonstrated that the reservoir of ability is much wider than was once imagined.

The task now facing schools is to raise their own expectations of what all children can achieve, and to become more effective in furthering their achievements. An approach which combines improvement in the overall conditions of learning in schools with flexibility to respond to individual pupils' difficulties may in future prove more successful than maintaining a separate category of special need. This will narrow the gap between what schools in general can provide and what those children with more severe needs require. It does not imply a doctrinaire approach favouring wholesale integration. There will continue to be a place for special schools and units which cater for children with severe and complex problems.

Our view of special needs is consistent with our general approach to school improvement. We place great weight on the capability of schools and the professionalism of teachers to deliver effective provision for all children, including those with special needs. This can be achieved only if each school is organised with that objective in mind. It means that schools need to be prepared to review every aspect of their provision and practice, from buildings and equipment to teaching styles and methods, classroom organisation and the curriculum, to ensure that there are no barriers to effective learning.

We see scope for improvement in a number of areas.

Funding special needs

The allocation of resources for special needs has been described as the single most important challenge.[28] In the present policy climate it seems likely that more and more resources will be tied to individual pupils who have statements, thus leaving less for the larger group of pupils who have special needs but are not statemented. This situation will lead to a vicious circle with more parents and schools pressing for more pupils to be statemented in order to secure a declining amount of funding.

There are advantages in retaining a statementing process, or at least a central 'record' (the term used in Scotland) of children and young people with special educational needs. Children with severe and complex problems are entitled to a multi-disciplinary assessment which is subject to regular review. The statement process embodies this principle. It also represents a commitment to make appropriate provision and is a basis for monitoring how effectively this is done.

We believe, however, that the direct link between the statement procedure and the funding of special needs should be broken. Instead, better ways of auditing the range and nature of the special needs of schools should be examined. The aim should be to increase schools' willingness and ability to provide for all their children with special needs out of the resources managed by them, with additional resources for children with very severe and complex needs. This approach recognises that significant variations in the overall quality of provision available in ordinary schools greatly influence the number of pupils 'who find it difficult to thrive or whom teachers find difficult to manage'.[29] It also acknowledges that teacher attitudes and school values make a difference: some schools are more inclined than others to regard it as part of their ordinary workload to work with pupils who have special needs.

School funding formulae should be developed to enable more accurate calculation of the incidence of special needs. Proxy indicators, such as the proportion of children receiving free school meals, are too simplistic. Several education authorities have instituted a system by which teachers conduct an audit of the special needs in their schools. The results are carefully moderated to ensure objectivity. By adopting this kind of approach, funds are more accurately matched to the needs of schools. Additional resources are then targeted effectively to the small number of children with severe difficulties. The establishment of Local Management of Schools (Special) schemes, from April 1994, should increase the incidence of these approaches. LMS (Special) schemes are concerned with the identification of, and support for, all pupils with special needs, whether in ordinary or special schools and whether statemented or not.

Securing high quality provision
We have emphasised the responsibility of schools and teachers. In addition, it must be a statutory duty of Education and Training Boards (ETBs) – the organisations which we propose should replace LEAs – to secure access to high-quality education for all children with special needs. In Chapter 13 we advocate placing all maintained schools, including grant-maintained schools, under the

direction of ETBs. This will have the benefit of ensuring that every school provides as required for special needs. In setting up pilot projects to test the purchaser-provider arrangements which we propose in Chapter 13, we recommend that special attention be paid to how these arrangements affect special needs provision.

Special needs support services are at risk. Our recommendations in Chapter 13 for the continuance of a single education planning authority (the Education and Training Board) within local government will allow for joint initiatives to support children and young people with special needs and ensure that accountability does not become fragmented. This body would be funded to retain or purchase support services for individual schools or groups of schools.

Two further areas of policy and practice should be addressed. The first of these is the school curriculum and assessment. The framework described in Chapter 4 will, we believe, create opportunities for teachers working with children with SENs. It emphasises progression, recognition of positive achievement, and flexibility for schools to develop and pursue learning programmes to meet their particular needs.

We stress assessment by teachers. Nursery and primary teachers in particular should be so trained that they are confident in the use of assessment procedures to identify particular learning needs as they arise and from the earliest stages.

We advocate the use of broad value-added techniques to measure pupils' progress, rather than relying solely on examination and test results. Schools should be given credit for good work with their least able pupils, an aspect of school performance to be measured and celebrated with as much interest as the success of the most able. This will be an incentive to teachers to persevere with children who have special needs.

Our recommendations in Chapter 5 for investment in information technology will enable schools to open up the curriculum for children who might otherwise be excluded from learning to their full potential.

Finally, we see scope for improvement in initial and in-service teacher training. 'The slogan that every teacher is a teacher of children with special educational needs is true in principle, though it is far from being accepted in practice.'[28] A significant component of special needs training should be compulsory in the initial training of teachers for the primary and secondary phases. Schools should be encouraged to invest in staff development to keep teachers up to date with practice, perhaps pooling the expertise of clusters of schools, and increasing outreach work by special school teachers. Our recommendations in Chapter 8 for strengthening initial training and continuing professional development should help improve the capability of ordinary schools to respond effectively to special needs.

Schools Active in Their Communities

Schools are not the only educators of children or even, some would say, the most influential ones: families have an all-pervasive influence on the learning of children and so do local communities. An excellent education involves a partnership between pupil, school, family and the wider community.

By building good community links, schools expand their capacity to provide stimulating and relevant learning. Over the past ten years the Schools Curriculum Award has celebrated excellent work of this kind by 1,000 schools across the UK, operating in many different situations, from attractive countryside and affluent areas to council estates with high unemployment.[30] To qualify for the award, schools have to demonstrate that their curriculum is accessible to *all* their children, and that they draw upon their communities as a resource for learning, as well as giving something back to the community in return. In our view, the school of the future should see its role as being at the heart of the community. The Schools Curriculum Award shows how this philosophy can be put into practice.

Involving parents

The first and most important link is with the home. According to the pupils who took part in the Commission's survey,[13] most parents are very supportive of their children's education. When schools fully exploit opportunities to involve parents in a productive way, parents, schools and children all gain. Evidence suggests that these opportunities are often missed or underused.[31] Sometimes this may be due to the lack of a clear school policy for parental involvement. Sometimes it may result from lack of teacher training, or from insufficient non-contact time for teachers to devote to this work. The circumstances of lone-parent families and dual-career families may make it difficult to establish successful links. Parents whose own experience of school was negative are often hard to interest in active school involvement. Schools must nevertheless persevere in their efforts to develop good links with parents.

Recent Government policy has emphasised the role of parents in strengthening the accountability of schools through such mechanisms as the Parents' Charter, which sets out parents' basic rights in relation to school performance. Parents' attitudes towards schools have undergone substantial change since the 1960s and 1970s: from 'deference, puzzlement and helplessness' and towards an acceptance that they have 'a formal right to information and access concerning their children's schooling, and to a share in decisions regarding this'.[32]

This change is broadly to be welcomed. However, treating parents mainly as consumers exercising legal rights is a limited approach. Good home/school links embrace the idea of joint commitment to a common purpose. The work of Parent Teacher Associations can contribute much towards this goal. Some schools have developed written home/school agreements which set out the mutual expectations and obligations of schools and parents as a way of promoting a sense of shared responsibility for a child's progress.

School/work links

Links with the economic community are particularly important. Since the 1980s, stimulated by the CBI's Business Education Task Force, numerous initiatives have helped to enhance links between schools and the world of work. High-quality links can increase pupils' motivation, as shown, for example, by the beneficial influence of Compacts on attendance, behaviour, and staying on rates. Employers involved in Compact schemes work with schools to provide incentives and support to help pupils improve their performance. Such links are also, as the CBI emphasises, central to the development of the UK's manufacturing base.

School/business contacts are already extensive: a recent survey indicated that 92% of secondary schools and 56% of primary schools had links with local business.[33] Some parts of the country were more active than others: in two areas, East Anglia and the East Midlands, all secondary schools had business contacts. East Anglia also involved 76% of its primary schools in this activity. Contacts were promoted for a variety of purposes, from curriculum development to company visits and from teacher second-ment to work experience for pupils (the latter involving 91% of secondary pupils in their final year). Schools also provided services for local business, such as design, market survey and translation services.

Interest now focuses less on the extent of these links and more on their quality. Good practice will ensure that an enriching experience of the world of work is an integral part of the curriculum entitlement of every pupil. We endorse the aim of combining 'broad educational goals with the needs of a skilled and adaptable workforce',[34] and believe that our curriculum proposals will encourage progress towards this end.

Adding value after school

Schools often possess underused resources in the form of buildings and facilities such as sports fields, gymnasia and art rooms which are closed after school hours. It is claimed that over a school year as much as 70% of schools' capacity is unused.[35] We would like to see this capacity exploited for a wide variety of purposes, from providing a safe place where children can do homework until their parents return from work, to offering educational and recreational after-school activities for children and the local community. Pupils would benefit by 'adding value' to their learning in school; the skills of the community would be brought into the school; and expensive plant would be turned to cost-effective use.

Community education

Many schools provide community education programmes offering educational, social and recreational activities to meet a whole variety of community needs, from parent and toddler groups to open-learning centres for adults and sports activities for senior citizens. Some schools involve adult learners in daytime classes alongside pupils. We would wish to see well-resourced community education programmes becoming more widespread.

Steps Towards School Improvement

Starting inside schools

Recent Government policy has emphasised the external scrutiny of school performance based on indicators such as examination and test results. Attention has focused on the idea of the failing school and mechanisms to correct failure.

Public accountability is important. Regulation and inspection have a key part to play in encouraging and maintaining high standards in schools. However, we would wish to see this balanced by recognition that sustained commitment to raising achievement must come from within schools and that headteachers, working together with their staff, bear the major responsibility for school effectiveness. Successful schools are those which reflect on their own practice and devise and implement changes in response to the needs of their pupils. Some of the most valuable strategies for improvement are those initiated by the school community itself: by the head and teaching staff supported by the governing body and the wider community of parents.

We therefore place considerable weight on self-evaluation by schools, linked to planning for future development and the effective use of the school budget to fund recognised priorities. Schools need to examine information and data relating to a wide range of indicators of effectiveness. Not only examination results, but information on pupils' progress in such areas as attendance, behaviour, extra-curricular activities, and attitudes to school should be considered. Although many schools may feel that they suffer from an overload of information, it can be argued that too little of it is constructively interpreted and used for improvement purposes.

Improving leadership and management

At the start of this chapter we identify 'strong, positive leadership' as a key feature of successful schools. There is evidence that leadership needs to improve. For example, Scottish inspectors judge that overall leadership is unsatisfactory in only 4% of secondary schools, but that in a further 24%, weaknesses, such as lack of direction or poor relationships, outweigh strengths.[19] In England, HMI observe that although there is more good than poor management, the range in quality is very wide. In Chapter 8, we consider these issues in detail and make recommendations concerning the training of teachers throughout their careers, and procedures for the selection and appointment of heads.

Governing bodies can develop their role helpfully. Governors who are genuinely in touch with the community can act as 'eyes and ears, ambassadors, go-betweens and interpreters'[36] for the school, as well as adopting a constructive but critical approach to evaluating the school's performance. They can be a valuable source of support and inspiration.

Catalysts for change

Schools which are failing may not be fully aware of their weaknesses. Those which are meeting customary expectations may not realise that they could build even further on their strengths, or develop new capabilities. External catalysts for improvement will always be needed. In Chapter 13 we describe the role of national and local inspection as a spur to school improvement. Under our proposed local inspection arrangements, Education and

Training Boards as purchasers of schools' services would monitor performance on a regular basis to ensure that required standards are being met and would provide feedback to assist in school self-evaluation and development planning, and in assessing the impact of policies for change. Although inspection is a regulatory and quality assurance function, it can thus be seen as part of a partnership with schools aimed at continuing improvement.

Local Education Authorities act as catalysts for improvement, sometimes funding projects jointly with Training and Enterprise Councils. Sheffield City Council's Raising Achievement and Participation Project (RAPP) focuses on 14-18-year-olds and includes a bursary scheme, mentoring, and the development of a database to track pupil destinations and achievement. Knowsley LEA has a wide-ranging programme to raise levels of attainment across the borough by working in collaboration with schools and the community, setting targets but also providing support. Central to this LEA's thinking is the need to promote a climate of shared responsibility for the drive to improve achievement.

An important contribution which education authorities can make to raising the level of performance in schools is to use data gathered in monitoring to identify differences between schools and to try to understand the underlying causes. Many differences in performance are likely to be relatively small. The main focus of attention should be on identifying 'schools that are doing a good deal better or worse than might be expected' and establishing what other schools can learn from them.[37] Figure 7.1 lists a set of key questions for monitoring and evaluating secondary schools. It illustrates the range of factors which might lead to one school performing better than another. Answers to some of these questions may be more qualitative than quantitative and can be gleaned only by observation and interviews rather than data collection.

Figure 7.1 Key questions for monitoring and evaluating secondary schools.

Core area	Key question
Clarification of values	What are our schools fundamentally about? What concerns do they share in common and in what ways do they differ significantly?
Academic progress	What is the extent of variation between schools in terms of the academic progress their pupils are making?
Other outcomes and forms of progress	What is the extent of variation between schools in terms of other aspects of pupils' experiences and development?
Teaching processes	What is the extent of variation between schools in terms of pupils' experiences of teaching and learning?
Key resources	What is the extent of variation between schools in terms of pupils' access to key resources known to be associated with growth in learning?
Equal opportunities	To what extent are differences in the above experiences related to pupils' characteristics or the context of the particular school they attend?

Source: Gray, J. and others, 1991.[37]

External consultants, including school improvement experts based in higher education institutions, provide another important source of stimulus and support, often working closely with local education authorities.[38] Examples of work involving higher education institutions includes the Two Towns project based at the Centre for Successful Schools at Keele University. This project has targeted disadvantaged inner city schools and has sought, over a four-year period, to challenge low expectations, poor staying on rates and limited progression to higher education. Cambridge University Institute of Education's Improving the Quality of Education for All Project is collaborating with schools in Yorkshire and the South-East to produce and evaluate a model of school development and a programme of support.

The Commission's view

These examples serve to illustrate, first, that a national inspection framework, though necessary, is not enough on its own to promote continuing improvement. A range of partnerships is needed. Secondly, there is no single recipe for improvement. Initiatives which succeed in generating the enthusiasm of schools and teachers proceed from the differing strengths, weaknesses and goals of individual schools and their communities. National and LEA-wide performance indicators are a guide and counterweight to school aims but are only part of the picture. Thirdly, school improvement is not a 'quick fix'. Resources and effort need to be committed over a significant period in order to achieve results. It may be necessary to change the culture of a whole school before improvements in performance become visible.

The Commission makes the following recommendations:

1 Government and inspection agencies nationally and locally should recognise the central role of the school in evaluating its own performance and making improvements in response to the school's own needs.

2 School budgets should include an element designed to enable schools to buy external advice and support.

3 Schools should be funded to allow for continuing staff development. Classroom-based methods may be particularly worthwhile, rather than expensive one-off courses. For example, it may be a matter of ensuring sufficient non-contact time for teachers to work in pairs to help extend their repertoire of teaching methods.

4 Successful school improvement projects should be evaluated and disseminated in a more systematic way. This may be an appropriate role for the Council

for Innovation in Teaching and Learning described in Chapter 5.

The physical environment

Schools where the physical fabric is deteriorating and books and equipment are outdated or in poor supply do not provide an environment conducive to high morale and successful learning. Although there have been recent improvements, more still needs to be done. This is particularly the case in primary schools in England, where in 1990–91 HMI judged that accommodation was less than satisfactory in 40% of schools, and library provision varied widely 'but was rarely very good'.[39]

In 1990–91, the Government spent an average of £57 per pupil on books and equipment in all English schools and £79 on repairs and maintenance.[40] In the same year, expenditure on books and materials in independent preparatory day schools was similar, at £60 per pupil, but higher in senior day schools, at £93 per pupil.[41] Independent schools spent far more than maintained schools on repairs and maintenance to buildings and grounds, at £161 per pupil in preparatory day schools and £322 in senior day schools. Exact comparisons cannot be made between the independent and maintained sectors but the figures indicate the relative advantage of the former. The Government should accept responsibility for increasing funding to a point at which it is possible for the Inspectorate to report that provision for all aspects of the physical environment in all schools is at least adequate.

Raising Achievement in Deprived Areas

Evidence of underachievement

Underachievement is an acute problem in deprived urban areas. Although schools serving very disadvantaged communities can be highly effective in enabling their pupils to make good progress, some of the lowest levels of achievement are to be found in these areas. Even in highly effective schools, the level of social deprivation in a child's immediate home area can substantially depress achievement below the level one would expect on the basis of that child's previous attainment and family background. Commissioners themselves have visited schools in deprived areas and observed some of the problems at first hand.

The Policy Studies Institute (PSI) has reported that in several deprived authorities in England over 20% of young people left school without graded results in the period 1987–90, compared with 9% in England as a whole.[42] A survey by the Careers Services presented figures on the proportion of school leavers in England and Wales in 1992 who were known to be neither in employment nor in education or training.[43] While the average was about 9%, the figure was over 15% for several areas defined as deprived in the PSI report; in two it exceeded 20%. Staying on in full-time education is also less popular in a number of these areas, falling below 50% compared with 66% for England as a whole. We note however that in most of the metropolitan districts in England, full-time staying on rates for 16-year-olds have improved, in some cases markedly.[44]

In deprived areas, multiple disadvantages combine to make educational success difficult to attain. People living with the effects of poverty, long-term unemployment, poor housing, a lack of good amenities, high levels of crime, vandalism and, increasingly also, drug trafficking are severely disadvantaged. We share the anxiety of many that we may be witnessing the emergence of an underclass: people for whom the problems of unemployment and poverty are so great that they lose a sense of belonging to the mainstream of society and of sharing its aims and aspirations, and instead become increasingly isolated. As we indicate in Chapters 2 and 3, social cohesion is threatened by the gap in incomes between the richer and poorer sections of society and also by the division between those who possess the skills increasingly required by the labour market and those who do not.

Briefing No. 16 for the Commission argues that a concerted national policy would offer the prospect of raising standards in these areas,[45] and we agree. In particular, we support the range of possible solutions there proposed.

A new approach to funding

The Commission advocates a change in approach where deprived areas are concerned.

There needs, first, to be a better approach to funding. We outline the problems in Chapter 13. Secondly, we believe that Education and Training Boards must be given flexibility to target funds for improvement. They should adopt a strategic approach to this task. Some schools in disadvantaged areas perform extremely well but may require above average funding in order to retain experienced staff or to maintain a high level of specialist learning support for pupils. Education and Training Boards must assess the cost of making high-quality provision in all schools in their area, identifying those which give particular cause for concern, allocating additional funds for improvement where necessary and monitoring progress against agreed targets. Thirdly, although an improved funding formula should achieve a closer match between resources and the needs of areas and schools, for some Boards in deprived areas it will be desirable to ensure sustained growth in funds at predictable rates over a period in order to help schools to develop plans for improvement.

Attracting excellent teachers

Schools where teaching presents some of the toughest challenges must be able to recruit some of the ablest and most experienced teachers in the profession. It is vital that schools in deprived areas should be able to select and retain teachers and heads who are committed to working in this kind of environment; who believe strongly in the capacity of every pupil to make progress; and whose expectations of pupils are correspondingly high. We would therefore argue for incentives commensurate with the demands being made.

Appropriate salary rewards for good teachers in deprived areas are important, but additional measures are needed in order to demonstrate that the skill and professionalism of those who choose to work in disadvantaged areas are valued highly. Professional development is vital as a source of new ideas for dealing with problems as well as a way of renewing commitment and enthusiasm for a demanding task. Resources should be made available for regular staff development, preferably tailored to the specific needs of teachers, heads and potential heads in deprived areas. There should be opportunities to spend time away from school on secondment or sabbatical. Professional development vouchers might be a worthwhile option.

Preparation for work in inner city schools should be available as a well-developed component in initial training, and, since new teachers tend to take up posts in the geographical area where they have been trained, consideration should be given to establishing more centres of initial training in inner city areas.

Encouraging innovation

Encouragement should be given to local innovation whether by schools, by partnerships involving schools and other agencies such as youth clubs, church organisations and voluntary groups, or by Education and Training Boards. Examples of innovatory projects could include business units such as design studios sited within schools to work with groups of pupils; after-school enrichment programmes and homework clubs; alternative curriculum programmes; or, indeed, new types of schools or learning centres, established on an experimental basis. Alternative learning centres attached to schools could, for example, prove particularly beneficial for those young people who, according to HMI, 'find the constraints of schools too daunting and prove too great a challenge for even the most imaginative school.'[27]

The Pattern of Schools

Diversity and choice?

The UK is a long way from having a common system of schooling. Whilst maintained co-educational primary and comprehensive secondary schools are the norm, many pupils have a different type of schooling. In 1992 in England, about 11% of secondary pupils and a very small number of primary pupils in maintained schools were educated in single-sex schools, although these figures have been declining.[46] Twenty-three per cent of pupils of secondary age were in non-comprehensive schools, with around 150 grammar schools in 28 authorities educating 3.4%. There are no grammar schools in either Scotland or Wales, but there were 70 in Northern Ireland in 1991, educating 38.6% of pupils of secondary age.[47] Many maintained schools have voluntary status, usually linked with a religious foundation. In 1992, 6.6% of pupils in the UK were in independent schools.[48] The Government has increased the variety of schools in England and Wales by creating two new types of school, grant-maintained schools (allowing some to become selective) and City Technology Colleges. Further diversification is permitted by the Education Act 1993 with the creation of Technology Schools and Technology Colleges, and schools specialising in particular subjects. Similar opportunities have also been made available in legislation for Scotland but no school has so far wished to use them.

Variations between schools in achievement by pupils are higher than in other countries. It may appear from examination results that the type of school that a pupil attends is of great significance: in 1992, 86.9% of grammar school pupils obtained five or more grades A–C at GCSE, as compared to 74.5% for independent schools and 34.3% for comprehensive schools.[49] This tells us more about the intake to these types of school than about their effectiveness. Indeed, differences in attainment between schools of the same type are far greater than differences between the various types of school.

A further factor widening the variation between schools is recent legislation which aims to give parents more choice of school. Although in practice this 'choice' is only an expression of preference, we know that it has increased social segregation in schools and widened differences in their performance.[50] There is a serious danger of a hierarchy of good, adequate and 'sink' schools emerging within the maintained system.[51]

Meanwhile, Britain has a small but influential independent school sector which provides some of the best education in the country as well as some that is indifferent. This sector, having shrunk in both relative and absolute terms throughout much of the century, is now expanding.[52] The boundary between the independent and maintained sectors has also become increasingly blurred with the development of new categories of school such as the City Technology Colleges, the introduction of the Assisted

Places Scheme (under which some places in some independent schools are bought for able pupils out of public funds) and the increasing questioning of the assumption that private contributions from parents and others should not be used to support statutory provision in maintained schools.[53]

Independent schools in various forms exist in many advanced countries and in some they represent a bigger proportion of provision than in the United Kingdom.[54] In this country, however, the existence of the independent sector is often a particular source of controversy. Its admirers point to the outstanding achievements of the best schools in the sector, citing not only their academic record but also their success in developing opportunities for pupils in a wide variety of fields and their emphasis on moral values. Its critics acknowledge the educational merits of the best schools in the sector but regard the sector's existence as itself contributing to and helping to perpetuate social divisions which they see as damaging to society. We do not try to reconcile these views. As we see it, the task for the future will not be to concentrate on producing a highly educated élite but to achieve higher learning outcomes for all, and particularly for those in the middle and lower bands of attainment. This argues for a national education system in which all schools, maintained and independent, are committed to similar goals (though they may achieve them by different routes) and play their part without jeopardising the success of each other. We therefore commend the trend towards collaboration and sharing of facilities between schools in the independent and maintained sectors.[55]

At present, there is a conflict between, on the one hand, moves towards greater diversity and choice of schools and, on the other hand, an ideal of equal access for all children to high-quality education. Laudable principles for schools may often work against each other: serving a local community, catering for all abilities as in the comprehensive ideal, or encouraging choice of school. For example, a community school where the neighbourhood is not socially mixed may not have a broad enough social or ability range to operate in a truly comprehensive manner. Choice, when exercised, is often used to escape from the local school, working against the community school ideal. Similarly, those parents who are exercising their choice are tending to use it in favour of schools with other pupils of an 'appropriate background'.[56] These conflicts are not necessary. In the rest of this chapter, we argue for a pattern of schooling that puts them into the past.

Diversity in schools
There will always be differences in the general ethos promoted by individual schools and in their approach to achieving their educational objectives. Such distinctions are likely to become more pronounced as a result of the increasing autonomy of schools. Moreover, the wide-ranging curriculum we propose in Chapter 4 will be such that secondary schools will provide varying options and courses to meet differing local needs and wishes. Indeed, the Commission would not wish schools to be precluded from developing particular strengths or specialisms, provided that access to a broad and balanced curriculum is guaranteed for all pupils. All schools, including independent schools, will, under our proposals, provide the national curriculum but will have scope to differ in the overall balance of their remaining provision.

Access to the breadth of the curriculum will be encouraged by links between neighbouring schools (including independent schools) and colleges enabling exchanges of both students and teachers. Closer partnership between the maintained and independent sectors will be made easier by extending inspection arrangements for the national curriculum and our proposed General Education Diploma (described in Chapter 4) to the independent sector. If an Education and Training Board feels that a particular aspect of the curriculum is not sufficiently catered for in its area then it will be able to invite schools and colleges to submit proposals for putting this right.

Increased selection by ability must be discouraged if we wish to promote a less divisive society. This entails ensuring that all schools are able to teach effectively the full range of pupils which they admit. The big question-mark against this is whether all pupils can be suitably challenged in schools which cater for all abilities. HMI have argued that very able pupils 'are often insufficiently challenged by the work they are set' and may be underachieving even if they obtain better than average results in tests and examinations.[57] It has been demonstrated that with imagination, good planning and support, schools with a broad intake can provide very successfully for gifted children. When specific attention is given to the needs of these children there is often a general enhancement of the quality of teaching and learning and a raising of the expectations and standards of all pupils. Indeed, in Scotland, where the maintained system is entirely comprehensive, more pupils qualify to enter higher education than in England and Wales.

The Assisted Places Scheme, whereby government pays some or all of the fees of pupils to attend independent schools, takes able pupils out of maintained schools and thus restricts the range of ability in the latter. It also gives a signal from government that many maintained schools are not thought adequate to cope with the education of able pupils. Our vision is that the improvements we propose for maintained schools, such as an enriched curriculum and flexible organisational and teaching strategies, will allow all pupils to make the best of themselves. As our vision comes to be translated into reality, there will be no need for an Assisted Places Scheme. Accordingly, we believe that it should be phased out in appropriate stages.

Our proposals in Chapter 4 envisage choice for pupils within schools rather than between schools. The broad-based, non-age-related and modular curriculum for 14–18-year-olds will allow all pupils to take increasing responsibility for their own learning programmes. Schools themselves will have more freedom to organise teaching to get the best out of every child, perhaps moving a pupil up a year for a particular subject, or providing extra learning support. Expertise, or provision for some options such as technical subjects or less commonly taught languages, may have to come from another phase: in the case of primary schools, from a secondary school; and in the case of secondary schools, from a college or university.

We believe a radical approach is consistent with the recommendations for a well-managed learning support system set out earlier in this chapter. It offers a flexible way of responding to each pupil's needs, which will change from time to time and differ between areas of study. It also avoids the potential risks inherent in setting or streaming pupils by ability, which, if organised in an inflexible way, may limit the expectations of both teachers and pupils.

Choosing a school
For the majority of pupils and parents, a crucial factor in choosing a school is how near they live to it, and catchment areas are still used by most LEAs and also, so far, by most grant-maintained schools. The benefits of neighbourhood schools include greater likelihood of a mutually enriching relationship with the community and minimisation of time-wasting and often expensive travel time

for children. However, children and parents now expect to have a large say in deciding which school the child will attend, and to know that their choice will be rejected only for a very good reason. The most conclusive will be that the school has more applications than it can accept and that priority has been given to other applications strictly in accordance with its admission rules.

It would not be desirable to attempt to remove these expectations. But on the basis of evidence from this country and abroad, it is absolutely clear that relaxing constraints on choice can have unacceptable consequences.[58] Schools are not typical consumer goods in the marketplace. Their popularity or unpopularity is partly driven by who their customers are. Differences in the ability and motivation of parents and their children to take advantage of choice (or even move house) can result in bandwagon effects and lead eventually to a two-tier system, perpetuated by the funding system where money follows pupils.[59] Signs of this pattern can be seen in Northern Ireland, where a system based on selection at 11 has been retained. With open enrolment, the proportion of pupils attending grammar schools has increased from 37% in 1989 to 39% in 1992.

The choice of many parents is extended by independent schools, which they usually perceive as having better outcomes, whether academic, social or cultural. Independent school pupils, on aggregate, achieve significantly better examination results and are much more likely to go on to higher education and eventually to reach senior positions in society. Prominent among the reasons for this is the fact that independent schools are on the whole much better resourced than maintained schools and have much more favourable pupil-teacher ratios.

We propose a system which responds to the individual

needs of children and also addresses wider issues of equity, the efficient use of resources and the difficulties faced by less popular schools. The decision as to which school a child should attend must result from collaboration between the pupil (with parents acting as agents), the schools, and the ETB, which will act as the admissions agency. The choices made by pupils and parents will partly be informed by improved availability of individual guidance and advice for all pupils and parents. This guidance and advice will be one of the functions of the Community Education and Training Advice Centres (CETACs), which we describe in Chapter 13.

The ETB will have the right to fill 10% of the places at each maintained school according to well-defined and published criteria, drawn up in consultation with the CETAC. Otherwise, pupil choice of school will have primacy in the sense that first preferences will be automatically accepted when the school is not over-subscribed. In cases where schools are over-subscribed they will draw up simple, clear and published criteria, such as proximity to the school, attendance of a sibling, religious faith and other special needs. These will be applied in their established order to all those pupils who have given the school first preference, until their 90% share of places is filled. As with all other schools, the ETB will have the right to fill the remaining 10% share of places in over-subscribed schools. In cases where parents feel disappointed about the decision that has been made they may use their right of appeal to an appeals board, whose ruling will be final.

Conclusion

Our vision of successful schooling is based on the best of current practice. The concept of what constitutes a 'school' may however change in future years. Peter

Mortimore, Deputy Director of London University's Institute of Education, has said that: 'there is a general agreement amongst academics and practitioners in many countries that schools of the future may have to be very different in order to prepare young people for life in the twenty-first century.'[60] One report envisages secondary schools operating flexi-time, with pupils working much more independently as individuals or in small self-supporting groups, meeting regularly with tutors to review progress.[61] Age would become irrelevant to the organisation of classes, as pupils and adults from the community shared classes according to the level they had reached. Each school would have a high-quality resource centre, linked into a national network via satellite and computer, with resource experts to prepare materials according to teachers' specifications.

The Commission anticipates that, in time, the organisation of schooling is likely to be more diffuse, with the boundaries between schools, the workplace, the community, and continuing education and training providers becoming much less marked than at present. Even so, schools will remain the central focus for young people's education, though increasingly working in partnership with other educational institutions, as well as with a range of organisations and people outside the school. We therefore expect that most of the features of effective schooling identified at the start of this chapter will continue to be important for the foreseeable future.

What is certain is that the far-reaching social and economic changes outlined in Chapters 2 and 3 will make the job of schools increasingly challenging. Other trends, such as the greater autonomy of schools in managing their own affairs, coupled with an awareness of the need for collaboration, have the potential to bring about improvement. We believe that, taken together, our recommendations in this and other chapters will help more schools to achieve success.

Notes

1   See for example:
(i) Mortimore, P., 1993. School Effectiveness and the Management of Effective Teaching and Learning. Paper for the International Congress for School Effectiveness, Norrköping, Sweden.
(ii) HM Inspectors of Schools, Scottish Education Department, 1988. Effective Secondary Schools. HMSO.

2   Foxman, D. and others, December 1992. Standards in Literacy and Numeracy. NCE Briefing No. 10. National Commission on Education.

3   Department for Education, June 1993. GCSE and A/AS Examination Results 1991/92. *Statistical Bulletin* 15/93, Table 5.

4   DFE, 1993. Communication to National Commission on Education.

5   Adult Literacy and Basic Skills Unit (ALBSU), 1993:
(i) Basic Skills Support in Colleges. Assessing the Need.
(ii) The Basic Skills of Young Adults.

6   Pyke, N., 1993. 'Cheap Talk Allows Pupils to Catch Up.' *Times Educational Supplement*, 19 February, p.8. (Article on the use of a 'talking computer' to aid reading recovery.)

7   Office for Standards in Education (OFSTED), 1993. Reading Recovery in New Zealand. A Report from the Office of Her Majesty's Chief Inspector of Schools. HMSO.

8   Council for the Accreditation of Teacher Education, March 1992. Training Teachers to Teach Reading: A Review. CATE.

9   Mortimore, P. and Blatchford, P., March 1993. The Issue of Class Size. NCE Briefing No. 12.

10   Central Statistical Office, 1993. *Regional Trends* 28. HMSO, Table 5.2.

11   Sources:
(i)   DFE, June 1993. Statistics of Schools in England January 1992. *Statistical Bulletin* 18/93, Table 7.
(ii)   DFE, 1992. Statistics of Education. Schools. Table A15/92.

12   Centre for Educational Research and Innovation, 1992. Education at a Glance. OECD Indicators. Organisation for Economic Co-operation and Development. Table P16.

13   Keys, W. and Fernandes, C., 1993. What **Do** Students Think About School? A Report for the National Commission on Education. National Foundation for Educational Research.

14   O'Keeffe, D. and others, June 1993. Truancy in English Secondary Schools. A Report Prepared for the DFE. Department for Education.

15   Rutter, M. and others, 1979. *Fifteen Thousand Hours. Secondary Schools and Their Effects on Children*. Open Books.

16 HM Inspectors of Schools, 1992. (i) Using Ethos Indicators in Primary School Self-Evaluation. (ii) Using Ethos Indicators in Secondary School Self-Evaluation. Scottish Office Education Department.

17 Scottish Central Committee on Guidance, 1986. More than Feelings of Concern. Guidance and Scottish Secondary Schools. A Position Paper. Scottish Consultative Council on the Curriculum.

18 Watts, A. G., July 1993. Promoting Careers: Guidance for Learning and Work. NCE Briefing No. 15.

19 Scottish Office Education Department, 1993. Standards and Quality in Scottish Schools 1991–92. A Report by HM Inspectors of Schools.

20 Audit Commission and Her Majesty's Inspectorate, 1992. Getting the Act Together. Provision for Pupils with Special Educational Needs. HMSO.

21 Mittler, P., March 1992. Children Who Have Been Failed by the Education System. Written Evidence to the National Commission on Education.

22 Wedell, Klaus, May 1993. Special Needs Education: The Next 25 Years. NCE Briefing No. 14.

23 Swann, W., 1991 & 1992. Centre for Studies in Education:
    (i) Segregation Statistics. English LEAs. Variations between LEAs in Levels of Segregation in Special Schools, 1982–1990.
    (ii) Segregation Statistics. English LEAs. 1988–91.

24 Evans, J. and Lunt, I., 1992. Developments in Special Education under LMS. Institute of Education, University of London.

25 Advisory Centre for Education, 1993. Findings from ACE Investigations into Exclusions.

26 DFE, November 1992. Exclusions. A Discussion Paper.

27 OFSTED, 1993. Education for Disaffected Pupils. A Report from the Office of Her Majesty's Chief Inspector of Schools.

28 Mittler, P., 1992. 'Educational Entitlement in the Nineties.' *Support for Learning*, 7 (4), pp.145-151.

29 Lunt, I., 1993. Some Issues Concerning the Resourcing of Special Educational Needs. Written Evidence to the National Commission on Education.

30 Schools Curriculum Award, 1993. *Report from the Trustees 1991–1992.* Longman.

31 Jowett, S. and others, 1991. *Building Bridges. Parental Involvement in Schools.* NFER-Nelson.

32 Jones, G. and others, January 1992. A Willing Partnership. Project Study of the Home-School Contract of Partnership. Royal Society of Arts.

33 DFE, April 1993. Survey of School-Business Links. *Statistical Bulletin* 10/93.

34 Confederation of British Industry/London School of Economics, February 1992. Education Business Partnerships. The Learning So Far.

35 Education Extra, 1992. Foundation for Arts and Sports in Schools. Communication to the National Commission on Education.

36 Sallis, J., 1993. 'Community Partnerships to Strengthen Teaching and Learning.' In: Learmonth, J. (ed.). Teaching and Learning in Cities. Whitbread PLC, pp. 226–231.

37 Gray, J. and others, 1991. 'Developing LEA Frameworks for Monitoring and Evaluation from Research on School Effectiveness: Problems, Progress and Possibilities.' In: Riddell S. and Brown S. (eds.). School Effectiveness Research. Scottish Office Education Department, HMSO, pp. 35–46.

38 See for example: Hopkins, D. and Ainscow, M., 1993. 'No Room for Hit Squads'; Myers, K. and Stoll, L., 1993. 'Mapping the Movement.' *Education*, 16 July, pp. 50–51.

39 HMI, 1992. Education in England in 1990–91. The Annual Report of HM Senior Chief Inspector of Schools. Department of Education and Science.

40 DFE & OFSTED, February 1993. The Government's Expenditure Plans 1993–94 to 1995–96. HMSO, Cm 2210, Table 12.

41 MacIntyre & Co., March 1992. Independent Schools Cost Survey 1990/91.

42 Willmott, P. and Hutchinson, R., 1992. Urban Trends 1. A Report on Britain's Deprived Urban Areas. Policy Studies Institute.

43 Slade, R. (comp.) and Yates, J. (ed.), 1993. School Leavers' Destinations 1992. An Analysis of Young People's Career and Educational Choices. ACC Publications.

44 Department for Education, 1993. Participation in Education by Young People aged 16 and 17 in Each Local Education Authority and Region of England: 1988–89 to 1991–92. *Statistical Bulletin* 12/93.

45 Barber, M., July 1993. Raising Standards in Deprived Urban Areas. NCE Briefing No. 16.

46 DFE, June 1993. Statistics of Schools in England January 1992. *Statistical Bulletin* 18/93.

47 Department of Education, Northern Ireland.

48 Central Statistical Office, 1993. *Regional Trends*, 28. HMSO. Table 5.1.

49 DFE, June 1993. GCSE and A/AS Examination Results 1991/92. *Statistical Bulletin* 15/93.

50 Adler, M., 1993. An Alternative Approach to Parental Choice. NCE Briefing No. 13.

51 Walford, G., 1993. Selection for Secondary Schooling. NCE Briefing No. 7.

52 DFE, June 1993. Statistics of Schools in England January 1992. *Statistical Bulletin* 18/93.

53 Mountfield, A., 1991. State Schools: A Suitable Case for Charity. Directory of Social Change.

54 Walford, G. (ed.), 1989. *Private Schools in Ten Countries: Policy and*

Practice. Routledge.
55 Davison, R., 1992. Good Neighbours. Independent Schools Information Service (ISIS).
56 Willms, J. and Echols, F., 1992. 'Alert and Inert Clients: the Scottish Experience of Parental Choice of Schools.' *Economics and Education Review*, 11 (4).
57 HMI, 1992. The Education of Very Able Children in Maintained Schools. A Review by HMI. HMSO.
58 Carnegie Foundation for the Advancement of Teaching, 1992. *School Choice*. Carnegie.
59 Miliband, D., 1991. Markets, Politics and Education. Institute for Public Policy Research (IPPR).
60 Mortimore, P., 1991. 'The Nature and Findings of Research on School Effectiveness in the Primary Sector.' In: Riddell, S. and Brown, S. (eds.). School Effectiveness Research. Scottish Office Education Department, HMSO, pp. 9–19.
61 Eraut, M. and others, 1991 Flexible Learning in Schools. A Handbook Developed from the Research Project 'The Effective Management of Flexible Learning in Schools'. Employment Department.

8
Teachers and Teaching

Introduction

The new deal in the classroom that is necessary to realise our vision for the future of education is described in Chapter 3. Given that 'the most crucial factor at the heart of high quality learning is high quality teaching',[1] that new deal requires a simple but immensely powerful aim. Every pupil should be entitled in each lesson to be taught by a teacher with the knowledge, training, competence and commitment to teach that lesson well. This may seem an impossible ideal. Yet it is precisely this that is implicit in the entitlement to be taught the national curriculum which the law now lays down, during the compulsory phase of education. We show in this chapter how far we have to go to realise the ideal at present and we propose ways of moving nearer to it in the future. We cannot emphasise enough the importance of resolute action to that end.

Teaching Today and Tomorrow

A day in the life of a teacher in 1993 might typically begin with typing up a handwritten worksheet, photocopying it dozens of times, setting up a display board for the pupils and then programming the video for an educational broadcast. After taking the class register and collecting dinner money the teacher might deal with a welter of disciplinary or welfare problems. When the class moves on, the classroom will have to be tidied up and prepared for the next class. Perhaps, between counselling one pupil and providing careers guidance for another (in a secondary school), the teacher might deal with the malfunctioning computer. At the end of the day, letters must be written to parents, and time spent in the school office on management of the school's budget, perhaps involving raising funds from local businesses. On top of all of this, the teacher must somehow find the time and energy to do what he or she was trained to do, namely teach! Are these the conditions for high quality?

The problems raised by this question are expressed more solemnly by the OECD:

> Education's responsibilities, and hence those of teachers, have become more extensive and complex than in the past. More is expected from them in contributing towards, or even resolving, a whole array of economic, social, and cultural problems, while perceived shortcomings in these different domains commonly inspire the charge 'youngsters failed by school and teachers'.[2]

Teaching will always be affected by its context, whether this is a stable and healthy environment conducive to learning, or one presenting teachers with particular difficulties, perhaps undermining the task, through problems of economic deprivation, illness, family break-up and social disorder. Either way, too much of teachers' time is spent on activities that are peripheral to lesson preparation and pupil development, detracting from their role as professional educators. When developments in educational technology, rising participation, increasing expectations of education itself and the impact of rapidly changing legislation are added to the equation, it is easy to see how we have lost sight of what it is to be a teacher.

Morale and motivation

Morale is low in the teaching profession. A survey of teachers in England and Wales conducted for the Commission showed that only 9% of qualified teachers (not including heads or deputies) were very satisfied with their current post, against 37% who were not satisfied or not at all satisfied (the remainder being 'satisfied').[3] The introduction of the national curriculum, the new framework for assessment and the frequent changes to both, often at very short notice, have created a huge increase in teacher workload, especially through administration and paperwork. Few teachers enjoy this; it is not what they entered the profession for. The effects are shown in the increase in the number of resignations due to ill-health, which have nearly trebled since 1979,[4] and in the findings of research studies showing a disturbing incidence of job-related stress amongst teachers.[5]

The influence of better ways of learning

Developments and innovations in technology and teaching methods will have significant implications for the types of skills required by teachers and how they should be trained.[6] Chapter 5 argues that the scope for raising the quality of teaching through the use of new technology is as yet uncertain, but potentially enormous. Widespread adoption of independent learning methods will change teachers' relationships with pupils and require teachers to devote more time to preparing and adapting a wide variety of resources for individual learners. Of course, it will remain important to distinguish between the learning methods appropriate to different stages of learning and to recognise appropriate assessment procedures. Teaching might involve less emphasis on instruction and imparting information (though these will still feature), and more on planning, review, individual guidance and feedback.

We believe that the essence and importance of the teacher's role will not be changed at all by these developments in the tools and methods of teaching. The teacher will not become a 'facilitator', responsible for putting pupils in contact with the resources they require and providing advice. The knowledge and skills of the teacher – in particular, the teacher's understanding of the subject taught and how children learn – will remain central to the whole process. The developments do, however, have interesting implications for the enhancement of teachers' professionalism. Experts in the preparation of technology-based learning may be able to design resources according to teachers' specifications. Information technology will aid teachers' detailed knowledge of and insight into individual children's learning processes and free teachers from some of the more routine aspects of assessment.

We emphasise the increased importance of teachers continuing to be 'learners' and even researchers themselves, keeping up to date with both the knowledge base of their subject area and with advances in understanding about the techniques and technology of teaching and learning.[7] It is likely that they will increasingly need to work in co-operative relationships not only with colleagues in their own institutions but with a variety of professionals elsewhere. New technology will contribute to making it possible to 'open up' classrooms and lecture theatres to outside influences and put teachers and pupils in touch with resources and people in other institutions both in this country and abroad.

Twenty-first century teachers

In our vision, a teacher in the twenty-first century will be an authority and enthusiast in the knowledge, ideas, skills, understanding and values to be presented to pupils. The teacher will be an expert on effective learning, with knowledge of a range of classroom methods that can be intelligently applied and an understanding of appropriate organisational and management styles, conditions and resources. The teacher will have the capacity to think deeply about educational aims and values, and thereby critically about educational programmes. The teacher will be willing to motivate and encourage each and every pupil, assessing progress and learning needs in their widest sense, even when this involves them in areas outside formal education. The teacher will in the first instance be an educator, not only of the 'subject' being taught but also aiming to extend the intellectual, imaginative, inquiring and critical powers of his or her pupils, and to encourage them to question their wider personal and social values.

The more time that teachers can spend on teaching, and pupils on learning, the better. Given the inevitability of the pressures described earlier in this chapter, if quality and standards in education are to be raised and teachers are to have higher expectations of their pupils, we will need higher expectations of teachers themselves. In general, these expectations should relate to the teacher as an educator rather than in any extended capacity. Indeed, one of the central arguments of this chapter is that to deal with many of the increased demands, teachers will need to draw on a range of expertise and support: from external agencies (for example, for counselling); from those who support the learning process (for example, classroom assistants, teaching associates and parents); and from those to whom teachers could delegate many of the administrative tasks that often take up so much of their time.

In the light of our vision for teachers in the twenty-first

century, we next examine the quality of the profession today and find that all is not well. We then consider ways of raising the quality of entrants, and examine the training and development that they should receive throughout their careers. We discuss a range of ways in which the professional status of teaching might be raised, including better use of support staff. Finally, we propose some improvements to the way in which the profession is led.

The Quality of Teaching Today

It was generally agreed that there was a crisis in the supply of teachers in England and Wales in the 1980s and at the beginning of this decade, especially (but not exclusively) in certain 'shortage' subjects in secondary schools: modern languages, maths and sciences.[8] There was also concern about the related problem of the quality of teachers.[9] The Education Select Committee's inquiry into the supply of teachers for the 1990s received 'significant evidence that, while schools are still able to fill most vacancies, the number and quality of applicants for each post advertised has been declining'.[10] These problems have been greatly reduced in the last two or three years; the recession has been a major factor, although improvements in teachers' pay may have helped.

However, not only do the shortage subjects remain but a Briefing for the Commission prepared by the Institute of Manpower Studies warned more generally that 'there is no room for complacency about the future'.[11] The school population will grow over the next decade, partly for demographic reasons and partly because of the trend for more young people to continue in full-time education beyond the age of 16.[12] Meanwhile, economic recovery can be expected to make more difficult the tasks of remedying and avoiding the recurrence of teacher shortages, especially in certain subjects and in certain parts of England and Wales.

The challenge for the future must be to ensure a supply of high-quality entrants even in times of economic prosperity when teaching has to compete harder with other occupations. A golden opportunity exists now to raise the quality of teaching. Periods of low or no economic growth make teaching, like other public sector occupations, more financially attractive. Increasing numbers of graduates will boost the field of applicants to teaching. Initial teacher training (ITT) institutions should be able to be more selective, and thereby create a virtuous spiral with higher entry standards raising the status of the profession and thereby attracting even better qualified students. Before looking at ways of encouraging this process, we must look at the nature of the situation now and in the recent past.

Vacancies

There were 1,343 advertised vacancies for full-time permanent appointments in England in January 1993, equivalent to 0.4% of all teachers in post:[13] a substantial decline from the level of 1.8% in 1990.[14] Vacancy rates remain high in certain parts of the country, although local authority recruitment schemes and the discretion available to headteachers in awarding pay have eased these problems. There are also significant variations across subjects in secondary schools; for example, the vacancy rate for language teachers is double the secondary school average. There are, however, some problems with relying on vacancy figures for measuring the extent of teacher shortages. Not only are vacant posts a normal part of the process of recruitment, but schools can employ various means to deal with shortages such as filling a post with a temporary or supply teacher or a teacher qualified in another subject, or even abolishing the post completely. To have a more meaningful picture of teacher shortage we need to look beyond these figures.

Hidden shortages
When teaching is carried out by a teacher unqualified in a particular subject it is described as a hidden shortage. In 1992, 27% of tuition in secondary schools in England was undertaken by non-specialist teachers (where the subject was neither the main subject nor a subsidiary subject of the teacher's qualification).[15] This is shown in Figure 8.1 for years 7–9 (11–14-year-olds) in the core and foundation subjects of the curriculum.

Figure 8.1 Tuition in years 7–9 by non-specialist teachers, 1992, England.

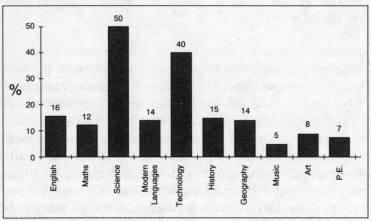

Source: Department for Education, 1993.[15]

A recent study found that 40% of secondary teachers thought that their academic background was well matched to no more than half or to only a small amount of the teaching they were required to carry out.[16] The teacher's own mastery of the subject closely affects the quality and intellectual challenge provided. We feel strongly that teaching with inadequate academic backgrounds is unacceptable, now and in the future. Not only does it fail this generation of schoolchildren but poor teaching can often discourage pupils from pursuing a subject or from considering teaching as a career when their time comes.

Suppressed shortages

When schools reduce or abandon tuition in a subject, or in more extreme cases when the requirements of the national curriculum are changed in response to lack of appropriate staff, this is known as a suppressed shortage. There are no figures available to quantify this but it is likely that it has applied to the teaching of modern languages and to craft, design and technology, subjects which will be of increasing importance.

Turnover

Resignations as a proportion of employment (turnover rates) provide another indicator of the state of the profession. Just over half of turnover arises from movement to other teaching jobs. The latest figure for England and Wales was 9.5% (in 1991); lower than in the previous three years.[17] Rapid turnover rates result in instability, slow rates result in stagnation, and establishing a satisfactory rate is very much a matter of balance. We are in no doubt that a series of high turnover rates over a succession of years prevents quality learning. Whilst the current overall level is acceptable, it was totally unacceptable immediately before the current recession and remains too high in particular regions (see Figure 8.2) and amongst large groups of teachers, for example, young teachers, language teachers and male primary teachers. We conclude that there have been, and to a lesser extent remain, problems associated with the retention of teachers which could damage the education of children.

Figure 8.2 Teacher turnover rate, 1985/6–1991, Greater London.

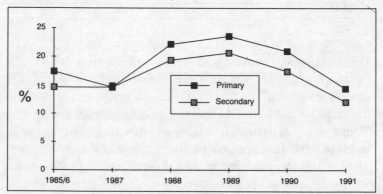

Source: Local Government Management Board, 1993.[17]

Quality of those entering teacher training
Teaching should attract intelligent and broadly educated recruits of the highest standard. Various sources suggest that the standards of those entering teacher training are not as high as they should be. Table 8.1 shows 'A' level scores of those entering undergraduate teacher training courses compared to other undergraduate degree courses (this does not take account of the fairly high number of non-standard entrants to these courses).[18] Two observations should be made. First, in both sectors, but particularly in universities, the average score of those entering teacher training has been lower than in other courses. Secondly, whilst over the five-year period the average score of those entering higher education has remained constant, in universities the average score of those entering teacher training has fallen slightly.

Table 8.1 'A' level score for entrants to initial teacher training (ITT) and other first degree courses, 1986-91, England.

Average point score

	1986	1987	1988	1989	1990	1991
ITT (university)	16.5	15.4	14.7	14.5	14.2	14.4
Other courses (university)	22.4	22.2	22.2	22.3	22.4	22.3
ITT (polytechnic/college)	10.5	10.8	10.3	10.7	10.6	10.3
Other courses (polytechnic/college)	12.0	12.0	12.7	12.7	12.8	12.0

Source: Department for Education, 1992.[18]   (N.B. A = 10 points, B = 8 points etc.)

Table 8.2 shows those entering post-graduate courses by degree class for primary teaching and three shortage secondary subjects in universities in England and Wales in 1991.[19] Undergraduate degree results in all higher education institutions in 1990 are shown in the bottom row to enable a rough comparison.[20] In both primary and the shortage secondary subjects the high proportion of lower second class degrees will be noted, as will the extraordinarily high level of third class degrees for the shortage subjects.

Table 8.2 Entrants to university PGCE courses by degree class, 1991, England & Wales.

Percentages

Sector Subject	Higher degree	1st	2:1	2:2	2 (undi-vided)	3rd	Pass/general	Other grad eqv	Total
Primary	0.8	1.9	37.4	45.4	0.6	4.4	7.9	1.6	100
Maths	3.9	4.9	20.6	32.4	1.5	20.1	14.0	2.4	100
Chem.	9.3	5.6	20.9	30.2	0.3	17.3	11.6	4.9	100
Physics	6.0	3.8	22.0	29.3	1.1	19.0	14.4	4.3	100
All graduates		7.2	38.0	36.6	0.2	3.1	14.9	-	100

Sources: Universities Council for the Education of Teachers, 1993;[19] Department for Education, 1993.[20]

The Commission's survey of the career choices and perceptions of undergraduates tells a similar story.[21] Table 8.3 shows the extent to which undergraduates were considering school teaching according to their expected degree result.

Table 8.3 Extent to which undergraduates were considering teaching, 1992, United Kingdom.

Percentages

Expected degree	Have chosen/ applied/ am applying	Considering applying	May consider as a last resort	Would not consider	Did not reply	Total
1st	9.4	13.1	37.5	39.4	0.6	100
2:1	11.7	17.4	33.1	36.4	1.4	100
2:2	18.4	18.1	28.6	34.3	0.6	100
3rd	27.4	12.9	29.0	29.0	1.7	100

Source: National Commission on Education, forthcoming.[21]

Again, it was noted that the standard of those intending to go into teaching (this time self-evaluated) was much lower than other professions. Clearly, the teaching profession is not attracting entrants of high enough quality and a golden opportunity is now being missed to raise standards, a subject to which we return.

Quality of practising teachers
The Commission has observed some outstanding teaching in this country but it has also noted evidence of real shortcomings. HM Inspectorate found that of the 22,500 sessions in 3,250 primary schools that were inspected, 30% were deemed poor.[22] Of the 18,000 sessions in 2,400 secondary schools that were inspected, 27% were deemed poor. This cannot be acceptable. HMI's verdict for particular groups of pupils and particular types of areas is even more worrying. They emphasised a failure to challenge pupils sufficiently, particularly in the case of less

able pupils. Much lower standards were noted in areas of disadvantage, where, for example, 45% of sessions for 8–11-year-olds were deemed poor.

The poor quality of some lessons may be attributed to teachers not being qualified in the appropriate subject area, but there is also evidence of more general problems with teachers' support of learning. We commissioned a survey of the views of pupils in the early years of secondary school. It found that 44% of year 7 pupils and 45% of year 9 pupils indicated that they never talked individually to their class teachers about their work, and 42% of year 7 pupils and 41% of year 9 pupils indicated that they never talked individually to other teachers about their work.[23] Only 55% of year 7 pupils and 50% of year 9 pupils indicated that all or most of their teachers praised them when they did their work well.

We have been impressed by the expertise and dedication of many of the individual teachers whom we have met. But the barrage of evidence is alarming and leads to a clear conclusion that the quality of a significant minority of teachers is unsatisfactory and that the overall quality of the profession needs to be raised.

Recruiting to Raise Quality

Promoting an attractive career
Raising the quality of the teaching profession to meet the demands of the twenty-first century depends greatly on those who are now entering or will shortly enter initial teacher training. An increased range of employment opportunities, particularly for women, will require teaching to compete hard with other professions for graduate recruits. As with the fall in vacancies described earlier, the recent rise in applications to teacher training courses, particularly post-graduate courses,[18,19] may be a short-term response

to the economic climate. It is vital that we consider the long-term attractiveness of the profession and aim to draw on the widest range of talent and skills to staff the profession, regardless of gender, race or disability. Perceptions of teaching as a career are not nearly as high as they should be. Figure 8.3 is derived from the Commission's survey of undergraduates. The black points indicate the students' ratings of 15 criteria in their general career choice and the white points indicate the students' perceptions of the extent to which teaching fulfils these criteria.[21]

Figure 8.3 Rating of career criteria and perceptions of teaching in fulfilling them, 1992, United Kingdom.

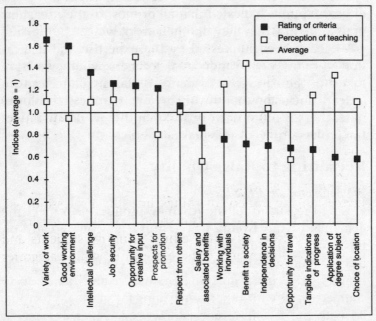

Source: National Commission on Education, forthcoming.[21]

In general, teaching was rated highest for those criteria which were considered relatively unimportant by the undergraduates (opportunity for creative input being the exception). On the other hand, the survey results give some room for optimism, with teaching rated above average for four of the five most popular criteria. Those undergraduates already intending to go into teaching rated it much higher for these criteria. The profession offers considerable scope for working with individuals in an independent, creative way and the salaries offered are now much more competitive. We conclude that much more attention should be paid to the way in which teaching is promoted to those considering their career options. Perceptions of teaching have been damaged by the media,[21] which along with politicians, should be more keen to publicise success stories in teaching rather than denigrating the profession. The teachers' unions also have a responsibility for the public image of the profession which they have not always discharged well.

The more attractive teaching is seen as a career option the more it will attract high-quality potential teachers. Similarly, a higher quality of entrants will raise the status of the profession and in turn contribute to its attractiveness. Meanwhile, its positive attributes must be boosted and promoted.

Routes into the profession
Increasing the variety of routes into the profession will not in itself raise quality. But some flexibility is desirable to attract mature students, ethnic minority students and non-standard entrants.[24] There are three main categories of entrants.

1 *Young entrants.* It is vital that young people, often not long out of school, should see teaching as a challenging career. Work experience has a very positive influence on perceptions of teaching[21] and should not be

used just to deal with short-term shortages.
Education authorities have, and will continue to
have, a key role in both promoting teaching and
recruiting teachers. They must reach out to sixth-
formers and undergraduates and offer attractive
recruitment packages. Teachers themselves have an
important role in presenting their profession
positively to young people – including their own
pupils.

2   *Mature entrants.* Undergraduate teacher training courses have a much higher proportion of mature
entrants (26 or over) than other first degree courses,
and almost half the entrants to post-graduate teacher
training are mature entrants.[18] Those with experience of other work have a particular contribution to
make. We commend positive efforts to attract
mature entrants through new and more flexible
routes into teaching such as the Articled Teacher
Scheme (shown to be of high quality but
expensive),[25] the Licensed Teacher Scheme (useful
for attracting teachers in shortage subjects when
carefully selected),[26] Access courses (described by
HMI as 'successful in preparing students for entry to
initial teacher training'),[27] part-time and two-year
courses for the post-graduate certificate in education
(PGCE) and distance learning courses (through the
Open University). Flexible employment contracts
would also address some of the needs of older
entrants.

3   *Returners to the profession.* There are over 350,000
qualified teachers who are currently 'out of service':
73% are women.[28] Many of these may return to
teaching: a government survey found that 17%
intended to return to teaching and 41% would consider it.[29] Indeed over half of entrants to full-time
teaching are returning after a career break.[30] This
proportion has risen substantially in recent years
(32.5% in 1980). These returners represent a valuable resource for the profession but they may have

special needs for employment arrangements such as
availability of part-time work, more flexible hours
and 'job-shares'.[29] Courses of retraining and refresh-
ment are also particularly important, given the rapid
pace of change in curriculum, assessment and other
matters. Some authorities have 'keeping in touch'
schemes which maintain contact with non-practising
teachers, restore their confidence and help transition
back into the classroom through carefully graded and
managed stages and in-service education and training
(INSET) support.[31] We commend this good practice
as essential for raising the quality of the profession.

A quality teaching profession should not have barriers to
entry for any group in society. Many of the individuals
and organisations that have submitted evidence to the
Commission have expressed concern that ethnic minorities are under-represented in the teaching force, in particular Afro-Caribbeans and Asians. This is a worrying problem today but also for the future, as it means a lack of role
models to influence ethnic minority children who might
otherwise have been interested in teaching. The 1985
report of the Committee of Inquiry into the education of
ethnic minority children (the Swann Committee) found
that: 'teachers from ethnic minorities are regrettably and
evidently a minority in themselves.'[32] It recommended that
government should record and publish statistics on the ethnic origins of all teachers in employment. This recommendation was echoed by Government's subsequent Working
Group in 1987.[33] It is regrettable that, despite this, the
Government has failed to publish any statistics of the ethnic
origins of teachers either in post or in training. This failure
prevents the profession and the public from having an
accurate picture of the ethnic composition of the teaching
force, from setting recruitment targets, and from monitoring progress.

We have attempted to gain a rough picture of the current situation. A 1988 survey by the Commission for Racial Equality found that only 2% of teachers were of ethnic minority origin, whereas the average ethnic minority population in the UK stood at around 5.5% and, in most of the eight areas surveyed, was higher than this (one 26.6% and one 33.5%).[34] Of applications to university undergraduate teacher training courses in 1992, 2% were from Asian students and 1% were from black students. In the same year, 24% of applications for medicine were from Asian students and 7% of applications for law courses were from black students.[35] As far as post-graduate teacher training is concerned, the Commission's survey showed that only 4.1% of the Asian undergraduates had chosen or were applying for teaching, as compared to 13.8% for the whole sample.[21] More than any other group, Asian students rated highly career criteria for which teaching scored lowest and were negatively influenced in their perception of teaching by family and friends.

Much greater effort is needed to attract ethnic minority teachers into the profession. Programmes like Teaching as a Career (TASC) should do more to target materials on young potential teachers from ethnic minorities, encouraging a positive view of the status and value of teaching. It is also probably fair to assume that, if teacher training did more to equip teachers to teach in a multicultural society, ethnic minority pupils would be more likely to become interested in teaching earlier.

Ensuring quality
Recent Government proposals for non-graduate primary teachers are a retrograde step. Not only do they diminish the importance of the early years in education but they are contrary to the trend in most industrialised countries

and threaten to create a two-tier profession.[36] The Commission recommends that teaching continues to be an all-graduate profession. All secondary teachers should have a degree in their specialist subjects, as is already the case in most countries, including Scotland and Northern Ireland. All entrants to teacher training courses should undergo a rigorous selection procedure with a clearly planned interview judging such attributes as personality, motivation, commitment, communication skills, inspirational qualities and potential, and with tests assessing competence. Our proposals in Chapter 4 for a broad based school curriculum will provide a better foundation for students going on to teacher training.[37] We would expect that those training to be primary teachers should have a GCSE (grade A–C) or equivalent in English, maths, a science and a modern foreign language as well as the standard entrance requirements for the course.

These recommendations could cause some short-term recruitment problems, although that is by no means certain. Universities which have raised entrance qualifications have found that they become more, not less, desirable. In any event, the quality of teaching is the paramount consideration and long-term recruitment, as well as status, can only benefit from raising the quality of entrants.

Training and Development

A career-long process
From the point at which teachers are accepted for initial teacher training to the point at which they retire, their training and development must be seen as a continuum. Our theme of education and training as a life-long experience is at least as important for teachers as for anyone else. Their professional careers will need to be managed in

a coherent and unified way to meet and maintain the level of quality in the profession that we judge to be desirable. As boundaries between schools and colleges become more fluid, we hope that teachers will see themselves as having entered the education service rather than a particular phase. We realise that our proposals for the training and development of teachers cannot be achieved without extra resources. This issue is addressed in Chapter 14.

Initial training

Initial teacher training (ITT) provides the foundation upon which the career of the teacher is based and is thus the foundation for very many pupils' learning. Getting ITT right is therefore of the highest importance. This cannot be judged in terms of the degree to which ITT turns out teachers prepared for the whole of their working lives since that would ignore what can be achieved through subsequent training and development. However, expectations about what can be achieved in ITT must be high. A rigorous period of training and education is essential for anyone entering a profession, not least teaching, and this is reflected in the fact that most industrialised countries are increasing the amount of training that teachers receive.[38]

ITT at present is in a state of flux with:

- diversification of training routes (primarily a response to teacher shortages), with growing numbers of entrants on part-time and other non-conventional courses;[39]

- a move towards basing training more in schools rather than in higher education institutions with Government stipulations about the amount of time that trainees must spend in schools[40] and pilot schemes for training based wholly in schools;[41]

- courses responding to criteria set by the Council for the Accreditation of Teacher Education (CATE)[42] by becoming more 'practical' rather than 'theoretical'.

Recent Inspectorate reports have presented a very mixed picture of the quality of current initial teacher training. They judged only 50% of new teachers to be well equipped for their post, with 19% less than satisfactorily equipped (although the figures given by headteachers were 73% and 8%).[43] In the training of primary school teachers, work in the higher education institutions on subject studies was described as 'generally sound'; 'good work was common' and staff 'were generally well qualified and experienced'.[44] There are, however, severe problems with the extent to which primary teachers are prepared for teaching the national curriculum. For example, less than a third of new teachers felt well prepared to teach reading. This is a particular problem on post-graduate courses, where only 22% felt well prepared. 'Time allocated to training to teach reading, writing, numeracy and science was being cut,' and 'there is insufficient time adequately to train primary student teachers to teach all the non-core subjects of the basic curriculum.'[22] These are very serious issues, given our concern that all pupils should receive sound teaching in the basic subjects. University PGCE courses for secondary teachers were described as satisfactory for most subjects, although some problems in maths, science and modern languages were cited.[45]

The Commission has received a substantial amount of evidence that the PGCE course for primary teachers cannot provide an adequate training for teaching the national curriculum effectively.[45,46] Government proposals to extend the length of the course by two weeks[37] will do no more than scratch the surface of the problem. The

Inspectorate, in a visit to two German regions, noted that the greater length and depth of teacher training there is regarded as an 'investment in quality' and 'does not appear to deter applicants'.[47] Whilst supporting the move to more school-focused training in primary as well as secondary schools, we are concerned about the view of HMI and others that primary schools 'do not generally have the capacity or the range of expertise needed to take on significant additional training responsibilities without considerable support'.[48] As a result of these concerns, the Commission recommends increased funding for the training taking place in primary schools and the extension of primary PGCE courses to fill a calendar rather than an academic year.

There seems no doubt that the most successful teacher training occurs when there is a genuine partnership between school and higher education institution, each playing a distinctive part according to strength, reinforcing the work of the other[49] with a 'clearly conceived relationship' for integrating this work.[46] From this partnership local bodies cannot be excluded. They can play a valuable role in the selection of suitable schools for teaching practice, where HMI have argued that 'there is a strong case for greater involvement of the LEA, and of advisers in particular'.[50] Once trainees have become secure in their subjects as we recommend, classroom skills are at the heart of teacher training. These skills can be acquired only by solid, continuous experience in a school working alongside experienced practitioners. However, to place all the responsibility for training on schools is impracticable and ignores the theoretical base: students can plan work and approach classes with more confidence if they have some knowledge of how children learn and which methods have been found successful in different circumstances. Theory and practice should mutually reinforce each other.

Quite apart from this, the teachers and schools acting as mentors to trainees need time, training and support, all of which must be adequately funded.

We see the roles of higher education institutions to be to:

- operate a system of admissions to ITT, to assess and support students and to administer and validate qualifications for entry to the profession so that quality is ensured across the system;

- provide breadth of perspective going beyond particular circumstances of individual schools and areas and providing access to a full range of educational research;

- develop knowledge and understanding in trainees, not just about teaching the national curriculum, but also about how children learn, about stimulating better ways of learning, about providing pastoral and careers guidance, and about assessment, management, equal opportunities and cultural awareness;[51]

- allow economies of scale in such essential training facilities as information technology, libraries and, of course, staff expertise;

- initiate profiles of students which will stay with them for the rest of their careers, and which will be continuously updated;

- provide support and training for mentors;

- provide consultancy, critical perspective in professional development, advanced degrees for teachers and educational research for the whole system.

We see the role of schools as providing:

- practical experience for pupils in the classroom,

opportunities to learn and apply skills, and a context for reflection;

- experienced teachers, whom students can witness in action and work alongside;

- an understanding of how a school functions and relates to the community;

- well-trained mentors, with sufficient time allocated in their own timetables to give advice and support to trainees;

- input into the assessment of trainees' suitability for teaching.

Induction

Initial training is only the first stage in the preparation of the teacher and is unlikely to anticipate the wide diversity of situations that will be faced. Much of the learning process will be best developed once the teacher is in post and it is essential that schools do not have too high expectations of the capabilities of new teachers. The Inspectorate has judged the performance of new teachers to be as good as that of teachers in general,[44] but nearly half of the secondary schools surveyed gave newly qualified teachers jobs which made more demands on them than were appropriate, fewer than half provided conditions which encouraged the full professional development of the new teacher,[52] and the quality of arrangements for induction were unsatisfactory or poor in about one third of LEAs.[22] The quality of experience during the first couple of years in post is crucial not only in developing skills, knowledge and understanding gained from initial training, but also in influencing attitudes to the career as a whole.[53] We note that in 1991, 38.4% of those leaving teaching for another job had been in post for under two years.[17] Of course, it is to be expected that some teachers will find in their first year or two that they have chosen the wrong career, but it is our impression that the main cause of such high wastage springs from over-burdening teachers when they first enter- the profession. A carefully managed induction programme is essential for creating a truly professional teacher.

This has been recognised for many years, but the system has only been tinkered with. Some authorities have excellent programmes, even by international standards, but such provision is not standard across the country, as the present Government guidelines are voluntary and therefore not always implemented.[54] HMI stated that: 'there were unacceptably wide variations in levels of support for new teachers, not only across LEAs but also across schools in the same LEA.'[22] This is corroborated by the NFER which found a large variation across LEAs in the number of days to which new teachers were entitled for induction activities, ranging from one to over 20.[55]

Opportunities for further learning following completion of initial training must be increased. Teachers, schools and authorities will differ in the precise content of the induction programme that is most appropriate, but a statutory national code of practice might provide a framework. We also propose that qualified teacher status (QTS) shall only be provisionally granted at the end of ITT and will be granted in full only at the end of a successfully completed induction period, normally of two years. We recommend that induction programmes should be funded by an earmarked grant from central government to Education and Training Boards (ETBs, the local bodies we propose in Chapter 13) and should ensure that each new teacher:

- has a probationary period, normally of two years, with an entitlement to a formal high-quality induction programme, provided by the ETB in conformity with the statutory national code, giving clearly defined roles to each of the partners;

- is allocated a mentor to advise and give support throughout this period, who has been trained for this role and given non-contact time (time away from pupils) to carry it out;

- has a detailed profile passed on from the training institution describing training undertaken, highlighting special expertise, skills, other personal strengths (including those gained before the training course) and areas for development, and informing the particular induction programme devised for that teacher;

- is entitled to a greater amount of non-contact time for continued training, planning, observation of experienced teachers, consolidation and reflection;

- is given opportunities to be observed and to receive feedback from the observer in structured discussion.

Information on the performance of new teachers during the induction period will provide valuable feedback for HE institutions and schools on the effectiveness of their training and selection.

Continuing professional development and appraisal

Teachers, like other professionals, develop throughout their careers. Not only will they wish to upgrade skills, knowledge and understanding, and perhaps take on roles of greater responsibility but they will also need to be updated in a rapidly changing education world. The Education Select Committee pointed out that opportunities for career development such as INSET and secondments 'can be as important to the mid-career teacher as financial incentives'.[10] The OECD has stressed that the need to keep abreast of developments in subject studies requires 'high quality continuing professional development'. INSET is being recognised by many industrialised countries as a 'high and permanent priority'.[2]

We endorse this view, but our own consultations amongst teachers in this country have revealed substantial gaps in this area. The bulk of INSET provision relates to priorities set nationally and keeps teachers updated about recent reforms, in particular in the curriculum. This has hindered personal development and the continuing development of teaching practices and strategies. There is also concern that the devolution of funding for professional development to schools may lead to schools 'recycling their own inadequacies'[47] unless they are able to question their own assumptions and engage with a wider range of experience. Advisory teachers have been shown to have a key role here,[56] as have universities and other external providers, including those outside the education world. The main point is that, whatever the purposes of INSET, curriculum updating, improvement of teaching methods or management training, they must ultimately lead to an improvement in the quality of learning for pupils in schools.[57]

We recommend the following:

1 All schools, as part of their school development plan, should have a policy for staff development with equal opportunities, regardless of gender, ethnicity or disability.

2 All teachers should have a personal development plan (PDP) in the formulation of which they should have had an active role and which should be linked to their profiles. This will outline their needs for training, responsibilities in the school, experience

outside the school (such as work experience, secondments and sabbaticals) and further qualifications. The plan will continuously evolve as INSET courses and other experiences are credited.

3 The system of teacher appraisal will draw on the profile and PDP of the individual teacher and will not only assess performance and progress but will also identify specific needs and plan for the fulfilment of potential.

4 Every teacher should be entitled to two days each year for INSET outside the school for personal development (not for training to cope with national initiatives).

One area that needs urgent attention is management training, where 'current provision does not match the requirements of the service'.[58] A report for the Government has argued that: 'the vitally important contribution of such factors as leadership, vision, culture, collaborative decision-making and the like, should surely figure prominently in training and development activities.'[59] Particular attention needs to be paid to management development opportunities for female teachers. Career breaks for family reasons, for example, are thought to disadvantage women in progressing to headships.[60] Another area needing attention is the use of information technology, where a Government survey has shown a particularly high proportion (47%) of secondary school teachers who were 'not confident'.[61] We emphasise the importance of training in these areas in other parts of our report.

Appraisal has now been introduced for all teaching staff. We welcome this initiative, which could help significantly to improve teaching quality. Properly used, appraisal allows the individual teacher to consider strengths and weaknesses, to receive credit for the former and discuss measures to address the latter. It links positively with professional development and should help to focus it on the needs of the individual rather than of the institution. It also offers the headteacher a means of tackling unsatisfactory teaching in the school. The profession as a whole is not finding it easy to adjust to this type of performance review, but appraisal should be seized as an opportunity to address weakness where it exists. In the last resort, the powers of dismissal do exist and should be used where necessary. The role of a General Teaching Council, discussed later in this chapter, should be important here.

The Conditions for Quality

A new structure for pay and progression
Career progression and rewards for experienced teachers are not sufficient to ensure recruitment, retention and motivation of high-quality professionals. The starting salary of the new teacher has almost caught up with that of other graduates and we hope that comparability will be achieved and maintained.[62] But of greater concern is the increasing gap throughout the career of the teacher, so that by mid-career most teachers are earning well below those in other professions.[63] Figure 8.4 shows that sporadic attempts to improve the position of teachers have not prevented their average pay from falling relative to average non-manual earnings, to a level only 2% higher.[64]

The position with respect to comparable professions is obviously much worse. It will not be satisfactory for a profession so vital to the future well-being of the country to continue to lose ground. These concerns are widespread: Figure 8.3 shows undergraduates' low perceptions of the promotion prospects for teachers; and the London

Figure 8.4 Average teachers' pay as a percentage of average non-manual earnings, 1974–1994, England and Wales.

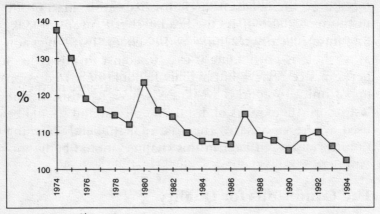

Sources: NUT, 1993.[64]

School of Economics (LSE) survey showed that 49% of teachers saw 'opportunities for promotion' as unsatisfactory or very unsatisfactory.[3] The School Teachers' Review Body (STRB) recognises this: 'more needs to be done to improve subsequent salary progression for able teachers'.[65] The Education Select Committee referred to 'very poor pay prospects in mid-career'.[10] It has been difficult for teaching skills to be rewarded or progression to occur without the teacher taking on additional administrative responsibilities and 'a major concern has been the lack of salary rewards for the teacher who wishes to remain in the classroom rather than taking on an administrative or managerial function'.[10] A study of secondary teachers' use of time found that 'the higher the salary status, the less the teaching'.[16] There were also problems with the use of incentive allowances which was haphazard and not necessarily linked with rewarding performance or attracting teachers in shortage subjects.[30]

New arrangements for 1993 have much to commend them, with the replacement of a complex array of incentive allowances, discretionary scale points and enhancements, by a single pay spine, in which progression depends on proven merit. We would, however, recommend the following features for the use of the spine:

- competitive and flexible entry points on the spine, above which a new teacher can only advance on the completion of the induction period;

- an advance of at least two points up the spine after the award of QTS (in line with the more rapid progression shown by other graduate professions);

- further multiple steps to motivate the teacher who has demonstrated high standards of classroom practice or who has taken on other teaching responsibilities.

Teachers and their work

Teachers' workloads have increased, partly due to the recent pace of change in education. The Chilver Report noted that: 'classroom teachers were often working well in excess of the minimum prescribed working year in order to achieve the standards they had set themselves.'[66] Recent studies show the average time spent on work during a term-time week to be between 50 and 55 hours for secondary school teachers[16] and 50 hours for primary teachers.[67] The survey of teachers we commissioned showed that not having a manageable workload was seen as a key factor leading to dissatisfaction by 69% of teachers.[3] Whilst any professional can expect to have a demanding workload, not all confined to officially allotted hours, there are three particular aspects of the workloads of teachers to which we have paid close attention: class size and non-contact time in primary schools and the case for increased use of non-teaching staff in both primary and secondary schools.

Class size constitutes a central factor in a teacher's workload by contributing to stress and fatigue, by generating further work outside lessons and, most importantly, by spreading more thinly the attention the teacher can give to individual pupils. Chapter 7 examines this issue in more depth and includes our proposals for the future.

All teachers need non-contact time for planning, lesson preparation, assessment and individual attention for pupils. Teachers in primary schools have little or no timetabled non-contact time and this was recently recognised by the STRB: 'We are concerned about the negligible amount of non-contact time available to most primary teachers within the timetabled school week. If this does not increase in the next year or two, we may be persuaded to overcome our reluctance to interfere with local discretion and to recommend a statutory minimum.'[66] The studies of teachers' time cited earlier found that Key Stage 1 teachers had on average 22 minutes per week of non-contact time[70] (whereas 80% of secondary school teachers had over three hours).[16] Sixty-eight per cent of primary school teachers considered this 'unsatisfactory' or 'very unsatisfactory' in the survey we commissioned.[3] This should be seen in conjunction with HMI's view that: 'By one route or another something around 10% non-contact time for each teacher is needed. Without it, many primary schools, particularly small ones, will be unable to implement fully the national curriculum and its related assessment and reporting.'[68]

Too much of teachers' time actually spent both with and apart from pupils is devoted to tasks secondary to their professional role. We believe such tasks should be delegated to non-teaching staff. It is to making this a reality that we now turn.

Support staff

'By under-investing in para-professionals, we have wasted part of the massive investment in teachers.'[69] This was written in 1978, a time when reformers rarely mentioned the subject of non-teaching staff. Since then, increasing powers for schools over their budgets and the introduction of the national curriculum have generated interest in the way that teachers spend their time. Examinations of the allocation of teachers' time found that the proportion of time actually spent teaching was 44% for primary teachers[68] and 31% for secondary teachers.[16] The figure for secondary teachers rises to 37% if registration, supervision and assembly are included, a figure roughly comparable to the 41% found by a teachers' union in a similar study.[16] A substantial amount of the time not spent actually teaching relates directly to the teaching process. However, it is clear that teachers spend too much time on relatively low level routine tasks, acting as 'clerical assistants, cleaners and secretaries', in '*ad hoc* and mundane duties' with an 'inefficient, ineffective and uneconomic use' of their time.[70]

Much of what teachers do in school does not require a qualified teacher to do it, for example, marking attendance registers, supervising the playground, issuing and collecting notes to parents, collecting money, photocopying worksheets and preparing displays. Although it is very important that teachers have contact with their pupils outside formal lesson time there should be far more people in schools who can support teachers by taking responsibility for some of these tasks, freeing teachers to implement their professional role. This would not only be a more effective use of resources but would also raise the morale of teachers. In a special study of non-teaching staff, in schools, HMI commented that: 'in the vast majority of primary and secondary schools the work of these staff is so valuable that important aspects of teaching and learning would be curtailed without their help.'[71] A large study for the Government found that: 'non-teaching staff are a valuable (and valued) resource. The work of such staff is cost-effective on educational criteria. There is considerable scope for further development of the innovatory staffing practices described.'[70]

We believe that teachers should be seen as managers of a range of expertise and support in the classroom. The Commission's vision of the classroom for the next century includes a significant growth in the number of classroom assistants, those staff without a graduate teaching qualification but with regular contact with pupils which is directly part of the educational development of the child, but always under the supervision of a qualified teacher. This type of staff is becoming very common, especially now that schools have control over their own budgets. We believe that there should be further expansion in the use of classroom assistants and perhaps qualifications, training and development to establish a much more coherent career structure for them.

Opening up schools
The work of teachers and the whole atmosphere of learning will be helped by opening up schools more to the outside world. We discuss this further in Chapter 7. There is substantial evidence that if they are properly prepared, then bringing parents, members of the community and other outsiders, whose knowledge or skills may complement those of teachers, into schools to help with the learning process can have a positive impact on school effectiveness.[72] The reasons for this are not only related to the introduction of specialist knowledge or skills but also to the improvement of links between the school, the parents and the rest of the community. There are many

examples of good practice in this area: the Pimlico Scheme, for example, brings engineering undergraduates into the classroom; the UNCLE scheme does the same with retired engineers; Ford's 'Industrialists in Residence' scheme seconds employees who are 'able to make a unique contribution' to schools;[73] the Paul Hamlyn Foundation has been funding two other pilot schemes. The opening up of schools can work both ways, with teachers interacting more with the community and being involved in out-of-hours extra-curricular activities both within and outside the school. We recommend further development and government support for schemes of this kind.

The working environment and resources

Many teachers work in an environment in which they are unable to perform to their full potential. A government study found that 38% of primary and 24% of secondary school buildings needed structural work and a National Audit Office survey subsequently showed that all 48 responding authorities faced difficulties with repairs and maintenance.[74] More recently, HMI found that accommodation was unsatisfactory in about 40% of primary and 30% of secondary schools.[22] The problems were particularly severe in primary schools where they noted lack of space for practical work, cramped teaching areas, library provision that was 'rarely very good' and about one-third of schools that did not have sufficient resources to meet the requirements of the core subjects of the national curriculum. These findings are yet another example of the neglect that has plagued primary education. HMI commented on the adverse effects on the quality of education caused by unsuitable buildings and the problems this causes in attracting to the teaching profession able and enthusiastic teachers.

Just to bring buildings up to an adequate standard for today would require a substantial injection of resources. However, the impact of new technology will present a significant opportunity to upgrade premises to meet the rather different needs of the future. For example, the implications of advances in communication technologies with data and telecommunications networking between educational buildings must be considered in all new planning. Extra space will be required for the increased movement of pupils and staff involved in individualised instruction and also for such facilities as library/resource areas, technical workshops and suitable places for the preparation of learning materials. For these reasons, it needs to be recognised that improvement of the working environment of schools should be a major priority for resources.

Better support for teachers from educational technology
There is potential for beneficial changes in the day-to-day work of teachers. Chapter 5 shows how advances in educational technology could aid the learning process. Developments, if exploited by the education world, could also provide increasing support for teachers in planning work, assessing pupils, recording achievement, interacting with each other and dealing with administrative tasks.[6] It is therefore essential that all staff are helped to become computer literate.

Leading the Profession

Low status and morale are exacerbated by weak leadership at all levels in the teaching profession, the largest graduate workforce in the UK. At the school level, senior staff have had responsibilities thrust on them for which they are ill-prepared; at the local level, LEAs retain 'the legal responsibilities of an employer, but with little power to manage the deployment of their staff'; and at the national level, 'personnel matters have been administered piecemeal', with a lack of any strategic focus.[75] All these issues need to be addressed if our vision for a high-quality teaching profession is to be achieved.

Preparation, selection and development of headteachers
Good leadership is one of the key features of successful schools (see Chapter 7). This has been emphasised time and time again, both by the Inspectorate, by researchers and by practitioners. It has always been the case, particularly in Britain where heads have a powerful role, but the major changes which are affecting schools will make even more significant demands. Such changes increase the importance of adaptability and place a premium on the ability to manage change. This is affecting all senior staff in schools, but is felt most by heads, whose roles and responsibilities have increased most of all. Most important, the increase in management tasks has not reduced the need for senior staff to provide curriculum leadership and to maintain concern for the development of professional skills throughout the school.

Government has stressed that successful implementation of its reforms depends on leadership of schools by experienced, dedicated and highly motivated heads. We agree with that judgement. However, the preparation, selection and development of heads in this country is haphazard. There is plenty of good practice but it must spread. Issues requiring attention include:[76]

- difficulties in identifying potentially good managers early enough in teachers' careers for them to be properly prepared;

- a rather *ad hoc* system of headteacher preparation in Britain which contrasts with other countries, in particular the USA, where there is compulsory certification;

- haphazard practices in the selection of headteachers in this country (e.g. poorly trained and informed selection panels), which compare very unfavourably with those of other large organisations, in both the public and private sectors, and with systems of selection of heads abroad;

- too few authorities with formal induction schemes for new heads (in 1988, only 25% of authorities provided formal programmes);

- too little commitment to management courses for heads and potential heads, with restricted resources and delegated budgets making heads reluctant to find the time or money for training for themselves and senior staff.

The following are recommended:

1 The preparation for headship, recognition of suitability and development of headteachers should be integral parts of general staff development. Preparation for headship needs to begin as early as initial teacher training with the recognition of the importance of leadership and management skills throughout all careers. Good potential headteachers need to be recognised early and encouraged to develop those skills which will stand them in good stead.

2 The work of the Council for Innovation in Teaching and Learning (CITL), described in Chapter 5, should include co-ordinating research into the development of educational leadership, including training and developing senior staff.

3 Heads should be entitled to appropriate preparation for their role, well before their first appointment. One of the principal responsibilities of the head is the development of staff and this must be stressed in their training. There should be better use of the period of deputy headship for preparation for headship with heads taking a more explicit, active and conscious role in career development of deputies, mainly through on-the-job experience but also through training and development.

4 There is a need to adopt a more professional approach to the selection of heads. School governors have an important role in ensuring that the successful candidate is appropriate for the specific nature of the school and is able to work constructively with them on appointment. They should, however, be better trained in this process than they are at present. The selection panel should have five members, three from the governing body, an adviser or inspector from the ETB and an external professional assessor from outside the area (for example from OFSET), all with equal voting rights. For every post there should be minimum requirements in terms of the information advertised, the information required from candidates and the practices involved in selection.

5 New heads should be entitled to an induction programme that not only addresses general issues of headship but is also geared towards the particular needs of the school, the locality, and of course the individual head. The headship mentoring scheme (where new heads can be paired with an experienced and established head) should also be made an entitlement and might be extended from one to two years. It is important that the mentors themselves should have received high-quality training and that when active, funding for cover is available to enable them to fulfil their role properly.

6 At the end of the induction period the expectation

should be that heads will require and be entitled to a certain amount of further training. Training requirements will be identified through appraisal, personal development plans and perhaps assessment of skills. In general, there should be a shift in the emphasis of headship development away from financial and marketing subjects which should be delegated, to more wide-ranging areas such as the development of school culture and creating a positive climate and ethos, curriculum and professional leadership, staff development, strategic planning and the management of change.

Government and the teaching profession

The teaching profession requires some direction from government. The proposals above will allow significant improvements to leadership of teachers and other staff at the level of the school and within Authorities. However, many of the problems of personnel management in the profession are a result of a lack of coherent vision at the national level. In Chapter 13 we propose a Teachers' Management Board which will bring appropriate expertise to bear on this within central government.

A General Teaching Council

It is important that those who are actually teaching have a degree of control over and responsibility for their own profession and involvement in the process of change. The Commission, in line with a wide range of individuals and organisations that have provided it with evidence on the teaching profession, recommends statutory self-regulation of the teaching profession through a General Teaching Council (GTC).[77] Most professions in Britain have such a body and Scotland has had a GTC since 1966.[78] A GTC south of the border might eventually have more extensive powers, but its initial functions should, we suggest, be:

- maintenance of a register of all teachers with qualified status;

- responsibility for professional standards of discipline and conduct, taking appropriate action in cases of serious misconduct and ill-health;

- a statutory source of advice on issues such as professional training and development, qualification levels of teachers, and changes in curriculum and assessment.

Conclusion

Whilst there is much excellent teaching by committed teachers, the overall quality of the profession is not high enough to deliver the new deal in the classroom which pupils need and are entitled to expect. A way forward has been suggested which in summary involves:

- a spiral of raised standards of entrants to teaching and the promotion of a high status profession;

- an entitlement for every teacher to rigorous training and development throughout his or her career;

- new arrangements for the pay, career progression and working conditions of teachers to establish and maintain a flourishing profession;

- a strengthening of the primary role of the teacher as an educator, in command of a range of expertise and with appropriate technological back-ups;

- coherent leadership throughout the profession, including self-regulation;

- equality of opportunity for all staff.

Notes

1   Bolton, E., (forthcoming). Speech to National Commission on Education Conference in Shrewsbury, 1992.

2   Organisation for Economic Co-operation and Development, 1990. The Teacher Today: Tasks, Conditions, Policies. OECD.

3   Varlaam, A. and others, 1992. What Makes Teachers Tick? Centre for Educational Research, London School of Economics.

4   National Association of Head Teachers, 1993. Press Release, 14 July.

5   (i) Centre for Organisational Research, 1990. Teachers and Schools: A Study of Organisational Health and Stress.
     (ii) National Union of Teachers and Institute of Occupational Health, 1992. Stress in Secondary School Teachers. University of Birmingham.

6   Wood, D., 1993. The Classroom of 2015. National Commission on Education. Draft Briefing.

7   OECD, 1992. High Quality Education and Training for All. OECD.

8   (i) Smithers, A. and Robinson, P., 1990. Teacher Provision in the Sciences. British Association.
     (ii) Association for Science Education and others, 1991. Only a Teacher ... ? ASE.

9   (i) Smithers, A. and Robinson, P., 1991. Teacher Provision: Trends and Perceptions and Staffing Secondary Schools in the Nineties. University of Manchester.
     (ii) Straker, N., 1991. 'Teacher Supply in the 1990s: An Analysis of Current Developments.' *Evaluation and Research in Education*, 5, 1 & 2.
     (iii) Booth and others, 1989. Teacher Supply and Teacher Quality: Solving the Coming Crisis. Cambridge Education Papers No. 1.

10   Education, Science and Arts Committee, 1990. The Supply of Teachers for the 1990s. HMSO.

11   Wilson, A. and Pearson, R., 1992. The Problem of Teacher Shortages. NCE Briefing No. 4.

12   Buchan, J. and Weyman, C., 1989. The Supply of Teachers: A National Model of the 1990s. Institute of Manpower Studies (IMS).

13   Department for Education, 1993. Teacher Vacancies at an All Time Low. Press Release, 14 May.

14   DFE, 1992. Teachers in Service and Teacher Vacancies in England in January 1992. *Statistical Bulletin* 20/92.

15   DFE, 1993. 1992 Secondary School Staffing Survey. DFE.

16   Campbell, R. and Neill, S., 1991. The Workload of Secondary School Teachers. University of Warwick.

17   Local Government Management Board, 1993. Survey of Teacher Resignations and Recruitment. LGMB.

18   DFE, 1992. Students on Initial Teacher Training Courses. *Statistical Bulletin* 12/92 (updated).

19   Universities Council for the Education of Teachers, 1993. First

Destination Survey of Students Completing University Courses of Initial Training for the Teaching Profession in 1992 in England and Wales. UCET.

20 DFE, 1993. Student Numbers in Higher Education – Great Britain 1981–82 to 1991–92. *Statistical Bulletin* 17/93.

21 NCE (forthcoming). Undergraduate Perceptions and Choices of Careers.

22 Her Majesty's Inspectorate (HMI), 1992. Education in England 1990–91. The Annual Report of HM Senior Chief Inspector of Schools. Department of Education and Science.

23 Keys, W. and Fernandes, C., 1993. What **Do** Students Think About School? National Foundation for Educational Research.

24 Barrett, E. and others, 1992. 'New Routes to Qualified Teacher Status.' *Cambridge Journal of Education*, 23, 2.

25 (i) Office for Standards in Education (OFSTED), 1993. The Articled Teacher Scheme. HMSO.
(ii) National Foundation for Educational Research, 1991. Evaluation of the Articled Teachers Scheme. NFER.

26 OFSTED, 1993. The Licensed Teacher Scheme. HMSO.

27 HMI, 1993. Access Courses and Initial Teacher Training. DFE.

28 Department of Education and Science, 1990. Projecting the Supply and Demand for Teachers. HMSO.

29 DFE, 1991. Survey of Out of Service Teachers. DFE.

30 DFE, 1992. Written Evidence to the School Teachers' Review Body. DFE.

31 Gooding, J., 1992. Teachers Renewed. St Mary's College.

32 House of Commons, 1985. Education for All. HMSO.

33 DFE, 1987. Working Group Report on Collection of Ethnically Based Statistics on School Teachers. DFE.

34 Commission for Racial Equality, 1988. Ethnic Minority School Teachers. CRE.

35 Universities' Central Council on Admissions (UCCA), 1993. Statistical Supplement to the 30th Report. UCCA.

36 DFE, 1993. The Initial Training of Primary School Teachers. Draft Circular.

37 Beardon, T. and others, 1992. School-Led Initial Teacher Training. Cambridge Education Papers No. 2.

38 Le Métais, J.,1991. Initial Teacher Training in the European Community. NFER.

39 Barrett, E. and others, 1992. Initial Teacher Education in England and Wales: A Topography. Modes of Teacher Education Research Project (MOTE).

40 DFE, 1992. Initial Teacher Training: Secondary Phase. Circular 9/92.

41 DFE, 1993. First Wholly School-Based Teacher Training Projects. Press Release, 4 March.

42 DES, 1989. Initial Teacher Training: Approval of Courses. Circular

24/89.

43 OFSTED, 1993. The New Teacher in School. HMSO.

44 OFSTED, 1993. The Training of Primary School Teachers. HMSO.

45 OFSTED, 1993. The Secondary PGCE in Universities. HMSO.

46 Alexander, R. and others, 1992. Curriculum Organisation and Classroom Practice in Primary Schools. DES.

47 OFSTED, 1993. The Initial Training of Teachers in Two German Länder. HMSO.

48 (i) HMI, 1991. School-Based Initial Teacher Training in England and Wales. HMSO.
(ii) Whitty, G. and others, 1992. 'Initial Teacher Education in England and Wales'. *Cambridge Journal of Education*, 22, 3.

49 Edwards, T., 1992. Change and Reform in Initial Teacher Education. NCE Briefing No. 9.

50 HMI, 1987. Quality in Schools: The Initial Training of Teachers. HMSO.

51 Mortimore, P., 1992. 'To Teach the Teachers: Teacher Training for Effective Schools.' In: Bashi, J. and Sass, Z., (eds.) *School Effectiveness and Improvement*. Magnes Press.

52 HMI, 1988. The New Teacher in School. HMSO.

53 General Teaching Council [England & Wales]. The Induction of Newly Appointed Teachers. GTC [England & Wales].

54 HMI, 1992. The Treatment and Assessment of Probationary Teachers. DES.

55 Earley, P., 1992. Beyond Initial Teacher Training: Induction and the Role of the LEA. NFER.

56 Harland, J., 1990. The Work and Impact of Advisory Teachers. NFER.

57 Cowan, B. and Wright, N., 1991. Managing for Schools and Staff Development. Sheffield Papers in Education Management.

58 School Management Task Force, 1990. Developing School Management: The Way Forward. HMSO.

59 Bolam, R. and others, 1993. Effective Management in Schools: A Report for DFE. HMSO.

60 DES, 1992. Statistics of Education: Teachers in Service, England and Wales, 1989 and 1990. DES.

61 DFE, 1993. Survey of Information Technology in Schools. *Statistical Bulletin* 6/93.

62 Association of Graduate Recruiters, 1993. Graduate Salaries and Vacancies. Press Release, 30 June.

63 New Earnings Survey 1992.

64 NUT, 1993. Submission to STRB updating 1989 DES figures with recent pay rises.

65 School Teachers' Review Body, 1993. Second Report. HMSO.

66 Interim Advisory Committee on School Teachers' Pay and Conditions, 1989. Second Report. HMSO.

67 Campbell, R. and Neill, S., 1990. Thirteen Hundred and Thirty

Days. University of Warwick.
68 HMI, 1991. Education in England 1989–90. DES.
69 Marland, M., cited in Mortimore, P. and others, 1992. The Innovative Uses of Non-Teaching Staff in Primary and Secondary Schools Project. DFE.
70 Interim Advisory Committee on School Teachers' Pay and Conditions,1991. Fourth Report. HMSO. See also Torrington and Weightman,1989. *The Realities of School Management*. Blackwell.
71 HMI, 1992. Non-Teaching Staff in Schools. HMSO.
72 See for example: Fullan, M., 1991. *The New Meaning of Educational Change*. Cassell; Mortimore and others, 1988. *School Matters*. Open Books; Rutter, M. and others, 1979. *Fifteen Thousand Hours*. Open Books.
73 Barber, M. and Brighouse, T., 1992. Partners in Change. Institute for Public Policy Research (IPPR).
74 National Audit Office, 1991. Repair and Maintenance of School Buildings. HMSO.
75 Keep, E., 1992. The Need for a Revised Management System for the Teaching Profession. NCE Briefing No. 2.
76 Hillman, J. The Preparation, Selection and Development of Headteachers. Paper for NCE.
77 GTC [England & Wales], 1992. Proposals for a Statutory GTC for England and Wales. GTC.
78 Maclure, S., 1993. A General Teaching Council for England and Wales? NCE Briefing No. 11.

9
Participation and Entitlement After 16

Introduction

Our system has concentrated for too long on the needs of the academically able at the expense of the rest. All young people reaching the age of 16, whatever their abilities, need to be able to see a clearly signposted way forward and to have an opportunity to build on what they have already achieved. All young people should feel that they will benefit if they go on to some form of structured post-compulsory education or training. There needs to be a framework for learning and a system of support which provides the necessary encouragement and the incentives to do so.

This means changing expectations not just about who and how many continue to learn, but about when they do it. We firmly believe that education and training should continue throughout life to play a key role in empowering individuals and enhancing their lives, just as the country's economic success depends upon using the capacities of people to the full. Learning, whether through education or training, does not and should not finish at 16, 18, 21 or any other fixed point.

This chapter, therefore, is about promoting positive attitudes towards learning among all adults, and providing equality of educational opportunity in the post-compulsory phase. Its main thrust is to extend the present narrowly-focused range of post-compulsory educational benefits and to outline a range of entitlements which will assist all adults, whatever their starting point, to go on learning. The privilege of mandatory financial support will no longer be reserved, as it is at present, mainly for those admitted to full-time higher education.

Extending public support for continued learning requires a new look at priorities and funding arrangements. This chapter is also, therefore, about striking the right balance in the use of public and private funds to encourage and enable people to participate, irrespective of gender, geography, financial situation, age, ethnic origin, or disability.

Trends in Participation

Encouraging signs

But do we need to take radical action to improve participation? Recent trends across the spectrum of post-compulsory education and training provision are, in fact, rather encouraging. In Figure 9.1 participation rates since 1979 are shown separately for 16-, 17- and 18-year-olds in England.[1] After a period of relatively little change in the mid-1980s the proportion of 16-year-olds has increased by 23 percentage points in the last five years (from 48% to 71%), including a 16 percentage point increase in the last three years. There remains a worrying loss between 16 and 17 and between 17 and 18, and for each group the proportion in part-time study has decreased. But, nevertheless, a sharp upward trend is observable overall.

The picture is improving in higher and further education too. The number of full-time students aged 18 and

Figure 9.1 Full-time participation rates for 16-, 17-, and 18-year-olds, 1979–80 to 1992–93, England.

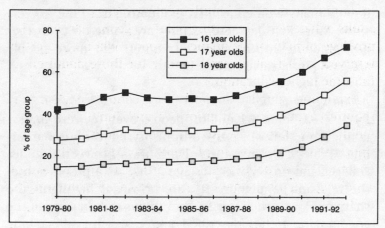

Source: Department for Education, 1993.[1]

over in the further education sector has grown by 82% between 1982–3 and 1991–2. Part-time enrolments have also increased, particularly among women. In 1991–2 there were over 36% more part-time enrolments by women (917,000) than by men (672,000). Government expenditure plans project further growth, and forecast an increase of 28% in the full-time equivalent number of adults in further education between 1991–2 and 1995–6.

The full-time participation rate in higher education for people in the 18–21-year-old group has risen dramatically from 12.6% in 1980 to an estimated 28.3% in 1992 in England and Wales. In Scotland and Northern Ireland the figure has already reached 34%. There are indications that, in spite of the Government's current desire to consolidate numbers over the next three years, their own target of 33.3% by AD 2000 will be substantially overtaken.

We welcome this. More striking still, more than half those in higher education are now mature students, whose numbers have increased by 77% since 1980.[2] There are now as many women as men graduating from the universities. More first degree graduates are going on to further post-graduate education and training, and more people are going into teacher training.

A long way to go

By 1991–2, some 3.1 million people over 16 were undertaking some form of post-compulsory education or training.[3] Table 9.1 shows their distribution between schools, colleges and universities, by age group, as a proportion of the relevant population. It also, however, highlights the sharp fall away after age 24, and shows that in spite of the encouraging trends described above we are still a long way away from being a nation which is committed to life-long learning.

Table 9.1 Participation in post-compulsory education (full-time and part-time), 1991–92, England.

				Percentages
Age	*School*	*Further*	*Higher*	*Overall*
16-17	34.5	34.6	-	69.1
18-20	1.4	14.4	18.5	34.3
21-24	-	5.9	8.6	14.5
25-34	-	4.2	3.0	7.2
35+	-	1.9	0.8	2.7

Source: Department for Education, 1993.[4]

This is of particular concern for the future competitiveness of our economy if we note the fact that nearly 90% of those who will be in the workforce in the year 2000 have left compulsory education already. It is even more crucial for the life chances of an individual when the clear relationship between unemployment and lack of qualifications is taken into account. The Labour Force Survey has shown that rates of unemployment were well above average among people without qualifications. In 1990, unemployment among those without qualifications aged 20–24 and 25–30 was 20% and 15% respectively, and that is twice the overall rates for those age groups. Furthermore, once unemployed, unqualified people were more likely than others to remain out of work for long periods. The 1991 survey gives further evidence that qualifications matter at the level of the individual. Table 9.2 shows the advantage which they give in the labour market.

Table 9.2 Unemployment rates by highest qualification, 1991, Great Britain.

	Percentages
Highest qualification held	*Unemployment rate*
Degree	4
HE below degree	4
GCE 'A' level or equivalent	7
GCSE or equivalent	8
CSE below grade 1	12
No qualifications	13
All persons	9

Source: Labour Market and Skill Trends 1993/4.[5]

National targets for learning

Recognising that education and training provision for the workforce in the UK still lags behind that of many of our international competitors, the Government, stimulated by the Confederation of British Industry (CBI), has recently adopted national targets for foundation and lifetime learning. We welcome this move which provides, for the first time, a yardstick by which to measure progress in upgrading the education and training both of young people and of people in work.[6] Their targets for lifetime learning are set out in Figure 9.2 and the foundation targets are discussed in Chapter 10.

Figure 9.2 National targets for lifetime learning.

---

1 By 1996, all employees should take part in training or development activities.

2 By 1996, 50% of the workforce should be aiming for NVQ/SVQs or units towards them.

3 By 2000, 50% of the workforce should be qualified to NVQ/SVQ3 (or equivalent).

4 By 1996, 50% of medium to large organisations to be 'Investors In People'.

Assessing where we are now in relation to the lifetime learning targets is not easy. However, the Employment Department confirms the message that there is a long way to go.[7] To meet the first two targets would require an increase of at least 5 percentage points per year in numbers taking part in training, and in the numbers aiming for vocational qualifications. To meet the third target would require a two percentage point increase each year. Between 1986 and 1991 the actual rate of increase was only just over half a percentage point a year, with just over 30% of the workforce being qualified to the required level by 1991. Better qualified people entering the workforce from school and college will not be enough to meet the target. Adults already in work will also need to be drawn in in much greater numbers. To meet the target for Investors In People over 6,000 organisations need to be recognised.[8] Currently only some 20% of this number are committed to action. The Further and Higher Education Minister recognised the scale of the problem recently when he said:

> The most challenging and difficult targets are the lifetime targets. If we are to achieve our aim of having 50% of the workforce working towards NVQs or units towards them within only three or four years, we must see a very dramatic increase indeed from the position now.[9]

The clear message which we draw from this brief look at what happens after school is that, in spite of some encouraging trends, there is a very big gap to bridge. Although the last few years have seen improvements both in staying-on rates and in levels of qualifications within the workforce, radical change is needed if we are to meet the challenges of the future.

Changing Attitudes

Many reasons have been given for the UK's relatively low levels of post-compulsory education and training. A range of structural barriers to participation has been identified. Restrictive entry requirements by educational institutions, reluctance by employers to take a long-term approach to investment in human resources, and failure on the part of Government to provide the necessary legislative framework have all been cited. To these may be added personal difficulties in finding the necessary time and money.

All these explanations have some force, but the truth is that underlying cultural and social attitudes and aspirations lie at the heart of the problem. This applies particularly to those who are already in the workforce. Evidence from a survey of adults found that 40% of the people not in training could not envisage undertaking training in the future.[10] Younger skilled and qualified workers were more likely to have positive attitudes to training, and older unskilled workers were more likely to have negative attitudes. Those with recent experience of education and training were more likely to see it as valuable and to envisage future additional training than those with no recent experience.

Veronica McGivney, of the National Institute of Adult Continuing Education, has noted that: 'certain groups exhibit a strong resistance to education because they perceive it as reflecting the values and aspirations of other social classes.'[11] Although lack of time and finance are the most frequently cited personal barriers to adult participation in post-compulsory education and training, research suggests that other factors play a determining role. Many people who leave school at an early age associate it with 'boredom, irrelevance and failure', and subsequent work experience may provide little evidence that further education and training will be of value to them. She cites a survey of attitudes to training[12] which found that unskilled workers did not see any connection between formal training and jobs such as labouring and cleaning, while semi-skilled workers did not see how it would help them to improve their performance or gain promotion.

A recent study by the London School of Economics (LSE) looks at participation in education in terms of an investment, and assesses the rate of return (through increased future income) which it brings at different levels and to young people from households with different occupational backgrounds.[13] It demonstrates, for example, that males from an unskilled household who undertake higher education can expect a real rate of return on their investment of 25%, in comparison with what they might otherwise have earned, and that females from an unskilled background who take 'A' levels can expect 13.5%. Their counterparts from professional backgrounds can expect 4% and 4.5% respectively. Why, then, they ask, if people from less skilled backgrounds can expect such high returns, are they represented to such a small extent in further and higher education? Their answer is that expected earnings differentials are not, at present, strong enough to overcome cultural and family influences, in particular the educational attainments and occupational status of the head of the household. In other words, attitudes work against greater participation.

This research supports our conviction that deeply rooted socio-cultural attitudes are leading to weak demand from potential adult learners. Many people from the lower occupational groups place low value on education, or feel themselves to be excluded from it. The feeling, in some groups within society that 'higher education is not for the likes of us' is still firmly entrenched. When lack of demand from employers is also brought into the picture the problem is further compounded, as David Finegold has demonstrated in his Briefing for the Commission, 'Breaking Out of the Low Skill Equilibrium'.[14] Until there is a collective will to change attitudes, and to drive home the message that as individuals and as an economy we must all keep learning to succeed, there will be little fundamental change.

Fundamental changes in attitude will not happen overnight. To accelerate the process we need to create incentives and to ensure that they are effective in motivating everybody in society to go on learning, irrespective of where they live, how old they are, what their ethnic background, gender or economic and personal circumstances are, or their existing level of achievement.

Incentives alone will not be effective. The education and training on offer must be appropriate to people's needs, and organised accordingly. If people cannot see the relevance of learning, their attitudes will remain damagingly negative. What is provided in the post-compulsory phase and how it is delivered is discussed in the next three chapters. Here we look at how people are currently supported and how these arrangements need to be changed to provide a much more comprehensive and equitable range of incentives.

New Patterns of Support

In proposing new patterns of support in the post-compulsory phase we look first of all at arrangements for 16 to 18-year-olds. We then look at how to provide incentives for people to go on learning after 18. Our post-18 approach is based on *levels of learning* as opposed to age or stage. It consists of three main levels: remedial and basic learning for adults; intermediate levels of learning up to and including the Advanced level GED and equivalents; and higher education and advanced vocational training.

Support for 16–18-year-olds

Provision for education and training in the years immediately after the compulsory school leaving age is highly unsatisfactory. In Chapter 10 we propose a new national foundation learning target: that 90% or more of young people will be working for a nationally recognised educational qualification at least until the age of 18.

Many young people will decide to enter traineeships of the kind proposed in Chapter 10. It is to be expected, however, that the majority will prefer to remain in full-time education. Our first priority must be to ensure that these young people receive the support they need. Those who choose to stay on at 16 remain dependent on their families for financial support. We do not propose to change this. However, real difficulties can arise for low-income and single-parent families and those drawing Income Support or Family Credit, if their children opt for full-time education. At the present time, educational support for this group of young people is discretionary, funding being administered through the Local Education Authorities (LEAs). There are two types of award: Section 2 awards for students in further education colleges, and maintenance allowances for those in schools. In 1990–91 expenditure on the former for

England and Wales was in the region of £50 million and for the latter £13 million. LEAs have discretion both as to whether or not to make an award, and as to the level at which the award is made. They may also decide, in the case of students in colleges, whether to pay only a proportion of the relevant fees, and whether or not to make a maintenance award.

We are concerned about the way this system is functioning. Where a young person lives can significantly affect his or her chances of getting support for staying on. Different LEAs operate different criteria. A number of factors can influence their policies, including the pattern of educational provision in the area and their generosity or lack of it. Some LEAs make no awards at all, others only in one of the two categories. Moreover, there are strong indications that cuts in local government finance are leading to a decline in the number and level of awards made.[15] Table 9.3 shows the very considerable variation between regions in the number and rate per thousand of awards to students in colleges and schools.

Table 9.3 Awards to 16–18-year-olds, 1990–91, in regions of England and Wales.

Region	FE college student awards		Maintenance allowances to school pupils	
	Number	*Rate per 1,000*	*Number*	*Rate per 1,000*
North	4,017	51	3,068	39
Yorkshire	11,988	93	4,957	38
North West	15,925	96	7,504	45
East Midlands	10,297	98	1,307	12
West Midlands	3,730	27	1,908	14
East Anglia	1,881	35	507	9
Greater London	5,450	35	7,482	48
Other S E	12,824	49	2,985	11
South West	4,032	42	1,210	12
England	70,144	59	30,928	26
Wales	5,904	78	4,352	57

Source: Department for Education, 1993.[16]

We recommend, therefore, that the current arrangements whereby LEAs have discretion should be changed and a new scheme, locally administered but with nationally determined criteria, be introduced to ensure that all young people are treated in accordance with the same criteria. We estimate that this would increase the current expenditure on discretionary awards in England and Wales from about £63 million to about £85 million.

We also want to ensure that by staying on, children of poorer families suffer no more than the loss of the difference between 'trainee allowances' and, where Social Security benefits are payable, the rate for dependent children in full-time education. This means that funds, administered locally, should be available, on a means-tested basis, to meet the costs associated with study for 16–18-year-olds in full-time education (books, travel, equipment, uniform, essential residence away from home, etc.).

Support after 18
Our next priority is to extend the scope of arrangements for support for people over 18 beyond the present targeting upon full-time higher education, to ensure that incentives to participate exist at all levels. We want to move towards providing support both for part-time study, and continued learning, both vocational and academic, from remedial education up to the equivalent of first degree. In the process the current statutory links between age and entitlement to funding for adult learning would be broken.

Current funding arrangements for those over 18 are discriminatory as between levels of learning and modes of study. Full-time attendance on a higher education course (whether for degree or diploma) attracts a mandatory award to cover tuition fees in full, a means-tested maintenance grant, and access to the Government's student loan scheme. Part-time attendance on a degree level course (except for initial teacher training) attracts no mandatory funding. Meanwhile there has been a damaging lack of financial support for those who wish to pursue a less academic route after school. At age 19 students lose all entitlement to state support for attendance on a sub-degree further education course, for example, a course conferring an RSA or City and Guilds qualification, or leading to an NVQ, GCSE or an 'A' level, whatever the mode of attendance. Discretionary awards from LEAs are becoming rare.

Adult basic education
As we point out in Chapter 1, a significant number of people in the adult population need education at a basic or remedial level. Research in recent years has indicated that one in eight young people consider themselves to have problems with writing, spelling or basic maths. The basic education of adults in literacy and numeracy, and English as a second language, has until recently been the only non-HE part of post-18 provision which has been free to the student. Even this is now under threat in some parts of the country.

Further education colleges may apply to the Further Education Funding Council (FEFC) for funding to support the teaching costs of such courses, and many LEAs operate targeted concessionary programmes so that individuals do not have to meet fee costs. To that extent support is available. We consider, however, that any arbitrariness which local discretion brings into the system should be removed, and that there should be a clear entitlement to basic education for all who need it, with fees being met from the public purse.

There is, however, a particular problem in convincing those who might benefit from courses of this sort to recognise that they have much to gain, and in giving them the confidence to come forward. The way in which colleges market themselves, their level of accessibility, and the extent of their outreach into the local community are key factors in making progress on this front.

Achieving the General Education Diploma

Not all those who stay on at school or college to the age of 18 achieve what they set out to do. In England in 1991–92, 73.5% of the total of 173,034 18-year-old A/AS level candidates reaching the age of 18 gained two or more passes at 'A' level. This is only 21% of the total age group. Of course, many of the remainder would have acquired at least some GCSEs. There were in addition some 35,000 BTEC First and 43,000 National certificates awarded to young people between 16 and 18 in summer 1992 and 120,000 qualified for City and Guilds awards. Thus there are many school leavers and many more in the population who can use what they have managed to achieve as building blocks for future progress. They should not be viewed, as they often are, as failures. They can learn to succeed and they should be given incentives to do so.

We propose, therefore, that action should be taken immediately to introduce an entitlement for anyone under 35 to the payment of fees for the completion of the GED, or acquisition of qualifications at an equivalent level ('A' levels, NVQ 3), subject to assessment and educational counselling for those with a previous failure at this level. Eventually, it should be extended to anyone at any age.

We wish to stress that what we are advocating here is support to reach a given level of learning, and not necessarily a given qualification. We wish to see academic and vocational routes intersecting, sharing equal esteem, and receiving equal support.

Fees are not the only financial constraints affecting potential adult learners. The National Association for

Educational Guidance for Adults draws upon an analysis of 1,699 counselling interviews to show that very practical problems, such as lack of child care facilities and transport, can be decisive for a significant number of people, particularly those not in the workforce, who may benefit most from being drawn back into educational or training activities.[17]

We recommend the early introduction of allowances for the provision of additional incidental (non-fee) expenses of undertaking education or training at basic or intermediate levels, such as travel, child care, and equipment, for those in receipt of Income Support, Family Credit, or Unemployment Benefit.

For those on low incomes or for the unemployed there is the added problem of contending with the regulations governing the benefits system. A particular problem for the unemployed is the interpretation of the requirement to be available for work (the 21-hour rule) which prevents participation in learning opportunities on a full-time basis while in receipt of benefit. In the 1993 Spring Budget, the Government went some way to recognising the inappropriateness of excluding the unemployed in this way by introducing the 'Learning for Work' scheme. This makes provision for selected individuals who have been unemployed for more than twelve months to undertake full-time education courses which are of 'vocational relevance and appropriate to labour market needs'.[18] We welcome this move and propose that its scope be extended beyond the present narrow focus on labour market needs. Unemployed people who wish to learn should have every encouragement to do so. The process of learning and the involvement in society which it brings have a positive value which far outweighs the concerns about 'scrounging' which the present rules are designed to meet.

If adults are to continue to learn they must have not

only financial support, but the time to study. For those in full-time work, who may also have family and other responsibilities, this can be a very significant constraint. Time and finance are the two most commonly cited barriers to continued learning by those who do not participate. The case for a statutory entitlement to a given number of days' educational leave has been made forcefully by the Institute for Public Policy Research.[19]

We consider that high priority should be given within the next five years to the introduction of up to one day a week off work, without loss of pay, for anyone under 25 who wishes to complete the GED or obtain a qualification at the equivalent level. Employers should also provide a minimum of five paid days' leave per year for recognised off-the-job education or training, whether offered as a part of an internally based initiative or through an external organisation, for all employees over 25, regardless of age, by AD 2000. We recognise that such a provision will cause particular problems for small employers, and in the case of part-timers. However, given the importance to the economy of small businesses, and the growth in part-time employment, we are convinced that the difficulties must be overcome. In some cases this could be achieved through the development of collaborative arrangements between large manufacturing companies and their suppliers.

Support in higher education

Ensuring that support for learning in higher education is designed to meet the needs of individuals and the economy in the future presents a different range of problems from those encountered at lower levels. There the problem has been a failure to place appropriate value on continued learning at non-advanced levels, and hence a failure to provide the necessary incentives. At higher education level, however, we are faced with the fact that a system which, compared with those in all other developed countries, invests very heavily in student support is, nevertheless, failing to meet the basic financial needs of the full-time students at which that investment is targeted. This failure is compounded by the fact that the support system excludes almost entirely the increasing numbers of those who wish to study part-time, and is aggravated by the rapidity of the recent and projected expansion.

Funding expansion

Student numbers have rocketed over the last few years in response to Government policy. This expansion has brought with it not only the need to meet institutional costs, but the requirement to foot the bill for student support, in terms of fees, maintenance grants and student loans. Government has put forward no funding strategy to underpin the costs of expansion, however, other than that of driving down unit costs and relying on a constant share of public expenditure, as increased by economic growth. In 1992–3 unit costs in the old universities were 83% of what they were in 1987–8, and in the former polytechnics they were 81%.

Government expenditure plans are set out in Table 9.4.

Table 9.4 Expenditure plans for higher education, 1993–4 to 1995–6, England.

£m

	1993-4	1994-5	1995-6
HE Funding Council for England (HEFCE), and other current	2,365	2,430	2,419
HEFCE capital	319	322	329
Student loans	223	285	334
Access funds	24	14	14
Mandatory awards: Maintenance	988	1,026	1,026
Mandatory awards: Fees	1,615	1,745	1,788
Total HE expenditure	5,534	5,822	5,910

Source: DFE and Office for Standards in Education, February 1993.[20]

The plans project a continuation of 'efficiency gains', through the planning period. In the hope of containing the escalating costs of student support, they also assume a consolidation of the numbers in higher education at current levels over the next three years before a further rise towards the end of the decade to reach the planned participation rate of about a third by the end of the century, which we welcome. In spite of this attempt at reining in, planned expenditure for the period from 1993–4 to 1995–6 shows that, whereas the overall increase in HE funding will be 6.8%, funding for student support will increase by 9.8%, leaving only a 2.4% increase for institutional running costs and capital expenditure.

However, all the indications are that demand will not be contained. Applications continue to rise, with a 9.3% increase in applications for entry in October 1993. The importance of student fees in the financial strategies of institutions, even in spite of sharp reductions by Government of the fees payable by students in the Arts and Social Sciences, mean that few institutions are in a position to cut back on recruitment.[21] In its submission on funding to the Government the Committee of Vice Chancellors and Principals (CVCP) pointed out:

> Market demand for higher education will be fuelled by the improvements in school staying on rates . . . the 25% expansion planned in FE . . . the demographic upturn in 18-year-olds in 1996, continued demand from mature students, and the underlying fact that recent rapid expansion in HE has raised awareness and expectations among students, parents and employers.[22]

Obviously, therefore, most difficult questions arise over funding for the rest of the decade.

Growing student debt

While numbers have been growing, so has dissatisfaction with the current arrangements for student support. Support for full-time higher education students in the UK has, as we have said, been generous by international standards. Chapter 14 shows that UK public expenditure on HE falls in the middle range of comparable countries. However, when the figures are broken down they show that the UK has the highest expenditure of all on student welfare and support.

Full-time home students who gain a place on a designated course at a higher or further education institution are automatically entitled to a mandatory grant. This means that course fees are paid in full irrespective of personal or parental income. At the present time these vary from £1,300 to £4,895 per year depending on the subject studied. In addition students are entitled to a means-tested maintenance allowance and have access to the Government student loan scheme which was introduced in 1990–91, and which will mean that the grant element will remain frozen at 1990–91 levels, while the loan increases to take account of inflation until it eventually equals the grant. None of these student support benefits is available as of right to part-time students, who may be eligible for a discretionary grant from their LEA. These, however, are increasingly rare.

In spite of this comparative generosity, the system is no longer working, even for the restricted group at which it is targeted. The value of the maintenance grant was at its peak when it was introduced in 1962–3. By the end of the 1980s its real value was approximately 20% lower than in 1962–3. The introduction of loans restored the combined value of the grant and loan to 1979 levels only. Moreover, this was accompanied by the withdrawal from students of a number of other benefits to which they had previously had access, including Income Support, Unemployment Benefit during the summer vacation, and Housing Benefit. It is clear, furthermore, that a significant number of parents do not make up their children's grant to the statutory level, thereby putting them in genuine financial difficulty.

There is ample and growing evidence of student poverty, and growing indebtedness. According to Barclays Bank the average student leaving college this year will owe £1,672. That is 22% higher than the £1,370 recorded last year. Students on professional courses have a higher level of debt than their counterparts in science, business studies or the humanities, having borrowed £2,680 on average.[23]

Social inequity
The financial strains on the system are not the only concern, however. It is also inequitable. We have already pointed to its inequity in scope, in that it does not extend to part-time students. It is also inequitable from the social point of view. Places in higher education in the UK have always been occupied by a disproportionately high number of people from families in the upper income brackets, and research shows that people from families in social classes I and II are currently about four times more likely to apply to university than those of classes III, IV and V, and also more likely to get in.[24] This is a pattern of participation which has changed little since the war in spite of the enormous expansion which has taken place since then. A recent article on social class and gender in higher education concludes:[25]

> The overall picture for social class is of unchanging service class advantage. The children of managerial or professional families are more likely to gain access to university, more likely to have obtained the most pres-

tigious qualification, a degree, at a university, and more likely to have qualified earlier in life than people from an intermediate or manual class background.[26]

The study deals with three 10-year cohorts, born between 1936 and 1945, between 1946 and 1955, and between 1956 and 1965. The most recent cohort was in higher education between the mid-1970s and 1980s. It may be argued, therefore, that since the analyses do not take into account the recent dramatic increases in participation, the picture they paint may not hold good for today. However, Table 9.5 shows Universities Central Council on Admissions (UCCA) statistics for students applying for entry to universities in October 1991 and 1992 which reveal that applicants and accepted students are still drawn predominantly from social classes I and II (the rough equivalent of 'service class').[27]

Table 9.5 Applicants and accepted applicants through UCCA and PCAS by social class, 1991–92, United Kingdom.

			Percentages in each social class						
			I	*II*	*IIIA*	*IIIB*	*IV*	*V*	*Not Known*	*Total 000s*
UCCA	Applicants	1991	14.8	43.7	10.7	11.8	6.4	1.0	11.5	207.3
		1992	16.5	40.5	11.3	14.4	6.7	1.5	9.1	241.6
	Accepted applicants	1991	17.4	46.0	10.3	10.7	5.8	0.9	9.9	106.7
		1992	19.6	42.4	11.0	12.7	6.0	1.2	7.2	118.0
PCAS	Admissions	1991	11.9	45.9	13.0	17.7	9.8	1.8	-	66.0
		1992	13.0	42.2	13.4	19.9	9.2	2.2	-	95.0

Source: UCCA Statistics Office/Polytechnics Central Admissions System.[28]

Home admissions statistics for 1992 from the Polytechnics Central Admissions System (PCAS), are also shown and indicate a similar dominance by social group II, but a slightly greater success in drawing in the manual and unskilled classes.[29]

Recent research into the distribution of subsidies (or 'benefits in kind') across families with different income levels tells a similar story.[30] Figure 9.3 shows that households in the top income bracket, on average, receive subsidies through higher education study away from home that are ten times greater than households in the bottom income bracket. Despite the fact that the top income groups take less advantage of state schools, they are still substantially favoured overall by educational benefits.

Figure 9.3 Education benefits in kind for quintile income groups, 1987, Great Britain.

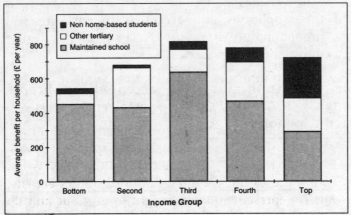

Source: Based on Figure 1 in Evandrou, M. and others, 1993.[30]

A new balance

Current arrangements are therefore unsatisfactory from a number of different perspectives. Because student support is mandatory, the associated funding commitment is open-ended. The call to expand has been enormously successful and has put severe strain on public funding at the expense of investment in institutions and their infrastructure. At the same time the combined grants and loan payments are failing to provide adequately for the living costs of full-time students. Meanwhile, no support either for fees or other expenses is available to part-time students, with the exception of those in teacher training. And better off groups in society are benefiting disproportionately, in particular from the payment of fees, which are not means-tested.

The time has now come for radical change in the way we fund students in higher education. A new balance between public and private funding is needed, so that as a nation we are able to devote a greater proportion of GDP to continuing education and training in all its forms. If we are not to inhibit the welcome increase in participation in higher and further education, nor to starve universities and colleges of the funds necessary to provide both a high-quality teaching environment and an appropriate research effort, there must be a shift in funding towards private sources.

There are a number of options for bringing private money into the system. At the institutional level, universities are already working hard and successfully to raise funds from employers and industrial concerns. Such funds, however, are usually raised in return for specific services, such as research and development or consultancy work. They contribute to the volume of an institution's activity, but actually represent money straight in and out and do not, in most cases, constitute additional funding to support the basic function of teaching. Funds raised from alumni are increasing, but are minimal in the budgets of most institutions. A culture where graduates are prepared to donate substantial sums to their former colleges and universities is yet to be created in this country. Some institutions are seriously considering introducing top-up fees, that is, charging more than the minimum rates for home students laid down by the Government.

Each of these options can provide a way forward for an

individual institution. However, they will not provide a satisfactory solution for the system as a whole. In our view, the only way in which new funds can be mobilised in sufficient amounts to achieve the shift we require is to seek a contribution from individual students in higher education towards the cost of their courses. This is a controversial proposal because it breaches the principle, of which we have been proud in this country, of providing free tuition, regardless of personal or parental income, to all those who gain a full-time place in a higher education institution. It also seems to fly in the face of the desire to see overall growth and much greater participation by groups which have not traditionally seen access to higher education as something to which they might aspire. Nevertheless, we are convinced that this is the way to go.

New Support Arrangements

Key features

Unlike the present scheme, the system of student support which we recommend will apply to all students in higher education, whether full-time or part-time. For this purpose we define higher education broadly to include all courses provided by higher and further education institutions which lead to qualifications of a standard higher than the GED, or under present arrangements GCE 'A' level, BTEC National Certificate/Diploma, GNVQ/NVQ/SVQ 3 or Scottish Higher Certificate. It will have a number of key features (there are more details in Appendix 2):

1 All higher education students will be required to make an annual flat rate contribution (HECON) towards the cost of their courses. The level of the contribution will be fixed by the Government as a percentage (say 20%) of the national average cost

of a course at that level (certificate, diploma, degree). In return, the remaining tuition costs will be met from public funds. In other words, all students will contribute the same amount, regardless of the different costs of their courses.

2 Students who are able to make their contribution in advance will benefit from a discount of, say, 15%. It will be open to employers or other sponsoring organisations to pay the contribution on the student's behalf. It will also be open to Government to waive the contribution where it wishes to encourage study in a particular field or by a particular group of students (for example, science teachers, mature returners to teaching etc.).

3 A new arrangement will be put in place to assist those students who are unable to pay their fee contribution in advance, to defer payment until after their period of study, and it will link repayments to capacity to pay. There will be arrangements to 'stop the clock', for example, for women at home with small children, or those who are unemployed.

4 A maintenance allowance (HEMA) will be available to those who require it, set at a level which permits a reasonable standard of living. Repayment of HEMA will be made through the same machinery as fee contribution repayments and will similarly be linked to capacity to pay.

The introduction of the HECON will be linked to a 20% rise in the level of maintenance payments available to students through the loan mechanism. The move to full repayment of the HEMA can be phased in by raising the ceiling of the student loan and gradually reducing the proportion paid as grant until the grant element is entirely replaced.

Issues and concerns
Our proposals raise a host of issues for individual students and their parents, for universities and colleges, for local authorities who administer the current arrangements, and for Government. We discuss a number of these below. We also, however, recognise that there will be detailed concerns about the operation of the scheme and its financial feasibility, and we address these more technical issues in Appendix 2.

Perhaps one of the first questions which will be asked about our proposals is why, if our aim is to raise more private funding for higher education, do we not simply suggest the introduction of a graduate tax?

This has some immediate attractions: in particular, the potential to provide a new income stream almost from day one; considerable redistributive potential; and the lack of significant set-up costs. It has less potential deterrent effect upon first-time entrants to higher education from groups where the culture is averse to the idea of debt. Over the long term, a tax can recover a greater amount from the private purse than a repayment scheme such as we propose, since taxation continues over a lifetime rather than ceasing once the principal sum plus any interest has been repaid. It also preserves the position in which tuition costs are experienced as free by full-time students in higher education and their parents.

However, we believe that the graduate tax is not a fair mechanism. In the much more complex and diverse post-compulsory education system of the future (see Chapter 11), the graduate, in today's sense of a person who has enjoyed three years' residential education at higher level in a college or university, will no longer be the dominant product of the system. Many of those who achieve graduate status in the future will do so after part-time or distance learning study. Many will choose to spread their study over a period of years progressing via a credit accumulation and transfer scheme, and may be supported by their employers, rather than the State. A significant number, whom we would wish to include in student support arrangements, will be following sub-degree courses which involve perhaps only one or two years' higher level study. The amounts which public funds contribute will vary considerably and the question of equity arises if the tax is to be applied regardless of mode and route. Tracking entry and exits to the system and assessing at which point individuals become liable to pay graduate tax will become increasingly complex. In these circumstances a 'pay as you go' repayment scheme, in which individuals are able to control their personal level of debt, and hence the risk to which they are committing themselves, is likely to be more attractive over the long term.

Implications for access

A major concern about changing support arrangements must be the potential impact upon access by full-time students. The extent to which a contribution and deferred payment scheme may present a psychological barrier is difficult to assess. The Government's top-up loan scheme is now in its third year of operation, and is becoming an established, if unpleasant, fact of student life. In 1991–2 36% of all eligible HE students took out loans. In the 18–21 age group 20% did so, but among 21–25-year-olds the proportion was 71%.[31] The average value of loan issued was £533. Evidence from other systems where new schemes have been introduced is scant, but it would appear that the Australian Higher Education Contribution Scheme (HECS), which was introduced in 1989, and which is in some respects the model for what we are proposing, has had no discernible deterrent effect upon traditionally under-represented groups.

The design of a deferred payment scheme is crucial to its acceptability to borrowers. There are basically two types of payment. Under mortgage payment schemes, like the present student loan scheme, repayments are made in equal instalments over a fixed period and usually represent a declining proportion of income. With income contingent schemes, where repayments are linked to capacity to pay, instalments vary according to the borrower's actual income each year, and represent a fixed proportion of that income. This reduces the burden considerably in vulnerable periods where, for whatever reason, earnings capacity is low. Nicholas Barr and his colleagues at LSE have been examining the practicality of introducing this type of loan in the UK. Using results derived from a simulation technique which models the impact of a number of different options and looks at their financial consequences, they show that it is possible to design schemes which both minimise the deterrent to young people to pursue higher education and raise additional income. Their results were modelled both for full- and part-time students and shown to perform well.[32]

A recent paper on the Australian experience with HECS suggests that the context in which a new scheme is introduced and the care which is taken to monitor its impact on vulnerable groups is also crucial in securing its acceptance. The paper states:

> The scheme was introduced at a time (1989) of significant reform and major expansion of the Australian higher education system; its ready acceptance owed much to its presentation as a means of helping fund the expansion of higher education which was considered necessary to meet national economic, social and cultural needs.
> Equity considerations were critical to the design of the HECS, and to ensure that access was not adversely

affected, and that there were no unintended consequences of this new scheme, the Government committed itself to regular monitoring by an independent body.
Reports to date have concluded that the scheme has
had little effect on the decisions of particular education-
ally disadvantaged groups to participate in higher
education.[33]

Securing investment

Whereas individuals will be concerned about the financial
burden which a deferred payment scheme imposes on
them, Government will be concerned about how funding
will be secured, and how much income might be raised
once it is fully implemented.

When the Government first proposed the current top-
up loan scheme it tried to involve the banks directly. It did
not succeed because there were a number of features
about that scheme which were unattractive. Most importantly there would have been no intermediary body to
administer the scheme and the whole burden of dealing
with individual students and chasing up debt would have
fallen on the banks.

It is important to try again to secure investment by
financial institutions, so that new funds are available from
the outset to begin to tackle the problems of expansion.
We are convinced that it is possible to devise such a
scheme. We describe this in more detail in Appendix 2.

New funds for the system

Appendix 2 indicates the immediate benefits which will
accrue from the introduction of such a scheme. There will
be a flow of new funds into the system from the outset
through advance payments of the HECON. We estimate
that this will be around £260 million for the UK. Deferred
payments, which will begin to accumulate significantly
after the scheme has been in operation for about five

years, will reach some £950 million by the time the scheme is mature. The funds required to meet maintenance grants and student loans, currently about £1.5 billion, will gradually be reduced as the existing scheme is phased out and replaced by HEMA. There will be costs to Government in underwriting these arrangements. These are itemised in the appendix. Extending the payment of fees to part-timers is difficult to estimate, but will be somewhere in the region of £240 million. Nevertheless, once the new scheme is fully in place, substantial funds should be available to meet the additional costs of expanding the system and extending the range of students eligible for support.

Conclusion

Our proposals for changed patterns of support for post-compulsory learning are ambitious. They involve a greater investment of GDP in education and training and call for a rebalancing of the private and public contribution. They rely on general assent to a proposition which we believe to be true – that is, that there is a fundamental partnership of interest in promoting post-compulsory learning. This includes all adults, employers, educational institutions, and local and central government. Each of these is a beneficiary of the system, directly or indirectly, and each has a stake in securing greater participation. Under our proposals, some sections in society will be called upon to make a greater personal contribution to the costs of the system in the interests of drawing in those who have hitherto not had sufficient incentive or encouragement to join in. In our view, we shall all benefit thereby, and shall begin to tackle the waste of human potential which has inhibited our economic and social progress.

Our proposals need further discussion and refinement,

but we believe that if all adults are to have a fair chance to learn to succeed and to continue to develop their talents throughout their lives, then we have pointed a way forward which is worth very serious consideration.

Notes

1 Department for Education, 1993. Participation in Education by 16–18-Year-Olds in England: 1979-80 to 1992-93. *Statistical Bulletin* 16/93. Note that participation rates show the percentages, for each of the age groups, of the estimated population of that age, in full-time education.

2 Mature students are defined as those enrolling for the first year of higher education courses at older ages than is the norm for such courses: thus first degree students and sub-degree students aged 21 or over and post-graduates aged 25 or over come into this category.

3 This does not take account of some 1.2 million enrolments by people over 18 in Adult Education Centres. Nor does it include those receiving training from employers, where this is entirely in-house.

4 DFE, 1993. Statistics of Further Education College Students in England 1970–71 – 1991–92. *Statistical Bulletin* 14/93.

5 Employment Department, 1992. Labour Market and Skill Trends 1993-94. Figure 6.8, p. 61.

6 Defined, for the purposes of the National Training Targets, as all 16–24-year-olds.

7 Employment Department, 1992. Labour Market and Skill Trends 1993–94.

8 Investors In People is a programme run by the Employment Department to encourage employers to invest in the skills which their businesses need. Funds are provided through TECs/LECs. Businesses entering the scheme have their current training and development practice reviewed. They then follow an action plan, and finally are assessed by external licensed assessors.

9 DFE, 1993. Press Notice 118/93, 15 April.

10 Training Agency, 1989. Training in Britain: a Study of Funding. HMSO.

11 McGivney, V., 1992. Motivating Unemployed Adults to Undertake Education and Training. National Institute of Adult Continuing Education (NIACE).

12 Fuller, A. and Saunders, M., 1990. The Potential Take-Up of Mass Training. Institute for Research and Development in Post Compulsory Education, University of Lancaster.

13 Bennett, R. and others, 1992. Learning Should Pay. London School of Economics (LSE).

14 Finegold, D., 1992. Breaking Out of the Low-Skill Equilibrium. NCE Briefing No. 5. National Commission on Education.

15 At the time of writing a research project was being undertaken by the National Foundation for Educational Research (NFER), commissioned by the Gulbenkian Foundation and the Sir John Cass's Foundation in collaboration with the Further Education Funding Council (FEFC) and DFE to collect statistics of English and Welsh LEA discretionary awards for 1990–93, and planned budgets for 1994; to gather qualitative information about changes in policy; and estimate future demand.

16 DFE, 1993. Student Awards in England and Wales: 1990–92 *Statistical Bulletin* 9/93.

17 National Association for Educational Guidance for Adults (NAEGA), 1992. Affording Adult Learning: Financial Barriers to Access and Progression. NAEGA.

18 The scheme will be operated by the Training and Enterprise Councils (TECs), which will decide, on the basis of individual guidance and counselling, the relevance of courses, which must be full time and may be for one year or a shorter period, to an individual's career prospects. The scheme will start in September 1993. Funding, which will cover fees, and other incidental costs such as travel, books and course materials, will provide for 30,000 opportunities in the first year.

19 Miliband, D., 1991. Learning by Right: An Entitlement to Paid Education and Training. Institute for Public Policy Research (IPPR).

20 DFE and Office for Standards in Education, February 1993. The Government's Expenditure Plans 1993–94 to 1995–96. HMSO, Cm 2210.

21 For 1993–4, fees for home students in Arts and Social Studies courses have been reduced from £1,855 a year to £1,300. Fees for science and engineering students remain at the 1992–3 level of £2,770. This has little impact on students, as fees are paid through the mandatory award in the vast majority of cases. It has a significant impact on institutional budgets, however.

22 Committee of Vice Chancellors and Principals (CVCP), May 1993. Public Expenditure Survey (PES) Submission.

23 *Times Higher Education Supplement* (THES), 1993. Student Apathy Mounts over Debt Burden. 9 July.

24 Smithers and Robinson, 1989. Increasing Participation in Higher Education. University of Manchester.

25 Egerton, M. and Halsey, A., 1993. 'Trends by Social Class and Gender in Access to Higher Education in Britain.' *Oxford Review of Higher Education*, Vol 19, No 2.

26 'Service' class includes higher and lower grade professionals and administrators and higher grade technicians. 'Intermediate' class includes groups of occupations which either offer relative security and some features of 'staff' status (e.g., rank and file employees in services), or some degree of autonomy and/or authority (e.g., small proprietors, lower grade technicians, and supervisors of manual

workers). 'Manual' class includes manual industrial and agricultural workers.

27 In assigning applicants to social class, UCCA uses the classification produced by the Office of Population Censuses and Surveys. This is a classification of occupations into six groups ranging from professional and similar occupations to unskilled manual work.

28 Universities Central Council on Admissions (UCCA) Statistics Office; Polytechnics Central Admissions System, Statistical Supplement to the Annual Report 1991–92.

29 PCAS figures do not include the number of 'not knowns' hence are not strictly comparable with those of UCCA.

30 Evandrou, M. et al., 1993. 'Welfare Benefits in Kind and Income Distribution.' *Fiscal Studies*, Vol 14 No. 1.

31 These figures do not include post-graduate students as they are not eligible for loans.

32 Barr, N. and Glennerster, H., 1993. Funding a Learning Society. LSE; unpublished paper.

33 Tracy, H., 1992. Financing of Higher Education in Transition. Department of Employment, Education and Training, Australia. Paper presented to a conference in Sofia, June 1992.

10
Traineeships

Introduction

Nowhere is the inadequacy of our education and training arrangements more obvious than in our attitude towards young people who leave school at 16 or 17.

This question is particularly important for the United Kingdom because we have always had a high proportion of young people who choose to leave school as soon as they can with the intention of starting work and as a result there has been low participation in full-time education among 16–18-year-olds.

The point is brought out by David Raffe in the Briefing which he wrote for us:[1]

> The low participation of 16–18-year-olds in education and training is widely seen as evidence of the UK's educational malaise. The UK fares badly in international comparisons; of the 13 OECD countries compared in a recent DES Bulletin, the UK had the lowest full-time participation rate among 16–18-year-olds in 1986. The UK rate was 33%, exactly half the average for the other 12 countries (66%). Such evidence as is available suggests that our lower participation is matched by lower attainment, especially in vocational skills.

Table 10.1, based on figures for 1990, gives a picture of

the extent to which young people aged 16–18 at that time participated in various kinds of education and training.

Table 10.1 Participation in full-time education and youth training for 16–18-year-olds, January 1990, United Kingdom.

	Males	Females	All
			Percentages
Full-time education	34	40	37
Youth Training Scheme/Programme	18	11	15
Others	48	49	48
Total	100	100	100

Source: Raffe, D., 1992.[1]

The table shows that by 1990 only 37% of 16–18-year-olds were in full-time education. In addition, some 15% were taking part in publicly provided training schemes for young people. Nearly half of all these young people, however, were in an 'others' category, of whom perhaps a third were receiving some part-time education or training.

Figure 10.1 compares participation rates of 16–18-year-olds in this country with those to be found in a range of other OECD countries.

Since 1990 there has been a remarkable rise in the proportion of young people staying on in full-time education, and in 1992–93 in England 71% of 16-year-olds and 55% of 17-year-olds were doing so. The most important reasons for this seem to be, first, that the idea is gaining ground among young people that their job prospects will improve if they get better qualifications and, secondly, that with rising unemployment the chance that a young school-leaver will immediately find a job on leaving school is much slimmer.

Unfortunately, for too many 16- and 17-year-olds who stay on in full-time education the outcome is disappoint-

Figure 10.1 Participation of 16–18-year-olds in education and training, 1990, international comparisons.

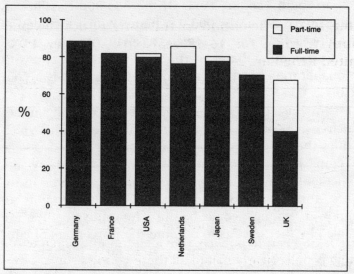

Source: Department for Education, 1993.[2]

ing. A study by the Audit Commission and HM Inspectorate[3] found that typically between 30% and 40% of students starting on a course were not succeeding and that there were many who did not even complete the course – 13% in the case of 'A' levels and 18% for vocational courses. The study underlined the crucial role of good guidance for young people; this should provide firm information about the value of particular qualifications and about the success rates achieved by students in the past.

The fate of 16- and 17-year-olds who have left full-time education in search of a job is not reassuring. Information from the official Labour Force Survey indicates that there were about 360,000 of these in Britain in the winter of 1992–93. About 21% were unemployed by the internationally recognised definition of unemployment, which excludes young people engaged in government schemes such as Youth Training (YT). Of the 284,000 classified as in jobs, only about 100,000 – a figure which includes all YT trainees of 16 and 17 – were receiving training. Given the fact that more than two-thirds of YT trainees end with no qualification even at the most basic level, it is a poor picture.

Meanwhile, pilot schemes have been running under which young people are given a 'training credit' which entitles them to buy education or training from a college or employer. This scheme is warmly backed by the Confederation of British Industry and is now to be introduced throughout the country. The scheme aims to 'empower' young people because in principle they are enabled by their credits to become the purchasers of education or training of their choice. In so far as it succeeds in doing this the scheme is to be welcomed. In practice, the approach has severe shortcomings. Training credits do not hold out much of an inducement to an employer to respond. Employers who do not want to engage a young person are not persuaded to do so by the fact that the young person has a credit to offer; and employers who do take on young people are not persuaded by the offer of a credit to alter their approach to training. In other words, whatever their theoretical merits, training credits are not likely to bring about a fundamental change in employers' behaviour.

The Legacy of the Past

We are prisoners of the past. Our relaxed attitude to the training of young employees was widely thought to be acceptable when qualifications were the exception, not the rule, and when full employment meant that virtually all school-leavers were absorbed into jobs within a few weeks of leaving school: as recently as January 1974 the number of unemployed school-leavers was only 4,500. Moreover, as noted earlier, our 'hands-off' approach extended into the training of apprentices. Excellent firms provided good apprentice training, but for many apprenticeship was much more a matter of serving time rather than a means of acquiring skills. Girls, moreover, were mostly excluded from apprenticeships, and where they were accepted, as in hairdressing, they were often regarded as cheap labour as much as genuine trainees.

We are prisoners of the past also in the sense that the past has left a legacy which has made it difficult to make changes needed for the future.

In the first place, there has been no proper structure of qualifications for young people starting work. It is true that such organisations as the City and Guilds of London Institute and more recently BTEC (the Business and Technician Education Council) have done valuable work in building up qualifications covering parts of the field. But until the establishment of the National Council for Vocational Qualifications (NCVQ) there was no institution which had responsibility for introducing vocational qualifications across the whole employment field. National Vocational Qualifications (NVQs) have so far been extended to cover four-fifths of jobs, and it is only now that the idea that all young people should be entitled or expected to gain a qualification relevant to their chosen work can be adopted as a realistic target.

Secondly, we do not yet have sufficient education and training provision to meet the needs of all young people. We welcome the decision of the Government to fund an expansion of further education by 25% over the period 1992–6. In industry, many good training officers and good instructors are to be found, but there is no British counterpart to the highly trained German *Meister* who, in addition to being a first-class craftsman and foreman, is also a highly qualified trainer. We lack a tradition of giving trainers and training a position of high status. Until this is properly remedied, attempts to reform training are bound to falter. In the present state of things, a modest but useful first step would be to reintroduce something like the old TWI – training within industry – short courses to teach trainers how to train.

Thirdly, we have not yet developed the concept in the United Kingdom that nearly all jobs, including many apparently humble ones, require skill and will be much better done by a trained than an untrained person. The work of the National Institute of Economic and Social Research has shown that treating jobs as skilled, and training accordingly, has led to great benefits in terms of higher productivity, of quality of output and of adaptability to change both in Germany and in other European countries. Direct comparisons with our own practice demonstrate how seriously our performance has lagged.[4]

Fourthly, our approach has led to raising the pay of untrained and unskilled 16- and 17-year-olds in ways which work against their longer-term interests. Instead of being given a trainee allowance or wage, 16- and 17-year-olds have typically received a wage approaching that paid to adults. This has seemed logical since they have been treated as productive workers from the outset. But there have been two very serious side-effects. First, this approach has played a large part over the years in inducing young people in large numbers to go for jobs as soon as they could legally leave school, and has therefore done much to bring about our low staying-on rates in education. Secondly, it has put pressure on employers - pressure which the trade unions have reinforced – to grant apprentices and other young people under training far higher pay than their contribution to output warrants, because many of these young people would otherwise be tempted into more highly paid jobs offering no training. As a result, the market for apprentices has been grossly distorted and the number of apprenticeships has declined sharply.

It has to be said, finally, that an important obstacle to change has been and remains the division of responsibilities between the Department for Education (DFE) and the Employment Department. Each Department has had, and retains, a vested interest in its own stake in the education and training of young people. The effects can be seen in the slowness of DFE to understand how deep-seated and injurious to the interests of the majority of young people its single-minded devotion to 'A' levels has been and in its long-term preference for full-time education as the route forward for all 16–18-year-olds. The Employment Department, for its part, for many years accepted that hundreds of thousands of 16-year-olds were going straight into work where they received neither education nor training, and was slow to recognise the necessity of building up a system of vocational qualifications suitable for young people generally. It must be doubted whether effective action to ensure that the transition from education to work is properly handled is possible as long as these two Departments, each with its own Secretary of State, remain separate.

One thing is certain. We can be sure that, without much more decisive action, the education and training of 16- and 17-year-olds will continue to be a hit or miss business, with far too many young people starting their working lives without proper preparation and without a good qualification.

National Vocational Qualifications – a stepping-stone for the future

The approach to qualifications developed by NCVQ undoubtedly helps to point the way forward. These qualifications are grouped at levels ranging from the most basic (NVQ 1) to craft level (NVQ 2), technician level (NVQ 3) and degree and sub-degree level (NVQ 4), potentially with further steps beyond (NVQ 5).

A strength of NVQs is that they are based on the actual requirements of the occupations to which they relate and are stated in terms of 'outcomes'. This means that a person who has acquired an NVQ has demonstrated that he or she is competent to do the job in practice. To an extent this strength is also a weakness. It places emphasis on jobs as they are currently organised, with no regard to how they might develop in the future. It also emphasises practical capability at the expense of the understanding of underlying principles and knowledge, so that, for example, while a bricklayer must be able to calculate how many bricks he requires for a length of wall, he is not expected to have a mathematical grounding which can be built on later. NVQs are intended for use both by young people and by adults. The shortcomings noted are especially important for young people who have a whole working life ahead of them. It is important that evidence of adequate theoretical knowledge should be made a requirement for the award of these qualifications as soon as possible.

Already the development of full-time General National Vocational Qualifications – GNVQs or Vocational 'A' levels at level 3 – covering a number of broad occupational categories is a welcome step forward. They promise, so long as they are developed as genuine high-quality qualifications, to provide a good route towards jobs at technician and equivalent levels. A GNVQ 3 is rated as equivalent to two

'A' levels or to an NVQ 3.

For the future, as we explain in Chapter 4, we propose that the new General Education Diploma should cover vocational as well as other education at Ordinary level (which equals NVQ 2) and Advanced level (NVQ 3). The flexibility made possible by the new Diploma will be a great advantage in providing appropriately for *all* young people, including those who wish to leave full-time education at 16 and 17. The approach to NVQs will need to be developed in the context of the new Diploma.

A New Learning Target for Young People

At this point, it is necessary to note the present targets for the learning of young people which were originally proposed by industry and which now also have Government support. They are set out below.

National targets for foundation learning

1 By 1997, 80% of young people should reach NVQ 2 or the equivalent (i.e. GCSE with at least 4 passes at A-C level).

2 Training and education to NVQ 3 level or the equivalent (2 'A' levels should be available to all young people who can benefit.

3 By the year 2000, 50% of young people should reach NVQ 3 or the equivalent.

4 There should be education and training provision for young people to develop self-reliance, flexibility and breadth.

The adoption of these targets was in itself a welcome step forward, as was the decision earlier in 1993 that DFE and the Employment Department should set up a National

Advisory Council on Education and Training Targets to ensure that they are met.

Progress so far does not suggest that it will be easy to meet either of the targets stated in hard numerical terms, that is the first and the third. In 1991, according to the Employment Department's publication *Labour Market and Skill Trends 1993–94,* 51% of 16–24-year-olds were qualified to NVQ 2 or the equivalent level, and this percentage has since been increasing at between 1 and 2 percentage points each year. The target of 80% by 1997 therefore looks distant. Again, 30% of 20–24-year-olds had reached NVQ 3 or the equivalent in 1991, and this percentage has been increasing by half a percentage point or more – but only in 1990 by over 1 percentage point – since 1986. The target of 50% by the year 2000 also looks remote.

These anxieties are greatly reinforced by a conviction that the targets themselves do not go far enough. It would be possible for the United Kingdom to achieve the targets and still be well behind the standards generally reached by other leading countries. The reason is that the definition of 'young people' being used is one that includes all 16-24-year-olds, whereas no world-class education and training system would now have a target which does not provide as a minimum for young people to continue with formal education and training at least until the age of 18.

We think it an essential immediate move for government and industry to adopt the further target for foundation learning set out below, and we so recommend.

New national target for foundation learning

By AD 2000, 90% or more of young people will be working for nationally recognised educational qualifications at least until they are 18 years old.

In principle, there are two main routes which 16–18-year-olds might take. One is to remain in suitable full-time education. The other is to undertake a standards-based traineeship - the modern equivalent of an apprenticeship - based on a contract with an employer but incorporating between 1 and 2 days a week of further education. Both of these routes have been well developed in Europe, apprenticeships notably in Germany's 'dual system' and full-time vocational education notably in France and in Sweden. Most countries make at least some use of both routes, and it is our recommendation that the United Kingdom should do the same.

A new form of traineeship

We explain in Chapter 4 how the framework of curriculum, assessment and qualifications might be developed in a way that would meet the needs of a wide range of young people. We propose here a new form of traineeship normally entered into at age 16 or 17. It would have the features set out on page 284.

It will be desirable for the Government and leading employers to consider together how effect can be given to this approach in practice and to agree on a framework for implementation. They should recognise from the outset that the reality is that the present approach, which seeks to leave the free play of market forces to govern the choices of young people and employers, is simply not going to deliver results of a world-class standard, for reasons made plain earlier in this chapter.

It should be recorded that some degree of statutory compulsion will be almost certainly necessary and desirable. In Germany, for example, young people who have left full-time education are obliged by law to attend vocational school part-time until the age of 18. In the USA – the home of voluntarism, some might assume – most

Recommended requirements governing traineeship agreements

1 Trainees will enter formal agreements with employers to undergo a 2- to 3-year period of work, training and further education.

2 Trainees will be required to work for a suitable vocational qualification within the General Education Diploma whether at Advanced or Ordinary level (i.e. the equivalent of NVQ 3 or NVQ 2 today).

3 Employers will undertake to provide the trainees with work for 3-4 days a week together with associated training on- and off-the-job.

4 Trainees will be released for 1 to 2 days a week in order to attend relevant vocational and general education provided at public expense in a college or other approved establishment.

5 Trainees will be paid 'trainee wages' fixed in the light of the hours they are working and the time and cost associated with the training provided by employers.

6 Standards of training and related vocational education will be safeguarded by inspection by the education and training inspectorate OFSET (see Chapter 13)

pupils are obliged by law to remain in full-time education till the age of 18, the completion of secondary education for those in the mainly state-funded schools having been made compulsory. In this country, there would probably be general support for obliging 16- and 17-year-olds who have left full-time education to attend further education $1^{1}/_{2}$ days a week, and we recommend that it be made compulsory by statute.

Employers should accept that the genuineness of their commitment to the 'skills revolution' proclaimed by the CBI in 1989 is at stake. If they fail to become involved, they will in effect be allowing the talent of much of another generation of young people to remain undeveloped and underused. They will also be showing that they do not really understand how important to employers knowledge and applied intelligence are becoming. An adequate response demands action and effort as well as rhetoric.

Employers should also realise that a well-organised traineeship scheme need not be costly to them. The cost of providing training and of paying a trainee wage will be largely offset by the value of the output of the trainee, especially as the young person gains experience and nears the end of the traineeship. There is in fact no good reason why large employers should not be happy to provide traineeships to many more young people than they eventually intend to employ, since this will not be costly to them in net terms.

In some parts of the country there will not be enough employers to provide high-quality traineeships for all the young people who will want them. The best solution in such cases will be for colleges to be enabled to offer education-based traineeships to young people, who will gain their practical experience of work from placements with employers in the area. In this way the involvement of employers, especially smaller employers who would not be able themselves to provide traineeships, can be obtained. The quality of the work experience and training offered will need to be monitored, and employers should meet at least the travel and other incidental expenses of trainees placed with them.

For the Government, traineeships offer a highly practical way forward. Traineeships are likely to be acceptable to many young people who, given this country's cultural traditions, will be glad to leave full-time education as early as they can and welcome entering the adult atmosphere of the workplace. At the same time they will be offered learning which has a clear relevance and which leads to a clear target, the acquisition of skills and a worthwhile qualification.

The only realistic alternative for the Government would be to try to persuade all young people to stay in full-time education to 18. That would not only have a much less satisfactory result but would also be very much more costly to the public purse: over three times so, since the Government would be incurring the cost of providing full-time (5 days a week) education at public expense, whereas the traineeship route would involve on average 1¹/₂ days a week of education at public expense.

Perhaps the most difficult practical issue to be resolved is how to set pay at a reasonable level. There are a number of options. It might be possible for employers and trade unions to reach an accord at national level on the major points of principle involved. The pay of apprentices is fixed by collective bargaining in Germany, where typically apprentices are paid about 30% of the adult skilled rate in their first year rising to 40% or so in the third year. Again, it might be possible for a consortium of employers to impose traineeship rates of pay unilaterally, emphasising that this was one aspect only of a new high-quality deal for young people. In the last resort, the Government might be drawn into intervening to set a statutory rate. What would not be likely to succeed would be to leave it to individual employers to take the lead piecemeal, since they would always be under suspicion that they were merely introducing a new form of cheap labour and would often fear that the young people they most wanted to attract would go elsewhere in search of higher pay.

Conclusion

We are convinced of the desirability of adopting a target whereby at least 90% of young people will by AD 2000 be working for nationally recognised educational qualifications at least until they are 18 years old. We consider that a traineeship scheme of the kind here outlined would make an essential contribution to meeting the target. Such a scheme will confer wide benefits. We stress, however, that those who stand to gain most are the young people themselves. It is the most practical way of ensuring that the vast majority of them will in future start a lifetime of work properly prepared and with a foundation of knowledge and understanding on which they can build as time goes on. Nothing less will be good enough.

Notes

1   Raffe, D., 1992. Participation of 16–18-Year-Olds in Education and Training. NCE Briefing No. 3.
2   Department for Education, 1993. International Statistical Comparisons of the Participation in Education and Training of 16- to 18-Year-Olds. *Statistical Bulletin* 19/93.
3   Audit Commission and HM Inspectorate, 1993. Unfinished Business: Full-Time Education Courses for 16–19-Year-Olds. HMSO.
4   National Institute of Economic and Social Research, 1990. Productivity, Education and Training: Britain and Other Countries Compared. Reprints of studies published in the National Institute Economic Review, with preface by Prais, S.J.

11
The Development of Higher Education

Introduction

This chapter is concerned with colleges and universities and the provision they make for higher education. It also looks at the growing importance of colleges of further education (FE colleges) in introducing young students and, increasingly, a broad range of older people to the idea of higher education, and preparing them for successful progression.

In a society in which knowledge and applied intelligence are central, higher education is at the heart of the country's well-being. Universities have a mission to pursue and transfer new knowledge; to help to manage and apply the international knowledge explosion set off by modern communications and information technology; and to educate and train to the highest levels people who will, to a large extent, provide the brains and backbone of industry and commerce, the professions, service organisations and political life in this country.

Recent years have imposed great pressures and strain on higher education institutions. Expansion has been the order of the day. More public funding has flowed into higher education, but financial stringency has grown; so have demands for greater accountability for public funds coupled with mechanisms which link funding with performance. This has brought in its wake a range of externally imposed procedures for assessing and maintaining quality both in teaching and research. Simultaneously, a new atmosphere of competition and managerialism has been introduced into a culture which has traditionally put more emphasis on co-operation between colleagues. Productivity has increased and unit costs have been cut, in many cases drastically, while expansion has not been fully funded. Finally, bringing together the universities and polytechnics into one sector has raised fundamental questions about what higher education is for and about the relationship between teaching and research.

Many institutions have responded with resilience and entrepreneurial zest to the climate of change, and have seized the opportunity to develop a new vision. Some have been more inclined to see change as threatening a fall in standards and the erosion of traditions of high-quality undergraduate education and research excellence. But the process of change will not stop. Managing effectively without sacrificing internationally recognised strengths is the challenge for coming decades.

There can be no blueprint here for the future of so complex and rapidly developing an enterprise as higher education. There are, however, important points of reference on which we need to state a point of view. We examine here in turn: the developing role of higher education in the twenty-first century; the changing mix of people entering higher education; the widening range of studies which students will wish to follow; the institutional diversity needed to meet new needs and circumstances; the question of professional training for university staff; and matters of finance.

Higher Education for the Twenty-First Century

We welcome the expansion that has already taken place in higher education and expect to see it continue both among young and mature entrants.

Expansion has brought much change, and further expansion will require more. There needs to be increasing diversity within the system, with a range of different types of institution each with its own mission and distinctive 'portfolio' of provision developed to respond to the needs of clearly identified client groups, whether local, national or international.

Flexible courses will increasingly be needed to accommodate the needs of more mature learners. Modular courses and credit accumulation and transfer arrangements, not just in this country but throughout Europe, will be important in allowing people to move in and out of higher education as their personal and employment circumstances require. Geographical mobility will be a fact of life.

Although the three- or four-year degree will remain at the heart of the teaching programme of many institutions, more one- and two-year qualifications are needed. These may be an end in themselves but may also form the basis for further progression. In particular, a closer matching of provision with the requirements of national and local labour markets is required.

There will be growing need for co-operation and collaboration between schools, colleges and universities, and for further development of close relationships with business, industry and public sector organisations. The local dimension in higher education will be important not only in ensuring a continuum of opportunity for students but in helping to gear the higher education system more closely to the world of work.

In research also, the need for co-operation and collaboration, both national and international, is becoming insistent. Certain institutions will take the lead in building on research strengths and exploring new areas. They will be the focus not only for their own staff but for those in other institutions where research is not central to the mission. The promotion of new knowledge, as well as its application and transmission, is central to the objectives of the system as a whole. British researchers must receive the encouragement and support they need in order to remain at the heart of international research networks.

Universities and colleges need, moreover, to be innovative in their approach to teaching and learning. Provision at all levels, including post-graduate, should include a greater degree of integration between academic and vocational content, lay greater stress on transferable skills and deliver outcomes not only in terms of knowledge and understanding but also of practical ability. There are many gifted teachers in higher education, but teaching itself does not yet have the status or the professional reinforcement it must receive in future.

The quality of the higher education system will be dependent on the professionalism of academics, support staff and institutional leaders and managers. A greater priority than hitherto must be given to all aspects of the managerial and professional development of the people who work in higher education.

The Changing Student Population

Expansion and the changing intake

Growth in student numbers is already forcing change. As we note in Chapter 9, participation rates have already outpaced expectations. Growth is likely to continue in spite of recent attempts by Government to put the brakes on.

Expansion is bringing with it a much less homogeneous student population. Eighteen-year-olds proceeding straight from school are no longer the majority in many educational institutions. People from different educational backgrounds, with different motivations and different requirements in terms of teaching methods, curriculum content and course structures are coming into the system at different stages in their lives. Inevitably, they make different demands on teaching staff and library and other support services.

In his Briefing for the Commission, Professor Halsey highlights some of the changes.[1] Women and part-time students now make up a much greater proportion of the total. The relative share of the higher education market claimed by the old universities and the new universities (the former polytechnics) has changed markedly. Table 11.1 shows how, within the overall 42% increase in higher education students in the UK between 1980-81 and 1990-91, the growth in participation by women in the new universities and in part-time courses has been particularly strong.

Table 11.1 Enrolments in higher education by type of establishment, mode of attendance and gender, 1980-81 to 1990-91, United Kingdom.

	Men		*Women*		*All*	
	1990–1 ('000s)	% increase since 1980–1	1990–1 ('000s)	% increase since 1980–1	1990–1 ('000s)	% increase since 1980–1
Old Universities						
Full-time	208	9	162	40	370	21
Part-time	82	37	72	76	154	52
Total	290	16	234	50	524	28
New Universities						
Full-time	190	50	187	85	378	66
Part-time	161	10	112	143	274	43
Total	351	29	299	103	652	55
All HE Total	641	22	533	76	1,176	42

Source: Government Statistical Service, 1993.[2]

More mature students

The age profile is also changing. For the first time, in 1990 more mature students entered higher education in Great Britain than young students. Between 1981 and 1991, the proportion of the 21–24-year-old age group entering higher education for the first time rose to 12.2% as compared with 7.5% in 1981. That represents a numerical increase from 17,300 to 36,600, out of a total of 281,100. In the same period, the number of first-year undergraduates over 25, of whom there were 47,600 by 1991, showed a similar rate of increase. Over 80% of mature students were in new universities. It may, nevertheless, be noted that, in spite of these increases in higher education, FE colleges are the major providers of education for the over-25s, and in the over-35 age group they have nearly two and a half times as many students as higher education.

Ethnic origin

As we point out in Chapter 9, children of working-class families continue to be under-represented in higher education.

Discussions of under-representation in higher education have often been accompanied by a concern that ethnic minorities may be experiencing difficulties in gaining access. Monitoring of the number of people from ethnic minorities applying for and being accepted into universities was first introduced in 1990. This has been helpful in refuting concern about under-representation overall. However, it has highlighted significant differences between ethnic groups in their comparative levels of participation, between levels of representation in different institutions, and in preferred areas of study. Figures for 1990–91 admissions, adjusted in the light of the 1991 census findings, show, for example, that as a whole ethnic minorities are well represented in higher education in relation to their percentage in the population of 17- to 21-year-olds. However, in the old universities several ethnic groups, including whites, are under-represented. Blacks and Bangladeshis are particularly poorly represented.[3] There is a range of possible explanations for this, apart from potential bias in the admissions process, including the tendency of minority groups to apply in greater numbers for subjects which are hard to get into, such as medicine and law.

Tariq Modood has recently examined the patterns of participation by different ethnic groups in higher education.[4] What he finds most striking in his analysis is the way in which race and ethnicity upset the overall pattern of distribution by social class. He notes that minority groups with a more disadvantaged class profile than whites produce much larger proportions of applicants and admissions to higher education, thus providing a counter-example to the view that class inequalities in higher education remain unchanged.

It is interesting by way of comparison to note the position in further education. Statistics for 1991–92 show, for the first time, participation rates for ethnic minorities in FE colleges. These are not analysed by class, but as Table 11.2 shows they indicate a relative under-representation, at all ages, of the white population, similar to that in higher education. The figures conceal striking gender differences in the participation by different communities, with black women represented in significantly greater numbers than their male counterparts, and the reverse phenomenon among Pakistanis and Bangladeshis. But even these women are participating in greater numbers, relative to their overall numbers in the population, than white men.

Table 11.2 Full-time participation rates in further education by ethnic community and age, 1991–92, England.

Percentage of relevant population

Age	White	Black Caribbean/ African/Other	Indian	Pakistani Bangladeshi	Other
16–19	12.6	29.3	24.0	21.0	17.2
20–24	0.8	4.3	1.0	1.6	2.4
25+	0.1	0.9	0.1	0.2	0.5
All over 16	0.9	3.7	2.2	3.3	2.6

Source: Department for Education, 1993.[5]

While evidence on the openness of higher education to all ethnic minorities must continue to be scrutinised, the unchanging class profile among whites and the relative under-representation of working-class men shows that we remain well short of the goal of attracting all who could benefit into post-compulsory educational provision at higher levels.

New routes to entry

As the composition of the student body shifts, routes to entry are becoming more diverse and the pattern of entry qualifications is beginning to change. The FE colleges have a pivotal role here. As Figure 11.1 shows, the numbers of 16-year-olds in England studying full-time in college have now overtaken those in schools. Government expenditure plans project a growth of 35% in the number of 16–18-year-olds in colleges by 1995–96, and it is expected that while 36% of all 16-year-olds will be in schools studying full-time, 45% will be full-time in colleges, with a further 9% studying part-time.

The trend towards college education for 16–18-year-olds has many positive features for students. Colleges can offer greater independence and a wider range of courses,

Figure 11.1 Full-time participation rates: schools and FE colleges, 1979–80 to 1992–3, England.

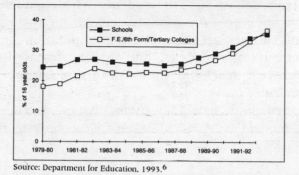

Source: Department for Education, 1993.[6]

adding the more vocational option of BTEC or the new GNVQs to the 'A' levels which schools normally provide. Their unit costs are lower than those of schools. There is no conclusive evidence on the relative success of different types of institution in terms of the achievements of their pupils in this age group. A recent Audit Commission report found that, overall, FE colleges performed very slightly less well than schools for 'A' level students, but that for individual subjects there were no important differences between types of institution.[7]

Although there may be benefits for students in going to college, the loss of a viable sixth form will have a significant impact on schools, and local plans need to take this into account. The presence in a school of a successful sixth form can be a strong positive factor, both in overall school performance and in attracting high-quality teachers. Quality and cost indicators would need to be decisively in favour of colleges to justify closing down a good sixth form.

Colleges are also attracting many older students into 'access' courses which lead on to higher education. In 1991–92 there were around 900 such courses, which typically include study skills and skills development in communications, numeracy and information technology. More than 80% of students who completed the courses took up a university place. An increasing number of colleges are also offering foundation years of higher education courses, and in some cases first and second year teaching, under franchise arrangements with partner universities.

Nevertheless, Table 11.3 shows that 'A' levels remain the dominant entry qualification, particularly in the old universities.

Table 11.3 Home acceptances for first degree courses by exam qualifications, 1991 and 1992, United Kingdom.

	Old universities				New universities			
	1991		1992		1991		1992	
	000s	%	000s	%	000s	%	000s	%
A levels	85.6	80.2	91.7	77.7	46.2	63.5	61.4	60.9
Scottish Highers	8.5	8.0	9.4	8.0	0.1	0.2	2.1	2.1
BTEC/SCOTVEC	4.9	4.6	6.6	5.6	9.1	12.5	13.2	13.1
Other	7.7	7.2	10.3	8.7	17.4	23.9	24.1	23.9
Total acceptances	106.7	100	118.0	100	72.8	100	100.9	100

Source: UCCA and PCAS.[8]

The more vocationally oriented BTEC qualification is beginning to establish its presence quite firmly, and its share is likely to increase. Some 30% of 16- and 17-year-olds in colleges, and 20% of 18–24-year-olds are pursuing BTEC qualifications as opposed to 14% in each age group who are doing A/AS levels. The new GNVQ programmes (vocational 'A' levels) introduced for the first time in 1992 are already proving popular.

Our proposed General Education Diploma at Advanced level (GED – see Chapter 4) would become a key route into higher education and will therefore need to gain the confidence of university selectors. As 'gate-keepers', selectors have often been seen as having a vested interest in maintaining the dominance of the 'A' level qualification. However, in recent years the majority of institutions have been stimulated to widen their entry criteria and selection arrangements. Many higher education institutions, with encouragement from a new 'Gate Committee' set up by the Committee of Vice Chancellors and Principals (CVCP), have guaranteed interviews to the first wave of applicants who have obtained the new vocational 'A' level.

These changes in the attitudes and practices of institutions and selectors are welcome, and give us confidence that the GED will quickly win acceptance. The GED will not be the only route, however. Accreditation of Prior Learning (APL) will assume increasing importance. 'Access' courses will continue to draw in those without formal qualifications, and some institutions may well follow the very successful example of the Open University, which has always taken students on a first-come, first-served basis without reference to qualifications.

Course Content and Structures

Subject choice

Just as the characteristics of students are changing, so are the choices they make about subjects and courses. Increasingly, they are rejecting specialised single honours courses in favour of programmes which combine two or more subjects. Joint degrees which include a language or an element of management studies are increasingly popular. In 1992, 16% and 20% of applications to the old and new universities respectively were for combined subjects; moreover, the number of applicants per place was higher than for single subject courses. Only 6% of applications were for single subject degree courses in engineering and the physical sciences.

Science, technology and engineering

Weak demand in science, technology and engineering has been an issue of concern for some years, although a recent study carried out for the German Government has indicated that Britain may be more successful in encouraging students to read scientific and technological subjects than some of its European partners.[9]

Concern stems partly from a belief that not enough potential scientists and engineers are inspired at school with enthusiasm for the subject; partly from the perceived level of difficulty of science subjects; and partly from the relative lack of status, uncertain career outlook and poor salaries which a future in science or engineering appears to offer. A recent report by the Royal Society paints a disturbing picture of the uncertainties of pursuing a career in scientific research.[10]

There will be a continuing need to encourage higher demand, but there must be a more co-ordinated approach for the different levels of the education system. Colleges are now successfully using the BTEC route to produce a growing stream of good quality entrants to university engineering courses. Collaborative arrangements at local level, drawing in not only colleges and universities but schools and employers, will be important in fostering more developments of this nature, not only in engineering but in other science subjects. Teacher training departments, in particular, need to consider how to use partners in schools and in industry to design programmes to attract good people into science teaching both at primary and secondary levels. In the long term, the influence of the greater emphasis both on science and the practical outcomes of learning in the GED should stimulate greater enthusiasm for these disciplines among schoolchildren.

Specialism or breadth?

Institutions need to take note, in planning courses, of the changing needs of employers and the impact these will have on graduate jobs. Many jobs for graduates now require flexibility and a wider range of knowledge and personal skills than before, and we expect this trend to continue. More people with a university education will find jobs in medium-sized and small businesses, where broad management responsibilities come earlier and require the ability to participate in a wider range of activities within the enterprise. The concept of a 'graduate job' as one entailing special training which leads to a faster track for advancement is receding. In future, people will be expected to move through a series of multi-dimensional roles rather than a series of rigidly defined jobs.

However, there remains a need for a smaller flow of highly-educated specialists. They will often be employed in professional firms; some will be in large organisations, but others will work independently as consultants or in small firms. There are also clear requirements for one- and two-year advanced vocational courses to meet specific employer requirements. Course planners in further and higher education must be alert to trends in the labour market and be quite clear about the outcomes their courses are designed to deliver. Students must have precise and accurate guidance about where courses are positioned.

The approach to teaching and learning we advocate at school lays stress on a mixture of outcomes in terms of knowledge, understanding and practical ability. We are of the view that this approach should be carried through into further and higher education. Such an approach is not incompatible with the need for some students to acquire a high degree of specialisation in their chosen field.

The Council for Industry and Higher Education has recently defined the long term needs of employers.[11] In addition to flexibility and adaptability, what employers will look for in their graduate recruits will be English language competence, foreign language skills, numeracy, data appreciation, teamwork, the ability to tackle unfamiliar problems and the desire to continue to learn. We consider that a 'profile of attributes' such as this is something which higher education programmes might reasonably be expected to deliver, and that institutions must provide an environment in which such attributes can be promoted. The Enterprise in Higher Education (EHE) programme, which has promoted the development of personal transferable skills in students, and the forging of links with employers to provide student projects and placements in work situations, has provided many useful examples of how this can be done.[12]

Levels of learning

An approach to course provision based on the levels of learning to be attained, and concerned with outcomes rather than process, will be the key to providing the more diverse and flexible range of courses which both students and employers need. This requires a framework of qualification levels for all post-18 education and training, building directly on the 14–18 continuum established by the GED.

The new framework should allow progression by a variety of routes through successive levels of learning and achievement, and provide cumulative awards which can dovetail with current higher education qualifications, while recognising achievement at intermediate levels. The traditional emphasis on length and location of study will decline in importance; part-time study will no longer be seen as second-best; and individuals will be able to choose their rate of progression and mode of study to suit their individual circumstances.

Maximum flexibility will be achieved if the framework is developed in association with modular courses. Students will have been prepared for this by the modular structure of the GED. Credit accumulation and transfer arrangements (CATS) extending across the whole range of post-18 educational institutions and also, in due course, across national boundaries will further promote flexibility. Many institutions have already embraced CATS and modularity, and what is in question is not the direction but the pace of change.

The CATS scheme introduced by the Council for National Academic Awards (CNAA), and now operated through the Higher Education Quality Council, requires students to accumulate 120 credits at three different levels to qualify for a degree. This operates within higher education only. A separate scheme put forward by the Further Education Unit proposes a common currency for all post-16 work, encompassing all levels and types of qualifications from Key Stage 4 of the national curriculum through to masters degrees and professional qualifications.[13] We agree strongly with this general line of development, though there are problems which still need resolution including, in particular, the alignment of NVQ levels 4 and 5 with existing higher education qualifications.

The framework which we propose should make use of the potential for APL and for the incorporation of in-house company learning into an overall programme of higher education. The validation and accreditation role of higher education institutions is likely to expand accordingly, very much to the benefit of students and employers generally.

The development of CATS, APL, and a single qualification framework raises many issues, and quality considerations are paramount among them. It is welcome, therefore, that much of the developmental thinking is taking
place under the auspices of the Higher Education Quality
Council.

We are convinced that the development of a single
framework for post-18 qualifications building on the GED,
in combination with credit-based systems, is the way forward. We do not underestimate the problems involved in
arriving at a high quality system which works for all, but
we also do not doubt that they can be overcome.
Excellent work is going on in both the further education
and the higher education sector. It is important that it be
brought to a successful outcome as soon as possible.

Organisational Change and Institutional Diversity

A unitary system
Recent organisational changes have brought together the
universities and the former polytechnics and colleges of
higher education into a single sector, and created a new
unified further education sector combining further education, tertiary and sixth form colleges. Over the last decade
a range of different institutional models has been developing, partly in response to client needs, but perhaps mainly
as a result of selective funding policies and the continuing
quest for efficiency gains by the Government.

Reorganisation has highlighted the existence of a number of honourable traditions in higher and further education each of which has great value. It has challenged the
misleading impression, which the former sectoral arrangements tended to reinforce, of a hierarchy of esteem in
which the 'old' universities, with their strictly academic

and research-oriented mission, were seen to occupy pride of place. While this view prevailed, the former polytechnics had to fight to demonstrate the worth of a different but equally valuable interpretation of the mission for higher education – a mission which placed greater emphasis on the application of knowledge and advanced vocational and technological education and training. The FE colleges, meanwhile, remained firmly within the ambit of local government, and were often thought of as a relatively unknown quantity. Emancipation from these stereotypes now permits a better understanding of the newer and more diversified models which are emerging.

Diversity of mission

We see increasing diversification as crucial. Not all institutions can carry out effectively all the tasks which the system as a whole needs to accomplish. All institutions must define their own strategic objectives clearly, in the light of an assessment of their comparative strengths and weaknesses so as to concentrate on developing their particular areas of excellence. Some will see full-time residential undergraduate education as their special strength. Others will prefer a wider range of students and provision, including one- and two-year vocational courses and outreach activity. Some will concentrate on strong research departments and post-graduate schools. Some will cover the whole spectrum of academic subjects. Others will concentrate on areas of special expertise.

There is room for a wide range of different combinations of activities in the system as a whole. What is important, however, is that institutions develop an explicit understanding of their distinctive contribution to the system, and actively plan their development in relation to a well-defined set of strategic objectives. In future, we expect to see institutions abandoning some activities or subject areas, however difficult this may be, in order to become stronger in those on which they decide to concentrate.

Diversity is, then, a crucial feature in the post-compulsory system of the future. There is nevertheless an obvious danger that the evolution of unified funding methodologies by funding councils will work against diversity, and that the system will tend to become 'a homogeneous continuum of a compound without contrasting colours or character'.[14] A factor which can work strongly against this is geography. Educational institutions form part of wider communities, whether local, national or international; and, in defining their objectives, they should take into account their positioning in this respect, and grasp opportunities to work collaboratively as a part of their community, with other institutions, with employers and public sector bodies.

We particularly wish to emphasise that universities and colleges have great potential to work for economic regeneration and to enhance the quality of life within their geographical spheres of influence. We hope that more institutions will give this prominence in developing their future plans.

The place of research

The debate which has accompanied the creation of the new single sector of higher education has been constructive in many ways. It has led to questioning of the basic purposes of higher education and exploration of what constitutes quality in this context. Most importantly, perhaps, it has uncoupled the concept of quality, in the minds of many people both inside and outside higher education, from its previous almost exclusive link with research excellence. The greater stress which has recently been placed on quality in teaching, and the importance of the concept of 'fitness for purpose' in education, is necessary and welcome.

In recent years funds for research in the old universities have been ever more closely linked to performance. As a result, there have been dramatic shifts in the pattern of allocations and some departments in some old universities no longer attract any funding for research.

These funding changes have been accompanied by pressure to increase research grant and contract income from other sources and by moves to concentrate research in 'centres of excellence'. They thus go directly to the heart of what many still feel to be the distinctive characteristic of a 'real' university – that its teaching and research activities are inextricably linked. The argument is put forcefully by Sir John Kingman, Vice Chancellor of Bristol University and former Chairman of the Science and Engineering Research Council:

> University graduates go out into a world of ever more rapid change, and they will be expected not just to respond passively, but to lead that change, or indeed on occasion to resist it when they judge it to be malign. How can we teach our disciplines so that our students develop that talent? Surely by presenting the subject as dynamic, as developing in response not to blind fashion but to refinement and discovery and deeper insight. I can see no other way of doing this but in a community of scholars involved in original and critical thought about the subjects they teach; in short, in a university which offers learning in a research environment . . . I believe strongly that:
>
> • the most able of our young people should receive their higher education in a research-led environment;
>
> • a major justification of the national research effort is the quality it adds to the learning experience of our students.[15]

This argument suggests that the new universities, which traditionally have carried out only a relatively small amount of research and have not been directly funded for it, have been of lesser value than that of the former university sector. However, the success of the former polytechnics in producing large numbers of well-qualified graduates, together with their innovation in teaching methods and curriculum development, is recognised by employers and in the formal assessments carried out by HMI. The example of the better liberal arts colleges in the USA also demonstrates that excellent undergraduate teaching can and does take place in institutions where research does not form a significant part of the overall activity.

Teaching in higher education involves the development of a pattern of understanding which is cumulative and hierarchical in nature. For a subject to be appropriate for undergraduate education it must have a theoretical underpinning which can be probed, tested and extended. To this extent teaching and research are natural bedfellows. Moreover, it is rarely if ever possible to identify in advance subjects or departments in which rising stars, capable of initiating original and innovative research programmes, may emerge. This does not, however, imply that all university teachers must be creative researchers actively engaged in pushing forward the boundaries of their discipline and therefore funded as such. This is not the case now, and was never the case in the past.

An atmosphere of inquiry and intellectual excitement
It follows that a range of academic staff with different qualities is needed. What undergraduates require is exposure to a significant number of teachers whose involvement in advanced work underpins their teaching. Increasingly, however, students will themselves become

independent learners and their relationships with academic staff will modify accordingly. Face-to-face contact between lecturer and student has been one of the highly valued features of the British system, and as staff-student ratios become lower, the teaching practices of the past will change. As the processes by which students learn are better understood and the potential of new technology in learning is exploited, the quality of the student experience will not necessarily be diluted.

Students do not have to be intensively taught by top-flight researchers. They do need to learn in an atmosphere of inquiry and intellectual excitement. In different universities the proportion of staff in different categories and their level of involvement in research already varies considerably. Within universities, and not only the new universities, some departments are already effectively 'teaching-only' departments. This is not a cause for concern if sufficient members of the department are engaged in advanced work and if the group as a whole creates an enthusiasm for learning. What is not acceptable is a department which merely recycles what is known, and fails to equip students with the spirit of inquiry which will inspire them to continue to learn throughout life.

Post-graduate provision

At post-graduate level the link with research is essential. This applies to taught masters programmes as well as research degrees. At this level, the need to extend disciplines, methodologies and students to their limits demands teachers who are themselves at the forefront of their own subjects and, increasingly, able to assimilate and apply what is happening where complementary disciplines meet. Where programmes confer professional or management qualifications, they also need input from leading practitioners.

Demand for post-graduate study is now strong. In 1991–92, post-graduate enrolments in Great Britain were 84% higher than in 1981 and 15% higher than in 1990. Enrolments are equally divided between full-time and part-time students, but the percentage increase since 1981 has been much faster for part-timers (123% as opposed to 57%). The largest expansion has been in taught courses, typically one-year masters courses, as opposed to the three-year doctoral programmes. The extent to which the recession has affected demand, as at other levels in education, remains to be seen.

In the past, the development of post-graduate education has suffered because it lies at the interface between the science and higher education policy areas.[16] The establishment of the Office of Science and Technology and the debate which that stimulated has now brought the organisation of research and the nature of post-graduate training to the fore in a way which is in itself welcome. In highlighting the needs in science and technology, however, the requirements of other disciplines should not be swept aside. It is to be regretted that the opportunity to establish a Humanities Research Council has not yet been taken.

The nature of post-graduate training

There has long been a tension between the requirement for research students to make an original contribution to knowledge and the need to provide structured training in research skills. Latterly, there has been a further concern that research degree programmes should also provide the wider skills which post-graduates going into employment need just as much as their undergraduate counterparts. The White Paper on science, engineering and technology has taken these concerns into account.[17] It not only links research and post-graduate work very closely to the processes of wealth creation, but proposes to take steps to make a masters degree a formal requirement for progression to doctoral work. This is seen as having a number of advantages:

- it will allow more students to be supported to the masters level, as a result of which they can acquire skills of value for a range of careers within industry or elsewhere;

- students will have an opportunity during this year to consider whether they have the wish and aptitude to proceed to research leading to a PhD degree;

- applicants for PhD training can be selected on a more informed basis by reference to their personal motivation, ability to benefit from PhD training and suitability for either an academic or non-academic career.

We acknowledge these advantages but draw attention to a real danger. If implemented, the PhD will effectively be turned into a four-year qualification. The White Paper states that: 'the new pattern will be achieved within planned resource levels.' The clear implication is that the number of students proceeding to doctoral work will fall, while the current trend towards taught courses will accelerate. The resulting reduction in the pool of highly qualified talent will exacerbate recruitment problems for universities, which already have difficulties in scientific and technological subjects in competing with industry for the best brains. It will also in the short term put yet further strain on academic staff by requiring additional formal teaching with no corresponding increase in funds. This is not a process which can go on indefinitely. Short-term funding exigencies must not be allowed to undermine an investment of such central importance for the long term.

Concentration of resources

Research, particularly equipment-intensive research in science and technology, will tend to concentrate more and more in a relatively small number of university institutions and, within institutions, in particular departments. This is inevitable given the funding pressures which the system now faces. It is likely, too, that those institutions will increasingly attract a larger proportion of the overall post-graduate research population. We do not see this as a bad thing. Research in many disciplines is not, and should not be, a solitary activity. This is particularly true for the young post-graduate setting out on a new project. We welcome the recent development in some universities of Graduate Schools. The Graduate School is an organisational model which is well understood in the USA but as yet not common in British universities, where, as a result, the post-graduate community, particularly in the arts and some social sciences, is often too fragmented.[18]

Issues of research and post-graduate education are a central concern for institutions at the forefront of the international research community. If they are to remain so, and it is important to our national competitiveness that they should, they must be adequately supported. In return, research-led institutions must be prepared to work collaboratively within the system as a whole to ensure that the boundaries between themselves and other universities are easily permeable. This is particularly important for the development and mobility of staff.

Professional Staff

The people who work in universities and colleges are the most important resource which the system possesses. This includes not only academic staff but the whole range of support staff who form part of the team which drives individual departments and research groups forward.

The academic profession is an ageing profession. The largest group is in the late forties and the rate of retirement will increase markedly over the next decade. The structure is also changing, with short-term contract staff now forming a much higher proportion of the total. Staff–student ratios have moved from around 1:11 in 1987–8 to 1:14 in 1991-2. New approaches to teaching and learning and the introduction of new technology are making new demands on academics and students. People are generally much more hard pressed than they were, with more administrative and teaching duties and less time for research, which in many old universities is still the main criterion for promotion.

These factors have contributed to a loss of morale over the last decade.[19] There has also been a relative decline in salary level, and this will bring serious recruitment problems if action is not taken to develop the profession and raise its status. It is a striking comment on the value that has recently been placed on university teachers that, while non-manual earnings in the UK have risen by 53% since 1979, academics' pay has risen by only 9% in the same period.[20] We support the CVCP when it says:

> No group of staff can expect to occupy a fixed place in the earnings league but a relative downward trend of this order is bound to lead to widespread problems of recruitment and retention especially at a time when it becomes necessary to replace a high proportion of staff.[21]

Academics must expect, however, that in a changing world their role will change and that they must show the same degree of flexibility and professionalism as their colleagues in schools or industry. This will require not only the co-operation of individuals but a much greater emphasis than has been given in the past to the active management of human resources in higher education institutions.[22] This applies at the level of the institution and at the level of the department, where a team approach to the successful delivery of the academic programme is likely to be more effective than the more traditional management style based on hierarchy.

At the institutional level, more thought needs to be given to job design and career development. The emergence of teaching-only universities, the introduction of new methods of teaching and the use of new technology in teaching all require that careful thought be given to how human resources are used, and whether the existing demarcation lines between academic staff and technicians, or academic staff and administrators, are still appropriate. The increasing tendency to devolve management tasks to the lowest appropriate level in the institution points up the need to develop further the few management programmes which currently exist for heads of departments.

There is no formal requirement in either further or higher education institutions for a teaching qualification. In universities, the doctorate has tended to be the passport to entry, but few doctoral programmes involve any training in either teaching or communication skills. The received view inside the profession is still very much that professionalism is rooted in knowledge of the specialist subject.

Some institutions now have a training requirement built in to their probation requirements, and it is increasingly common in further education to require staff recruited without formal teaching qualifications to take a part-time teaching certificate. The growth in both sectors of the use of part-time teaching staff, whose relationship to the institution may be peripheral and transitory, raises problems in respect of induction and training. It is important that institutions recognise the need to integrate part-timers fully into their staff development provision.

In a recent survey of students and teachers in universities and colleges there was positive feedback, although not total enthusiasm, from both groups for a proposal to introduce a national training programme for new lecturers.[23] More likely to be acceptable to institutions, however, is a procedure which allows them to maintain responsibility for their own professional standards rather than have regulation imposed from outside. This was, no doubt, one of the motivations behind the recent introduction by the CVCP Standing Committee on Educational Development of a national scheme for the accreditation of institutions' in-house training schemes for new lecturers. There is no set curriculum for this scheme, which lays out a range of objectives and underpinning values for a training programme and ensures standards through an external steering committee.

The new scheme is a step in the right direction. It has only just been piloted in eight institutions. The extent to which it will be capable of growing to an effective scheme for self-regulation by the universities of their professional teaching standards remains to be seen. We are strongly of the view that effective system-wide regulation is overdue, and that the changing demands on teachers in both further and higher education make a clear emphasis on teacher training, both for new and existing staff, necessary. We consider that a permanent appointment in either higher or further education should require the holder to have a qualification which attests his or her competence as a teacher.

Financing Expansion

Giving greater emphasis to human resource management,

developing a more targeted academic programme, taking advantage of new ways of learning and adapting to a changing student population all put pressures on teachers and managers in universities and colleges. They also bring with them financial pressures additional to those associated directly with increases in student numbers. We are deeply concerned about how expansion and change in the universities and colleges are to be financed. The system which we envisage will, inevitably, require greater investment. That means not only more investment by Government, but more investment by individuals and by industrial and business concerns. All this requires an overall strategy which aims to find the right balance between these different contributions and to provide a secure funding base for the future. That is essential if institutions are to plan their expansion rationally and to manage successfully the manifold changes in practice and culture involved.

At present there is no Government financial strategy for expansion other than a determination to drive down unit costs and minimise calls on the Exchequer. This is a process which can continue for only so long if it is not to lead to a serious deterioration in the quality of higher education. Our evidence is that, although this has not yet happened, some institutions are now dangerously close to being unable to provide properly for all their staff and students.[24] We think that the time has come when the Government should join with the higher education sector in a joint examination of the financial basis on which future expansion can be secured without putting at risk the value of the contribution which higher education should make to the long-term future of the country.

Investment in the infrastructure of higher education
As the number of students in higher education rises, pres-

sure on buildings, including residential accommodation, is becoming severe. Although there are indications that institutions could manage greater numbers in existing buildings if funds were available for adaptation, recent investigations into the management of higher education's physical plant and its capital funding have revealed a number of serious and unavoidable expenses. These range from the cost of implementing health and safety requirements and adapting buildings to allow for more efficient use of space, to tackling serious backlogs in maintenance of university buildings. This is particularly acute in the new universities where local authorities had tended to cut back on maintenance before the polytechnics were given corporate status in 1988. The CVCP identifies a requirement of £11350 million to make up the maintenance backlog and £45 million to meet health and safety regulations. Similar infrastructure problems may well be revealed in the colleges once the Further Education Funding Council takes stock of the sector's physical plant.

Investment is needed not only in buildings and maintenance, but in libraries, laboratories and scientific and computing equipment. Inflation in the costs of books and scientific equipment have run ahead of general inflation for many years. This has resulted in real cuts in the funds available for the basic tools of the trade. A CVCP inquiry into library provision is currently underway. This should provide firm evidence of the extent to which reinvestment is required. If the potential benefits of new learning environments are to be exploited, and institutions are to be enabled to maximise their outreach, then networking campuses to exploit information technology will be another key area for investment.

Capital investment will be needed if expansion is to be achieved successfully. In the past, institutions have not always used their plant to best advantage. Investment should, therefore, be linked to the introduction of measures to ensure more efficient and effective use of existing plant. In this context, we welcome the major inquiry undertaken by Lord Flowers into the organisation of the academic year. This has proposed the possibility of accommodating substantially more students without significant augmentation of existing space. Profound academic as well as financial implications are at stake. For this reason, the wide consultation process which is now taking place is essential if any resultant changes are to be effective both in containing the costs of expansion and maintaining quality both in teaching and research.

A funding shift
Indefinite continuation of the policy of funding the recurrent costs of expansion through efficiency gains cannot continue without leading to an unacceptable drop in the quality of both teaching and research. The case for substantial capital investment in expansion is strong. Our conclusion is that the only satisfactory long-term answer is to seek a shift in the balance of funding. This involves looking to a greater contribution from the beneficiaries of higher education; both employers and students.

Higher education institutions receive funds from a variety of sources. Public funding provides, on average, 67% of universities' incomes. Other funding comes from a range of income-generating activities (conference lettings, intellectual property rights, consultancy, short-course work etc.), from endowments and investments, and from business and industry.

Income from business and industry and from charitable sources has increased very significantly over the last decade, but, as the greater part of such funds is usually earmarked for specific research contracts and may not carry full overheads, it makes little contribution to general running costs and may even be a drain on other institutional resources. Views expressed in a report from the Council for Industry and Higher Education that: 'business cannot be expected to pick up the bills for the mainstream of higher education that the Government is unwilling to pay,' underline the fact that, while funding from this source should steadily increase, there are limits to the amount of the extra contribution to institutional funding which it will make.[25]

The proposals put forward in Chapter 9 are designed to bring about a funding shift by requiring more of students. We recognise that this alone will not solve the problem in the short term, especially if it is to be applied to broadening the scope of student support as well as to expansion. Greater government investment will also be required until the scheme is fully mature. Nevertheless, we see our scheme as providing a way in which government, individuals and institutional investors can all collaborate in order to ensure that universities and colleges are provided with a secure base from which to deliver the high-quality research, education and training we require from them in the years ahead.

Notes

[1] Halsey, A.H., 1992. Opening Wide the Doors of Higher Education. NCE Briefing No. 6. National Commission on Education.

[2] Government Statistical Service, 1993. Education Statistics for the UK, 1992 Edition.

[3] Article by Tariq Modood in *Times Higher Education Supplement*, 1993, updated in 6 August issue in the light of 1991 census findings.

[4] Forthcoming article in *Oxford Review of Education*, Vol 19, No. 2, 1993.

[5] Department for Education (DFE), 1993. Statistics of Further Education College Students in England 1970–71 – 1991–92. *Statistical Bulletin* 14/93.

[6] DFE, 1993. Participation in Education by 16–18-Year-Olds in England: 1979–80 – 1992–93. *Statistical Bulletin* 16/93.

[7] Audit Commission and OFSTED, 1993. Unfinished Business: Full-Time Education for 16–19-Year-Olds. HMSO.

8   Universities Central Council on Admissions Statistics Office; Polytechnics Central Admissions System, Statistical Supplement to the Annual Report 1991-92.

9   Cited in the *Times Higher Education Supplement*, 6 August 1993.

10 Royal Society, 1992. The Future of the Science Base. Royal Society.

11 Council for Industry and Higher Education, 1992. Investing in Diversity: An Assessment of Higher Education Policy. CIHE.

12 Tavistock Institute of Human Relations, 1990. The First Year of Enterprise in Higher Education: Final Report of the Case Study Evaluation of EHE. Tavistock Institute of Human Relations.

13 Further Education Unit, 1992. A Basis for Credit? Developing a Post-16 Credit Accumulation and Transfer Framework. FEU.

14 Opening remarks by Sir Ron Dearing to a conference of the Higher Education Funding Council for England, 6 April 1993.

15 Sir John Kingman, 1993. 'The Pursuit of Truth.' *Times Higher Education Supplement*, 18 June.

16 Advisory Board for the Research Councils, 1993. The Nature of the PhD: A Discussion Document. Office of Science and Technology.

17 Office of Science and Technology, 1993. Realising our Potential: A Strategy for Science, Engineering and Technology. HMSO, Cm 2250.

18 Burgess, R.G., 1992. A Graduate School in the UK: The University of Warwick Graduate School. ACU Bulletin of Current Documentation, No 106.

19 Halsey, A.H., 1992. *Decline of Donnish Dominion*. Oxford University Press, pp. 134–5.

20 Committee of Vice Chancellors and Principals (CVCP), 1993. Public Expenditure Survey Submission.

21 *Ibid*, para 35.

22 CVCP, January 1993. Promoting People: A Strategic Framework for the Management and Development of Staff in UK Universities.

23 Centre for Higher Education Studies, Institute of Education, 1993. Identifying and Developing a Quality Ethos for Teaching in Higher Education: Identifying Priorities.

24 CVCP evidence to the Commission.

25 Council for Industry and Higher Education, 1991. The Business Contribution to Higher Education. CIHE.

12
Learning throughout life

Introduction

In recent years the idea that lifetime education and training is desirable has become accepted, but too often it attracts a dutiful genuflexion rather than enthusiasm. The subject is commonly imagined to be of minor interest, though worthy.

The reality is that adults participate in learning on a very large scale – though this needs to be larger still. The topic is of such great importance that it should be receiving continuous and close attention from anyone concerned with education and training.

Why? Some pressing reasons are as follows:

- the increasingly rapid obsolescence of people's knowledge and skills, and the constant need therefore to renew and reinforce them;

- the ageing of our workforce and the impossibility of replenishing skills purely from intakes of newly trained young people;

- increasing polarisation between those with high levels of skill and access to jobs and those with neither;

- the increasing disadvantages of poor literacy and numeracy for adults;

- the fact that the educational level of parents, and mothers in particular, is one of the most significant factors affecting the educational achievement of young people;

- the opportunities for personal fulfilment which further education and training can offer;

- the need to recognise fully both the needs and the potential contribution of people currently prevented from playing a full part in the labour force and in society.

Together these reasons justify a thorough reappraisal of the country's approach to continuing learning. We use this term in preference to 'continuing education', partly because it is clearly essential that training should be coupled with education, and partly because the term embraces all sorts of learning, formal and informal, and is not limited to formal courses or to provision in colleges or training centres. Our interest here is with education and training which serves needs ranging from the immediate to the long-term, and from those of individuals to the corporate and communal.

Structured education and training are mainly the responsibilities of Government and employers, but continuing learning should be seen in the context of broader policies. It has the potential to generate large savings in public spending. Thus, investment in education and training can be a positive means of reducing costs – social as well as financial – in such fields as health, law and order and economic regeneration. The economic and social reasons for encouraging continuing learning should never be underrated.

The Scale of Adult Learning Today

Training by employers
The most important force behind learning for adults is the

provision by employers of training for their employees in order to maintain or raise competitiveness.

In 1986–87 private sector companies were spending some £11 billion on training (of which £2 billion was spent by firms with fewer than 10 employees). At that time public sector employers were spending £5 billion on training and the armed forces some £2 billion. The national outlay by employers was therefore about £18 billion. A total of some 8.6 million people received training, of whom the great majority were adults.[1]

Since 1986 employers have been increasing the number of employees they train – the proportion was about 40% higher in 1992 than five years earlier – so that a conservative estimate of employers' expenditure today might be £35 billion.

Further education in colleges and adult education centres
Table 12.1 shows the numbers enrolling as students in FE colleges in England in 1991. Over 1.6 million adults enrolled – but if young people of 16 and 17 are also included, the total number of students in FE colleges is seen to be well over 2 million.

Table 12.1 Enrolments on courses of further education in colleges, 1991, England.

Thousands

Type of course	Age of student						All adults (18+)	All students
	16–17	18–20	21–24	25–59	60+	Unknown		
Full-time and sandwich	270	112	27	53	1	2	195	465
Part-time	137	139	73	294	103	36	645	782
Evening only	41	80	98	412	81	50	721	762
Open/distance learning	5	6	6	26	1	2	41	46
Total	453	337	204	785	186	90	1,602	2,054

Source: Department for Education.[2]

Part-time and evening study are overwhelmingly the commonest modes of attendance among adults – about 85% of the total. Among younger people a majority are on courses with a vocational qualification in view. From age 25 upwards an overall average of 40% of people are on courses not leading to qualifications; the proportion rises with age and most of the courses in question are probably taken for recreational and leisure purposes.

Table 12.2 provides information about enrolments in adult education centres in England over the period 1987–91.

Table 12.2 Enrolments at adult education centres, 1987–91, England.

					Thousands
Type of course	*November in year shown*				
	1987	*1988*	*1989*	*1990*	*1991*
Part-time day	449	463	460	480	470
Evening only	941	929	916	872	822
All courses	1,390	1,392	1,376	1,352	1,292

Source: Department for Education, 1993.[3]

Adult education centres are defined as places of part-time learning mainly funded by local authorities to provide further education for adults. It will be noted that provision in adult education centres has been declining, and we refer to this later in this chapter. Despite the decline, there were still nearly 1.3 million enrolments at adult education centres in England in 1991, and this bears testimony to the extent to which these centres continue to attract public support.

To these figures must be added education for adults provided by universities and other higher education institutions. A total of some 930,000 students are involved.

Among students up to age 24, full-time and sandwich courses predominate, but from 25 upwards 70% are studying part-time. (This figure includes Open University students.)

There will be some duplication in these figures; for example, some students enrolled in further or higher education will have been sent on courses paid for by employers and therefore included in the figures relating to employers. Nevertheless, the numbers involved are very high – upwards of 10 million. The public and private expenditure too is very great: approaching £3 billion for public expenditure alone.[4]

Why This is Not Enough

Despite these figures, we have no reason to be satisfied with current levels of activity. It is not sufficient to provide us with a fully skilled workforce in international terms, as we point out in Chapter 1. Nor is it enough to ensure that those people who need access to learning actually receive it: those with poor basic skills, for example, or older people who have much to contribute to improving the quality of life in their communities as well as much to gain in personal fulfilment.

Training for work

If the figures for training given by employers do not increase, it is most unlikely that national lifetime learning targets can be met, as we note in Chapter 9.

Nor will the current level of activity be enough for the future, given the ageing structure of the labour market. This is illustrated in Figure 12.1.

It is clear that it will be necessary to train many more older workers than we have done hitherto. The task will be all the greater because there are many more older people who have inadequate qualifications or none at all, as Table 12.3 shows.

Figure 12.1 Projected change in labour market, 1991–2001, Great Britain.

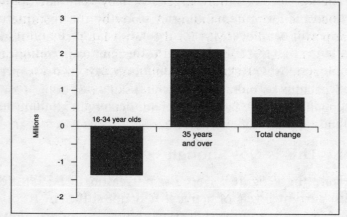

Source: Employment Department, 1992.[5]

Table 12.3 People of working age with no qualifications, Great Britain, spring 1991.

Age	Percentage
16–19	27
20–24	17
25–34	20
35–44	31
45–64 (women, 45–59)	44
All	30

Source: Employment Department, 1992.[6]

Training in basic skills
There is a further problem of fundamental importance. In the first chapter of this report we refer to a survey of literacy and numeracy among 21-year-olds which revealed that almost 15% had limited literacy skills and 20% only very limited competence in mathematics. However suc-

cessful our schools may be in teaching children these basic skills in future, there is an immense job to be done in helping people already at work to improve their competence in them.

The job becomes more urgent year by year as employers become more demanding. A study by the Institute of Manpower Studies (IMS) for the Adult Literacy and Basic Skills Unit (ALBSU)[7] showed how significant minorities of job applicants lacked basic skills and that this was most noticeable in numeracy and writing skills (see Table 12.4). Such individuals face greater difficulty in finding or retaining employment or else find themselves debarred from advancement at work.

Table 12.4 Distribution of employers' satisfaction with basic skill supply among applicants.

Percentages

| Type of skill | Level of satisfaction | | | |
	Less than adequate or completely inadequate	Only just inadequate	Fairly adequate	More than adequate
Numeracy skills	8	20	52	19
Writing skills	8	20	52	20
Oral communication skills	7	18	54	21
Reading skills	4	14	56	26

Source: Atkinson, J. and Spilsbury, M., March 1993. [7]

The IMS also argued that, while evidence suggests that on the whole employers' immediate requirements of their employees are satisfied, 'that is only because their demand for skills is socially and economically sub-optimal . . . if you aim low, you are unlikely to be disappointed.'[7] In other words, demand is constrained by supply, and employers may have embarked on a 'low skill route' and chosen their working methods and technologies accordingly. Nor are those who remain constrained by the limited skills of their employees likely to be able to expand their business horizons in future.

We are certain that an altogether sharper sense of urgency is needed in seeking to persuade and enable adults with weak basic skills to undertake appropriate training programmes. Any such adult who becomes unemployed must have a right to a suitable course; an early decision should be taken to waive the '21-hour rule' in such cases so that an unemployed person is entitled to draw benefit while undertaking a full-time course.

The Way Forward

If we are to address these problems and make an entitlement to continuing learning a reality, we must have a coherent policy which builds on employer training, supports colleges and other providers, develops individual opportunities and motivation and encourages community learning.

Training instigated by employers
The dominant reason why employers train in a society which relies largely on free market competition to stimulate and reward industrial success is that it pays to do so. We bring out in the opening chapters of this report the historical reasons why this country has under-invested in skills. There has been a 'low-skill equilibrium' for much too long. As a nation we depend on employers moving to a high-skill equilibrium for the future – a virtuous circle in which they produce high-quality goods and services which enable them to earn good profits, this being made possible by high investment in the skills of the workforce. The biggest incentive to train in the years ahead will be the

increasing difficulties which will be faced by employers who do not seek to create and benefit from this virtuous circle – they will be hard put to remain in business at all. It will be the verdict of world markets that will ultimately decide.

We do not propose in this report the imposition of a training tax on employers, even though this idea has some attractions as a way of stimulating attention to training and of generating funds for it, and even though in France it seems to be accepted and to bring benefit. Our own past experience of training levies and grants was not a success and it has left a legacy of distaste for such arrangements which would be hard to overcome.

We do, however, propose in Chapter 9 that employers should be obliged to provide employees with a minimum of five days a year of off-the-job education or training. If an employer does not make provision, as a part of his own training programme for off-the-job training, whether delivered in-house or through an external organisation, the employee will have the right to choose what learning he or she wishes to have. The employer will be obliged to pay the fees involved (subject to a maximum limit) as well as to allow the employee time off without loss of pay to attend the course or pursue the learning concerned. This we believe to be a minimum necessary obligation which employers should be required to observe, and a minimum necessary right which employees should be able to exercise.

Voluntary means of encouraging employers
Beyond these measures there are other voluntary means of encouraging employers to invest more seriously in human resources which need to be pursued with determination. We cite two examples.

The first is the Investors In People award. The award is

available to employers who apply exemplary standards in developing the capability of their workforce. Key principles embodied in the award are: public commitment by top management; a plan setting out business goals and targets and identifying the development needs of employees in relation to the plan; the earmarking of the necessary resources for training and development; practical implementation; evaluation; and continuing commitment for the future.

The principle of the Investors In People standard is excellent. The Employment Department's aim is that 50% of medium to large organisations – a total of about 6,000 – should reach the standard by 1996. If that aim is realised without any watering down of the standard set it will be a major step forward. Training and Enterprise Councils (TECs) have a key role and a key responsibility in this.

Secondly, there is the influence which TECs can bring to bear on smaller employers. Its importance is underlined by the fact that about 97% of employers employ fewer than 20 people and they account for 35% of non-government employment.[8] It will be particularly the smaller employers who provide extra jobs in the years ahead; it is estimated that firms employing fewer than 20 people created over a million jobs between 1985 and 1989.[9] TECs have a much greater likelihood of influencing and helping smaller employers to provide training than any previous government agencies, and it is highly desirable that they should be able to concentrate on this problem.

The encouragement of the desire to learn

Various companies are recognising the value of developing a desire to learn among their employees. Striking examples include Ford, Rover and Lucas. Each of these companies has run schemes which have encouraged employees to undertake whatever education and training they themselves choose to meet their own wishes, whether job-related or not. Many have, for example, chosen to learn Spanish or another foreign language for holiday purposes. Others have, nevertheless, chosen to take vocational courses, for example in mechanical engineering or word-processing. The common experience has been that these schemes are successful and have many benefits; that the self-esteem and confidence of those who take part in them rises; and that as a result those concerned become more interested in the job-related training opportunities which the company has to offer – a benefit both to themselves and to the company.

Seen beside the total cost of investment in job-related training which these companies make, initiatives such as these cost comparatively little and bring a very good return. We find it surprising that more medium and large companies are not following suit. The Confederation of British Industry and the TECs have a responsibility to stimulate much more active interest in their doing so. The public sector should not lag behind, and we would hope to see the Department for Education and Training (see Chapter 13), once set up, to be conspicuous for its own training performance, both as an Investor In People and as a provider of learning opportunities for its staff.

Basic skills and employers
There are excellent examples of companies which have, as part of their commitment to raising the capability of their workforce, sought to improve employees' basic skills. There are charitable companies such as Workbase which have special experience in providing the training involved. TECs should give encouragement to such schemes, and we think it would be a proper use of their funds to give grants to help persuade employers to commit

themselves to raising employees' basic skills.

Training on the Initiative of Individuals

A report on the Rover Group's programme to encourage employees to pursue education and training of their own choice quotes a manager as saying: 'The most dangerous people in Rover are those who have forgotten how to change. If they are hit by change, they fear it and resist it.'[10]

Perhaps the most critical task of all in the years ahead is to persuade a greater number of men and women that learning is for them, that it can improve their personal lives and that there are opportunities there for them to seize. The goal in the end is to create a learning culture, a society in which learning is the norm and the question people ask when the possibility of education or training arises for them is not 'why should I?' but 'why shouldn't I?'.

It is known that a great many people in jobs cannot envisage undertaking training in the future. The younger and the better qualified workers are, the more likely they are to welcome the idea of training; conversely older workers, particularly those with no qualifications, are more likely to have a negative attitude. Though attitudes are changing, progress has been slow.

And yet there are important signs that an apparent unwillingness to go on learning does not run deep and that there is an immense latent readiness to do so if only this can be aroused. That is the true lesson to be learned from the initiatives at Ford, Rover and Lucas.

Further proof of the latent readiness to undertake education or training was provided by the BBC's Second Chance Initiative in 1992. During a week devoted to programmes aimed at helping people to decide about returning to education and training, no fewer than 57,000 people called the Employment Department supported helpline and 42% of these subsequently took up opportunities for learning.

An essential part of improving motivation is to do something to reduce the barriers which stand in the way of a decision to undertake further education or training. The main barriers are well-known:[11]

- the difficulty of obtaining funding;
- finding the time to study;
- the risk of giving up a current job to take a full-time course.

On the other hand a major motivator is the desire to improve job prospects. About 60% of individuals taking the initiative to train have a change of job in mind.

Our recommendations in Chapter 9 go some way towards overcoming the barriers for those who seek to improve their educational qualifications up to and including the Advanced level of the General Education Diploma (GED). We propose the right to a day a week off work without loss of pay for anyone under 25 who wishes to raise his or her qualifications up to the Advanced level of the GED (or, in present terms, to NVQ 3 or the equivalent); and we wish to see fees for these courses met out of public funds for anyone under 35 whether or not they are employed. Those who are dependent upon unemployment or other State benefits must not be allowed to become worse off financially as a result of a decision to pursue further education or training.

FE colleges are leading the way in improving access for individuals who wish to pursue their education and, together with universities, adult education centres, community colleges and other organisations, often working in partnership, are providing a variety of routes to a wide range of courses and qualifications. We refer in Chapter 5 to the increasing flexibility with which courses can be provided, especially with the help of new technology. But it will not always be the educational establishments who are themselves the providers. They also have a role in securing, licensing and validating courses provided by others and should be encouraged to do so where this would be to the advantage of clients.

Learning in Communities

Expanding educational achievement and opportunity is a community issue. For many people, continuing education is the means by which they may find a sense of personal worth by contributing within the community, rather than taking. Many people come to adult education, for example, as a result of an issue affecting their personal circumstances which makes them feel the need to become more skilled or better informed.

Recent reforms in health and caring have improved understanding of the relationship between education and health and of the value of community-based initiatives such as women's health groups, parents against drug abuse and so on. There is a rich tradition of voluntary tutoring and peer learning which can be built on.

Education and training also play a supportive role for vulnerable individuals and groups. While colleges may provide a lead in the growth of community learning, they can be well supported by such voluntary initiatives and by business/education partnerships. Similarly, projects to promote social responsibility among young people have addressed the needs of communities as well as individuals, and have offered a wide range of curriculum activities while supporting, encouraging and restoring confidence. Such support is essential, especially where the effect of family and friends on attitudes, aspirations and levels of educational achievement is negative. We see such activity as important and worthy of development.

The diversity of need

Those providing education and training have to cater for a very diverse range of needs in the community. Colleges are becoming increasingly adaptable in the way they offer courses in order to improve access and encourage, for example, women returners, unemployed people or others who may lack confidence. 'Leisure' learning may be a very effective way of bringing people into a positive learning culture, and increasing the opportunities available to them for work and further training. This is particularly important in relation to equal opportunities for women and people from ethnic minorities. We applaud, for example, the many local initiatives which have attracted women who have poor spoken or written English because it is not their first language.

Education has to be relevant to people's lives. It must include understanding and skills in topics which are not always passed on from parents to children such as parenting and caring, or home management and maintenance. Individuals must be able to acquire skills such as communicating, negotiating, dealing with authority – all areas which we stress today's children should be taught but which previous generations may have missed out on. And community education plays a crucial role in enabling people to become involved in and appreciate many forms of artistic and visual expression.

People of all ages must be welcomed in. It is important for parents because of the strong association between their educational achievement and that of their children.

It is important for grandparents since the participation of older people in education is an example and an incentive to others. If they are excluded or discouraged, that is clearly a loss to them and to society – but it is also unlikely to encourage them to propagate the idea among young people that continuing to learn is both useful and enjoyable. When the involvement of whole families in learning within a community setting is common, we shall be well on the way to securing a nationwide learning culture.

The special relevance of these considerations is that so many of those over 50 have themselves had limited educational opportunities. Two-thirds of 'third agers' left school by 15 and 60% of those aged 50–69 have no qualifications, compared to only 18% of those in their twenties.[12]

Opportunities for adults to continue learning are best provided and managed locally, in a setting and with a purpose appropriate to the needs of the 'clients'. But this provision will best be encouraged if there is a national policy within which local initiative is encouraged. The best TECs provide a good example of how such arrangements can work.

Adult education

We note that enrolments in adult education are declining. To the extent that this truly reflects declining participation we regret it. The major cause is stringent control of local authority spending, coupled with some scepticism about the rationale for providing adult education for leisure purposes at public expense. There is indeed no particular reason why provision for those well able to pay for it should be subsidised, and we do not advocate that. On the other hand, many of those most likely to benefit cannot afford to pay the full cost.

Although local authorities have devised excellent schemes enabling pensioners and unemployed people to enrol on courses at less than the full cost, they then have to make up the gap in funding. Inventive as they have been at attracting sponsorship from charities or local employers and in conducting a wide range of fund-raising activities, this is not enough. They must have greater freedom to raise funds from the council tax and they are entitled to look to central government for encouragement and a measure of financial support.

Continuing education provides important opportunities for increasing skills and knowledge and providing personal fulfilment. It also promotes social exchange and mutual understanding at a time when social cohesion is weakening. In some recent initiatives for social and economic regeneration, the value of education and training in enabling disadvantaged communities to begin restoring a sense of local identity and of opportunity has been recognised. Greater recognition of the potential contribution which adult education in particular can make would be welcome.

Notes

1 Employment Department, 1992. Training Statistics 1992, pp.64–65.
2 Department for Education communication. Excludes enrolments at adult education centres; includes further education enrolments at colleges now funded by the Higher Education Funding Council.
3 DFE, 1993. Statistics of Further Education College Students in England 1970–71 – 1991–92. *Statistical Bulletin* 14/93.
4 DFE communication.
5 ED, 1992. Labour Market and Skill Trends 1993–94. Employment Department, Figure 1.4, p.5.
6 ED, 1992. Training Statistics 1992. HMSO, Table C1.1.
7 Atkinson, J. and Spilsbury, M., March 1993. Basic Skills and Jobs. A Report on the Basic Skills Needed at Work. Adult Literacy and Basic Skills Unit.
8 ED, 1992. Labour Market and Skill Trends 1993–94. Employment Department, para. 2.33.
9 *Ibid*, para. 2.37.
10 Metcalf, H., February 1992. Company Initiatives to Encourage Learning: Successful Practices in Employee Development. Vol 2: The Case Studies. Policy Studies Institute.

[11] Atkinson, J. and Spilsbury, M., March 1993, *op cit.*

[12] Schuller, T. and Bostyn, A. M., 1992. Learning: Education, Training and Information in the Third Age. Carnegie UK Trust, p. 87.

13
The Management of Education and Training

Introduction

The running of a national system of education and training is an extraordinarily demanding and complex task. The sheer scale of it is shown by Table 13.1. Moreover the nature of the task is continually changing as society itself evolves. It is not becoming easier. We shall require more and more from the providers of education and training in the years ahead, and the penalties for failure or incompetence will be greater. The system will need to be robust and also sensitive and above all able to encourage change and improvement while itself also being capable of initiating or absorbing change.

Table 13.1 Scale of education and training provision in the United Kingdom, 1990–91.

Number of students and pupils	- full-time and part-time	14.0m
Number of teachers	-full-time equivalents	700,000
Numbers of	- universities, polytechnics and colleges	750
	- secondary schools	4,800
	- primary schools	24,000
	- special schools	1,800
	- independent schools	2,500
Total public expenditure on	- education	£26.7 bn
	- training	£2.2 bn

Sources: See Note.[1]

It goes without saying that the system needs to be democratically accountable, but there are other accountabilities which need to be provided for. First, and most obviously, it must be accountable to students and trainees at every level, and to parents acting on behalf of children. Beyond that, however, it must enable others with a stake in the system to be involved in ways which recognise that stake, not to enable special interests to pursue selfish ends but to make it possible for those concerned to contribute the utmost of which they are capable to make the system perform well.

For example, a well-designed system will encourage professional teachers and trainers, and also educationalists, to contribute to the running of the system. We are struck by the extent to which the German and French education systems place responsibility on the shoulders of professional teachers. It contrasts sharply with the mood of distrust of the professionals which has grown in this country in recent years, not without Government encouragement. This mood has been carried too far and must be reversed.

This is not to say that a provider-dominated system will meet the nation's needs; quite the reverse. The system must be designed to enable those involved – pupils and students of all ages, parents, trainees and employees – to exercise informed choice and to press, as need may be, for quality to be raised. But a high-quality system depends also on fostering the professionalism and creativity of teachers and trainers.

A well-designed system will exert pressure on schools, colleges and other providers, but will also provide incentives and support. It must be *transparent* too, in the sense that it will be clear where responsibilities lie and possible to check whether the very large sums of public money going into it are being used efficiently and with good results.

Well-designed arrangements will also encourage co-operation between the various parts of the system where that is what students and trainees need. For example, there is an obvious need for the transition from primary to secondary school to work well for all pupils. At the same time individual schools and other institutions need the incentive and the degree of freedom to enable them to excel at what they do. A balance has to be struck at the right point.

There are further characteristics which a well-designed system should have. For example:

- it should embody the principle that decisions are best taken at the lowest practicable level;

- it should provide proper accountability, for example, by teacher to student, provider to local community, local to national level (and vice versa) throughout;

- it should recognise that the interests of users and customers are not necessarily best served by the exercise of choice in an education or training 'marketplace';

- it should promote reasonable consistency of standards throughout the country, though some local and regional variation is both necessary and welcome;

- it should seek the enhancement of quality at every point, and that requires both pressure and support from outside;

- it should accept that education and training are parts of a continuum, and have to be planned and managed as such.

In the rest of this chapter we concentrate mostly on how arrangements in England and Wales need to develop to meet the needs of the future. There will undoubtedly be ways in which advances in England and Wales can be applied to good effect in Northern Ireland also. Scotland is in various ways already further down the road than the rest of the United Kingdom; we refer to the position there in a concluding section.

Recent years

Arrangements in England and Wales have improved in a number of ways in recent years. Some important examples of improvements are:

- the introduction of the principle of a national curriculum as an entitlement for all children;

- the delegation of management to schools. According to HM Inspectorate, local management of schools (LMS) has achieved its objectives of giving schools control over their finances and, with it, greater flexibility. It is also proving to be 'a powerful lever for change and reconstruction in schools and LEAs alike' (including, for example, bringing greater openness on financial planning). (That is not to say that LMS has been well-managed in every case; hence the need for regular scrutiny and local accountability.);

- the requirement for educational institutions to be more open to public scrutiny and to publish information about their aims and achievements;

- greater involvement of parents and employers in school governing bodies;

- the development of a coherent framework of national vocational qualifications;

- the active involvement of employers in promoting training by means of the Training and Enterprise Councils;

- incentives for institutions providing post-compulsory education to respond flexibly to demand in their 'markets'.

Some changes have also taken place which are for the worse. Three in particular need mention:

- there has been a rapid growth of the power of central government which in important respects has undermined local accountability. It is true that some of the transfer of responsibility to the centre has been desirable, for example, in the case of those universities which until recently were polytechnics, and of the further education colleges. On the other hand the dwindling role for Local Education Authorities (LEAs) means that all sorts of decisions about schools which ought to be decided by people who are accountable locally will be taken by officials of bodies acting in the name of the Secretaries of State;

- schools are being developed in a way that encourages competition at the risk of undermining necessary and desirable co-operation. For example, there is a possibility that children with special educational needs may be marginalised;

- the framework within which schools work is becoming too punitive in conception; instead of offering schools help to overcome weakness, the accent is on punishing failure.

The future

In the rest of this chapter we show how a system for the future can be developed which meets the kind of requirements already described as well as overcoming present weaknesses.

Our starting point is provided by the essential need now to bring the Department for Education and those parts of the Employment Department which have responsibility for training into a single Department which we entitle here the Department for Education and Training. We explain our proposals in the next section of this chapter, and go on to discuss other changes which we think desirable, some of which follow as a consequence of the departmental merger and others of which are desirable in their own right to strengthen and improve arrangements.

We emphasise that we are not seeking a proliferation of extra bodies concerned with running our education and training system. That is not the way forward. On balance, what we propose will reduce the number of such bodies.

The Department for Education and Training

We propose that the Department for Education should merge with those parts of the Employment Department which are responsible for training to form a new Department for Education and Training (DET).

The rationale for the proposal is that vocational education has become part of the mainstream of educational provision in this country and that there are many drawbacks to divided responsibilities within that mainstream. As we say in Chapter 10, it is evident that an important reason for the extremely slow progress in providing 'a new deal' for 16–19-year-olds, the need for which was foreshadowed by Lord Callaghan in 1976, has been the division of responsibilities in England between two Secretaries of State and two Departments.

Increasingly, moreover, responsibility for provision for other young people and for adults has straddled the two Departments: the Employment Department is responsible for training programmes for unemployed young people and for adults, but much provision is made for the same clientele under educational programmes provided from educational budgets; in both cases colleges of further education are major providers. The result is an unnecessarily confused array of choice from the customer point of view, coupled with variations in the financial entitlements of trainees/students which have no justification in terms of their personal circumstances. From the point of view of the tax-payer, moreover, unacceptable differences in costs arise according to which programme is funding provision and what level of success the programme in question achieves.

There have often been attempts in the past to differentiate 'education' sharply from 'training'. In reality, there is no sharp division but rather a continuum, with some studies which can clearly be classed as education at one end - philosophy, say, or physics – and some at the other end which are clearly training, for example, instruction in the use of a particular machine or software package. There never was a clear dividing line in the middle, and doctrinal objections to the proposed merger on the grounds that the nature of the two activities is so different that responsibility for the two must be kept separate simply cannot be sustained. The important question is rather what is likely to lead to a well-managed system in practice, and on that there is now little room for doubt.

A distinction which does need to be maintained is between that training which must be the responsibility of employers and that which is funded by the State. It is clear that employers should be expected to fund that training (or education) which they wish their employees to undergo because it is for the benefit of the organisation. Employers have an obvious interest in ensuring that this investment of their resources is efficient and productive. We have no wish to see this general principle changed. Important questions do, nevertheless, arise at the margin, for example, where fear of poaching of people

trained in transferable skills may lead to insufficient training; market failure of that kind can be very damaging but
has to be dealt with pragmatically, and only as a last resort
with the intervention of the tax-payer. Other issues also
arise where the preparation of a young person for a working career is concerned; we make clear our approach to
traineeships for young people in Chapter 10.

Management responsibilities of the DET
As a result of the growth of the powers of central government in education, the DFE has acquired extensive management responsibilities formerly discharged elsewhere,
and these will be inherited by the DET.

Funding bodies have been set up for higher education
and for further education in England and Wales (as also in
Scotland and Northern Ireland). There is no evident need
for these arrangements to be disturbed. The power of the
centre is great in each case – the funding bodies are
appointed by and responsible to Ministers – but this is balanced by the funding bodies' membership, which recognises the interests of others, such as the institutions themselves and employers. Again, all of the universities, colleges and other institutions covered by these arrangements are relatively large and well-established bodies
with governing councils of their own which enable a
range of interests to be represented and brought to bear in
decision-making.

These new funding bodies are faced with challenging
tasks and rapid change, and must be given the opportunity to succeed. We emphasise, however, that success
should not by any means be taken for granted. Together
with the Government, they will possess very great
power. It will be right for the way that power is used to
be subject to constant and energetic scrutiny.

With schools, there is a different situation.

The Secretary of State and his Department now have a crucially important management role in relation to professional schoolteachers, of whom there are some 440,000 working full-time in maintained schools in England.

Schools are going through a sustained period of rapid change. Such change cannot, of course, be effected simply by management diktat and the issue of instructions, however much these can be said to be backed by statute and to represent the will of Parliament. Their implementation has to be planned and managed most carefully, with close regard to the amount of change which can be absorbed at any given time and to the provision of adequate training, in good time, to all concerned.

This is true no less of any other large enterprise, whether in the private or the public sector. All successful enterprises depend for their success on enlisting not merely the obedience or understanding of their workforces but their positive support and enthusiasm. In an undertaking whose workforce is as large and as highly qualified as that of education, the importance of this can hardly be exaggerated.

For this reason, we believe that it would be of great benefit to the Department if there were appointed what might be termed a Teachers' Management Board within the Department to assist the Secretary of State with this side of his responsibilities. We stress that this would primarily be concerned with *management* rather than *policy-making*. It would be composed of members with substantial experience in the education service together with members with senior executive and personnel management experience in industry. Branches in the Department which are concerned with various aspects of teacher employment would report to the Board.

The Board would be responsible, under the Secretary of State, for such matters as: plans to meet national teacher staffing requirements; national initiatives to stimulate teacher recruitment; the training provision required to implement national policies and arrangements for providing it; the dissemination of good personnel practice to Education and Training Boards (see below) and schools; and the design of the package of pay and conditions (including pensions) which teachers receive (though it would *not* replace or take over the responsibilities of the School Teachers' Review Body).

We take it for granted that the staffing of the Department will develop in a way which reflects its increased management responsibilities, together with the fact that HM Inspectorate is now no longer part of the Department. There must be substantial numbers of people at the centre who are familiar at first hand with working in schools and colleges because they are or have been teachers. There must also be some who have experience of inspection and of local administration in education or training, often on secondment to DET for a fixed period.

We consider that parallel changes will be needed in the Welsh Office.

Office for Standards in Education and Training (OFSET)
Inspection of schools has recently been made the responsibility of a separate department, the Office for Standards in Education (OFSTED). With the creation of the new DET, it will be desirable for the remit of OFSTED to be expanded to cover inspection of training provided under publicly-funded programmes, and its title should be amended to the Office for Standards in Education and Training (OFSET) to reflect that.

OFSET will thus become responsible for the regular inspection of publicly-funded education and training provision up to and including traineeships. As well as being responsible, as OFSTED is at present, for inspection of maintained and independent schools, its remit will extend to further education provision for trainees as well as other further education provision associated with the General Education Diploma (see Chapter 4). Its mode of operation in further education will be the subject of agreement with the funding councils responsible for further education.

Other bodies at national level

We make proposals for other bodies at national level at a number of points in our report. They are designed to fit in with the major developments here put forward. They include:

- the Education and Training Development Authority (ETDA). We propose in Chapter 4 that the School Curriculum and Assessment Authority and the National Council for Vocational Qualifications should merge to form the ETDA. This move is in any case desirable, but will be especially so with the establishment of the new DET;

- the Council for Innovation in Teaching and Learning. We propose in Chapter 5 that this body might be developed out of the National Council for Educational Technology. The new contribution which it will make will be to ensure that innovatory methods of teaching and learning, once proven, are widely applied with the minimum of delay;

- a General Teaching Council for England and Wales. Our proposals for establishing this are to be found in Chapter 8;

- an Educational Achievement Unit for the United Kingdom – see Chapter 4. A convenient home for this unit, which will require its own expert and independent board, may be found with OFSET as long as that remains a separate department.

Education and Training Boards

Under the legislation currently in Parliament, funding bodies for schools are to be set up for both England and Wales. These bodies will take over responsibility from DFE for funding grant-maintained schools in their respective countries. Each body will share with any given LEA the duty to secure sufficient secondary or primary school places in the area, from the point where 10% of those pupils are in grant-maintained schools. The funding body will assume this duty on its own when 75% of secondary (or primary) pupils in the LEA are in grant-maintained schools, though the LEA can apply to be relieved of this responsibility at an earlier point.

We find this proposed erosion of local accountability both unnecessary and in principle undesirable.

The reason that it is unnecessary is that the benefits of greater autonomy made possible by grant-maintained status are in principle available also under LMS. We want all schools to enjoy those benefits, but we also want to ensure that autonomy does not lead to putting the interests of the school ahead of those of pupils who would benefit by attending them, but whom the school would rather not admit lest its image or published results be adversely affected.

The reason that it is undesirable is that accountability for many decisions about local schools will be taken away from the locality and vested in a remote funding body which is accountable to the Secretary of State. The principle of 'subsidiarity' has often been invoked in recent times to mean that decisions which can perfectly well be taken by individual member states in the European Community should not be removed to Brussels. The same principle applies within the United Kingdom. What is best settled locally by democratically accountable bodies should be left there.

In our view, therefore, there is no place for the funding bodies for schools which will shortly be operating in England and Wales, and we would wish to see them removed.

We think it essential that there should continue to be an intermediate tier of locally accountable bodies between the DET and individual schools. There is no other OECD country where such a layer does not exist. We term the bodies we have in mind Education and Training Boards.

The ETBs will differ in important ways from LEAs. In particular:

1 Their constitution will differ. There will be a majority of members on each Board drawn on a politically representative basis from among elected local councillors, but they will also have strong representation drawn from other interests which have a stake in the work of the Board. We foresee, for example, that representation of churches will be important, and that Training and Enterprise Councils will nominate a number of employers to seats on the Board.

   The total membership of Boards must be kept within strict bounds to enable them to function effectively, and this means that room cannot be found for every local interest which would wish to be represented. Legislation should give guidance as to which interests should have preference in allocating seats; and there should be provision for a certain number of observers who may speak when invited but do not have a vote.

2 ETBs will be responsible, among other things, for strategic planning and for quality assurance. In discharging their responsibilities, they will be required to comply with duties and objectives laid down by the Secretary of State, for example, in relation to nursery education, special educational needs and innovation.

   The Secretary of State will be expected to monitor

the performance of ETBs and to warn one if it is failing in its duties or falling below an acceptable standard. As a last resort he should have power to replace one or more members of an ETB by nominees of his own or even, if circumstances warrant it, to replace the whole membership of an ETB for a limited period by nominees of his own.

3 The mode of operation of ETBs will differ, in that they will be formally required to operate on an arm's-length or 'purchaser-provider' basis in relation to the providers of education and training, whether they are schools, further education colleges, private training companies or any other kind of provider. It will be desirable to develop the arrangements progressively on the basis of carefully monitored pilots in different kinds of situation, for example, in a rural area, an inner city area and a commuter area.

The ETBs will, at any rate for the time being, be based on the current LEA areas and elected councillors will serve as their elected members. This is desirable for at least two important reasons. First, it should in principle be possible for local councils to decide to increase (or decrease) the amount of council tax they raise for educational purposes. Total reliance on national funding effectively removes that possibility. Secondly – an important advantage – it facilitates co-operation with other locally-provided public services, and in particular those provided by social services departments.

The size of the areas covered by ETBs may change in time. It will not be helpful if local authority areas are broken down into units too small to be economical and efficient for the purpose of planning and running education services. More helpfully, in the longer term it may be that a new tier of government at regional or sub-regional level will develop in response to developments in the European

Community, and that could eventually prove a suitable basis for ETBs. ETBs will clearly be able to make a major contribution to regional development plans.

Relationship between ETBs and schools

We have been struck by the enthusiasm which acquiring grant-maintained status has given some schools. We have also been impressed by the excellence of some maintained schools which enjoy the opportunities provided by LMS but prefer to remain within the LEA network. There is no evidence that a high level of performance is confined to one type of school or the other. Under the arrangements we propose, all schools will enjoy benefits similar to those available to grant-maintained schools but will be in a framework which promotes local co-operation where that is desirable and makes support available when it is needed.

Accordingly, the distinction between grant-maintained and other maintained schools should be removed: all would be given the same status.

It will make good sense also for City Technology Colleges to be brought within the aegis of ETBs. These schools have some notable achievements to their credit, and they should not be put at risk. Their current funding comes entirely from tax-payers, however, and they should take their place in the family of maintained schools in their areas.

A strong motivation towards the good performance of a school comes from the professionalism of teachers themselves, and especially from the lead given by its head-teacher and the management team, coupled with the direction imparted by its governing body. Beyond this, however, all schools need both pressure and support from outside. Some of the pressures will come not only from parents but from the desire of schools to be well regarded by the community and from better focused external scrutiny of their achievements and shortcomings. When a school has a weakness, it is highly desirable that it should receive support that enables it not only to identify but to remedy that weakness.

Key to this are good arrangements for inspection. We are encouraged to note that OFSTED sees its work as part of a broader framework 'explicitly linked to school improvement through action plans and schools' own development planning'.[2] We do not, however, think that a four-yearly cycle of national inspection is enough. We suggest arrangements on the following lines, which would resemble those now being developed in further education. Each ETB will employ its own inspectors who will be required to train to OFSET's standards and to be registered by OFSET. A named inspector will be allocated by the ETB to every school and will pay regular visits to it. Periodically, different aspects of a school's work will be inspected by an inspector (or inspectors) qualified in relation to those aspects. Every four years a fuller inspection by OFSET will take place. The whole cycle of inspections will be agreed between ETBs and OFSET.

We believe that this arrangement will work very effectively without any increase in the total cost of inspection. This can be done by reducing the weight and cost of the 4-yearly inspections now being introduced; that will be made possible by the increased inspection being carried out by ETB inspectors. It may also be possible to reduce the amount of inspection by introducing an accreditation scheme which gives, as it were, a 'kite mark' to the work of a school, or parts of it, on the basis of inspection for a stated period, provided that data relating to its performance continue to be satisfactory.

Finally, we stress that it will be important to enable schools, whether on their own initiative or on the recommendation of an inspector, to purchase independent advice to help them to overcome difficulties or improve aspects of their work that require it.

Governing bodies of schools

The governing bodies of schools have considerable powers. They are responsible for the appointment of headteachers (a matter we discuss in Chapter 8). They help establish, with the head, the aims and policies of schools. They are also responsible with the head for deciding how to spend a school's budget; in this they are accountable both in narrow financial terms and also in terms of getting best value out of the money spent. Their accountability is to the school and the community and also to the LEA or, in the case of grant-maintained schools, to the Secretary of State.

There are well over 300,000 school governors in England and Wales. We have no doubt that governing bodies vary very greatly in effectiveness.

A number of factors influence this. The powers of governors were much increased in 1986 and 1988, and adjustment to this both by governors and by heads takes time. Many people who might make excellent governors are deterred from serving by the difficulty of giving enough time to the task. Employers are obliged by law to give school governors 'reasonable time off' to carry out their duties but are not obliged to pay them. Governors need training in their duties, but the task of ensuring that every governor has sufficient training is immense; the problem is made more difficult still by turnover among governors, which can be high, especially among parent governors. It is not necessarily at all easy for governors to keep in touch with current feelings, whether among parents (where a link with the Parent Teacher Association can help) or in other 'constituencies'.

No precise definition of where the role of the governing

body ends and that of the head begins is laid down in legislation. It is clear enough, however, that the governing body has a general responsibility for the oversight of the school, but that operational decisions about running the school are for the headteacher and his or her colleagues. The relationship must be a flexible one to be worked out by those involved and we do not suggest that further clarification in the law is needed or would help.

Though we point out problems confronting governing bodies, we do not wish in any way to suggest that they should not exist or should not be encouraged and helped to carry out their responsibilities to the full. It is, however, clearly unrealistic to assume that every school will have a governing body which can be relied on to perform to the standards which would be expected, say, of the governing council of a university or the board of a large public company. We consider that the ETB will be a very desirable source of support to governing bodies in developing their ability to discharge their important role to a good standard.

The funding of ETBs and schools

The funding of LEAs and maintained schools has been put on a completely new basis in recent years. Formerly, local authorities used to decide what educational services they wished to provide. Rates were fixed in the light of that and automatically attracted extra finance from central government. From the point of view of accountability, this arrangement had the severe shortcoming that the proportion of spending covered by the central contribution, over which central government had little or no control, was far larger than the proportion provided out of local rates.

Under current arrangements, through a process called the Standard Spending Assessment, the share of the available central funding thought to be needed to meet the current spending requirements of each LEA is estimated by central government on the basis of various statistical indicators; 85% of that amount is included in the Rate Support Grant which goes to each local authority, the assumption being that the remaining 15% will be raised locally through the council tax.

This arrangement too has many shortcomings. There is no assurance that the total sum made available by central government for sharing is adequate. The statistical indicators used by central government for sharing out the funds are those that happen to be available and cannot accurately represent the full reality of local circumstances. There is also a historical element in them which itself introduces chance inequities and becomes increasingly removed from reality as time goes on. It is plain that something better is needed.

The design of better arrangements is a highly technical business and is not a task we can properly attempt. It should be given high priority by the Government. We are convinced that a satisfactory system for the future must have two features:

1 The amount of money from central government going to individual ETBs has to be based on the reconciliation of calculations which are both 'top-down', i.e., based on dividing up an amount which central government is prepared to allocate for educational purposes, and 'bottom-up', i.e., based on as objective and accurate an assessment as possible of the amount an ETB needs to enable education of a given quality to be provided in its area.

2 There needs to be real freedom in practice at local level to vary upwards or downwards the contribution made towards education from council tax. Moreover it would be highly desirable if, within pre-set limits, ETBs which contribute extra council tax towards the

cost of education receive a proportionately larger contribution from central government and vice versa.

ETBs and Training and Enterprise Councils

The long-term role of Training and Enterprise Councils (TECs) will need to be carefully considered in the new situation resulting from the creation of the DET and the Education and Training Boards.

TECs have two rather different sets of responsibilities. They are, in the first place, responsible for promoting better training by employers and for encouraging enterprise in their areas. Secondly, they have responsibility for running Employment Department programmes for unemployed people – both young people and adults – and the major part of their funding is for that purpose.

TECs have been set up relatively recently and not surprisingly their effectiveness varies. The best TECs, however, are judged to be having a significant impact on the amount and quality of training provided by local employers and especially by medium-sized and smaller employers. They also provide valuable help to entrepreneurs in setting up and developing new enterprises.

The establishment of TECs represented a new departure, in that the majority of each TEC's directors are themselves men and women engaged in business. This policy means that TECs are naturally oriented towards the needs of employers and are led by people who can be expected to have both the understanding and the drive necessary to ensure that the needs of employers are met. They have a key part to play in ensuring that the national targets for lifetime learning are met. In doing this they will be assisted by their role in persuading employers to apply the principles embodied in the Investors In People award (see Chapter 12).

TECs are known to be less enthusiastic about administering training programmes for unemployed people, since provision for unemployed people is seen as being a government responsibility and one which employers are not uniquely suited to carrying out. A major part of the funding for these programmes in any case goes towards providing allowances for trainees and much of the remainder is due to be absorbed into training credits for young people.

For the future, it is clear that the ETBs should take over responsibility for programmes for providing education and training for unemployed people, buying from TECs under contract any services which the latter are best placed to provide.

TECs will then concentrate on the tasks for which they are uniquely fitted, being funded to do so directly by the Government.

Community Education and Training Advice Centres
There is a consensus that high-quality advice about education, training and careers is needed by young people. As opportunities for education and training are greatly extended and the range of choice expands, this need will grow and will be felt much more widely among adults also. We propose that the need be met by the establishment of Community Education and Training Advice Centres (CETACs) serving both young people and adults. They will receive their funding from ETBs and be accountable to them for their performance.

There has always been a tendency to underfund careers work, but in addition too much advice is at present being given to young people by advisers whose point of view is coloured by that of the organisation that employs them. CETACs will operate as it were as 'citizens' advice bureaux' for education and training and they will be bound by their terms of reference to offer independent and impartial advice to those seeking their help. They will be developed out of the existing careers service. Their governing bodies will be composed of people with a range of backgrounds in education, business and community affairs which ensures that no one interest will predominate.

CETACs will operate at arm's length from ETBs. Their role will include:

- offering independent advice to individuals (or their parents) about educational and career opportunities;

- providing information and advice to parents and/or young people to assist them in making choices about which school or college young people might apply to attend;

- providing advice in connection with appeals to ETBs over such matters as school admissions or special needs assessments;

- advising young people or adults about the use of their entitlements to further learning and the grants or awards for which they may be eligible.

Scotland

The principles which underpin our recommendations for the management of education and training apply in all parts of the United Kingdom, but the form in which they will be implemented in Scotland will differ in some ways from the concrete proposals we make for England and Wales.

Overall, the task in Scotland could well prove to be more straightforward. Education and training are already the responsibility of a single Secretary of State. The present intermediate authorities, the education authorities, command widespread support. There are no grammar schools, and no equivalents of City Technology Colleges or grant-maintained schools. State schools do not have governors, but do have elected boards composed of teachers and parents. There are schemes for the devolution of resource management to schools but, in this and in other respects, neither school boards nor the public at large has wished to exercise the option offered by the Government of a major transfer of powers from the local authority to the individual school. The vast majority of school boards work in harmony with the headteacher.

Such considerations lead us to believe that it would be relatively easy to transfer training functions to the new intermediate authority that would replace the education authority in Scotland, and that the spirit of co-operation that we wish to promote in England and Wales among local schools, the teaching profession and other agencies would flourish in Scotland under the new arrangements.

At the same time, there are institutional and other factors which would affect the structure of reform in Scotland, and which must be the subject of further consideration in Scotland. Four such factors may be mentioned.

First, there is the impending reform of local government which could replace the present, mainly two-tier, structure headed by the twelve mainland and island authorities with a larger number of single-tier authorities. The uneven dispersal of population in Scotland has always required that any arrangement for local government pay attention to the balance between the size of an authority and its accessibility to those who elect it and use its services. It is clear that many of the areas envisaged as new local authorities in Scotland would be far too small to support the functions we intend for the Education and Training Boards in England and Wales. Conversely, to construct the equivalent to ETBs around larger areas, whether created from new local authority areas adjacent to each other or in some other way, could compromise other features we think important at the intermediate level of government, especially democratic accountability and the local determination of the level of locally raised expenditure.

Secondly, HM Inspectorate of Schools (HMI) in Scotland, though nominally independent, remains a key component of the Scottish Office Education Department (SOED), and is fully integrated into its work. HMI brings to the SOED a close working knowledge of teachers and schools of a kind that the Teachers' Management Board would supply to the new Department of Education and Training for England and Wales. There might, however, be a need in Scotland, no less than elsewhere, for senior executives from business, industry and the public services to contribute their expertise in human resource management alongside that of HMI.

As to the advisory function of HMI in Scotland and also its responsibility for the monitoring of standards, the scope of these functions would be adjusted in order that they broadly matched those of OFSET in respect of schooling, further education and training. A more fundamental question, however, is whether HMI can maintain public confidence in its monitoring of quality without a greater degree of visible independence of the sort that OFSTED represents in England and Wales. We are not well placed to answer this question. We can observe, however, that the arguments which led the Government to create in OFSTED an independent body for the monitoring of standards were apparently thought not to apply to HMI in Scotland. And we can record that public confidence in the integrity of quality control is so vital to the success of our proposals throughout the United Kingdom that the validity of the arguments which the Government thought cogent in Scotland, but not in England, should be kept under review.

This does not signal any criticism of HMI in Scotland or in England, or any wish to extend the work of our proposed OFSET to Scotland. Rather, it is to insist that there be measures and judgements of quality that are publicly transparent, valid and comparable across the United Kingdom. It is for this reason that we also propose the establishment of an Educational Achievement Unit (EAU). In Scotland, part of the work that we envisage for this unit is already carried out by the Assessment of Achievement Programme (AAP), a sample-survey approach to the monitoring of standards in schools steered by HMI along the lines of the former Assessment of Performance Unit in England and Wales. Provided that the functions and principles we attach to the EAU are met by Scottish arrangements such as the AAP, we would see no reason to disturb matters. In similar vein, careful thought would need to be given to Scotland's place in the proposed Council for Innovation in Teaching and Learning, especially in respect of issues that were close to the practice of schools in Scotland, such as the training and professional development of headteachers.

The third factor, then, that would affect the form in which our proposals are implemented in Scotland is those features of Scottish provision which are already close to the changes we are seeking. On the institutional front, the AAP is one example. A more striking one is the General Teaching Council for Scotland, established in 1966. But we also recognise that in matters such as the curriculum, and in the nature of the awards of the Scottish Examination Board (SEB) and of the Scottish Vocational Education Council (SCOTVEC), there is the potential for Scotland to take a different route towards the creation of a flexible, modular, comprehensive system of progression of a type which the General Education Diploma is intended to achieve in England and Wales.

Fourthly, there are other features of Scottish provision that are also distinctive. There would, for example, be a need to consider the role in education and training of the Local Enterprise Companies and of the bodies to whom they are responsible: Scottish Enterprise and Highlands and Islands Enterprise. We would also ask whether the role that we envisage for the Education and Training Development Authority in England and Wales could be adequately fulfilled in Scotland by the separate institutions of SEB, SCOTVEC and the Scottish Consultative Council on the Curriculum, or whether there should be some reformulation of their relationships with each other.

Finally, lest there be any doubt over our views on the implications of our proposals for the government and administration of education and training, both in Scotland and in Northern Ireland, we repeat our earlier assertion of the importance of the principle of subsidiarity within the United Kingdom: what is best settled locally by democratically accountable bodies should be left there.

Northern Ireland

Since 1972, Northern Ireland has had five Education and Library Boards (ELBs) with nominated members, replacing the democratically elected LEAs that existed before, and receiving all of their income from central government. It is generally agreed that the education system in Northern Ireland is over-administered and that the number of ELBs should be reduced. We would hope that eventually the model we have recommended in this chapter could be applied to Northern Ireland. We recognise, however, that this might be achievable only in the context of a broader political settlement.

Conclusion

Decisions about institutions must always be defined by the task in hand and the circumstances prevailing at the time. We are clear that existing arrangements must now be developed in important ways with the needs of the future in mind, and we propose how this should be done in this chapter. The changes we suggest will not on balance entail any extra cost.

We would not expect any particular institutional structures to stand still for long, but there does need to be an underlying stability and consistency of approach if systems are to be continuously and fully productive. We believe that it will be possible to build on our proposals as time goes on without sudden and disruptive changes of direction.

Notes

1   Sources:
   (i)   Government Statistical Service, 1993. Education Statistics for the United Kingdom, 1992 Edition. HMSO.
   (ii) Public Expenditure Analyses. HMSO.
2   Millett, A., 1993. In: *Times Educational Supplement*, 25 June, p.12.

14
Paying for it

Introduction

Our vision for education and training in the UK is ambitious but it is the minimum necessary for any reasonable set of economic and social goals that the nation should set itself. We have seen that, whilst particular examples of excellence can be observed in the current system, an aspiration for overall quality as high as any in the world will require some radical changes of approach.

Before discussing how we can pay for education and training in the future, and in particular how we can implement these changes, we need to have a clear picture of the current situation. How much do we spend? How is this spending spread across different phases of the system and different parts of the country? How much comes from the public purse and how much from individuals and companies? Are these amounts changing over time? How do we fare in comparison with our competitors?

Once we have answered these questions, we will be in a better position to look ahead and outline a pattern of resources that follows the principles of our vision: in the level of spending, how it is spread across the system and who is required to pay. This chapter undertakes this task and projects how the level of resources available in the future might be affected by the benefits of economic growth, the future costs of running the system, the scope for savings through efficiency and our proposals for alternative methods of funding.

The main question is how much our proposals will cost and who will pay for them. Many of our proposals will not cost any more than a change of attitude. These include enabling every individual to learn to succeed; a commitment to creativity, innovation and partnership; an accountable system of management; and development of a broader and more flexible post-14 curriculum. Some of our proposals do, however, require extra resources. These include raising the quality of teaching in the classroom; greater attention to the early years, with nursery education for all and smaller classes in primary schools; and a learning entitlement for life. We put a price on this overall package of proposals and end the chapter by showing how it could be paid for by our proposed pattern of resourcing.

Spending on Education and Training: Recent Patterns

Trends in overall public expenditure on education in the UK
For some time, observers of the education world have been confused by the discrepancy between apparently rising real expenditure and a perception 'at the chalk face' that severe financial cuts have been imposed. Table 14.1 shows that in cash terms, public expenditure on all levels of education for the UK has risen from £1.6 billion in 1965–66 to £26.7 billion in 1990–91. The effects of general inflation can be removed from this rise using the GDP Deflator, an index reflecting prices in the economy as a whole. The table shows changes in expenditure adjusted in this way. This still leaves a rise of 84.4% over the 25-year period, that is an average annual increase of 3.4%, an amount which might seem substantial. The bottom line of

the table shows that the young population has fallen over the period, suggesting an even greater amount of spending per person. But this ignores the rapid increases in participation rates that have taken place in the system. While there have been fewer young people overall, a much larger proportion of them remain in the system longer. Later in this chapter we look at the question of how much is actually being spent on each pupil or student.

Table 14.1 Public expenditure on education, 1965–66 to 1990–91, United Kingdom.

	1965–6	1970–1	1975–6	1980–1	1985–6	1990–1
Cash terms (£ billion)	1.6	2.7	7.0	12.9	17.3	26.7
Real terms (1990–1 prices using GDP Deflator)	14.5	18.8	25.3	23.7	23.2	26.7
Average year-on-year change over 5 years (%)	-	6.0	7.0	-1.3	-0.4	3.0
As % of GDP	4.6	5.2	6.4	5.5	4.8	4.8
As % of public expenditure	12.1	12.7	13.0	11.9	10.7	12.0
Population aged 0–24 (000's)	20,818	21,613	21,022	20,621	20,062	19,262

Sources: See Note.[1]

Table 14.1 also shows education expenditure as a proportion of total national income and as a proportion of total public expenditure. This gives us the first explanation for the confusion described earlier. While the country has been getting wealthier over the period (real gross domestic product rising by 75%) and government has been spending more (real public expenditure rising by 43%), education's share of this growth has not risen. Indeed, it is a source of concern to the Commission that it has fallen since the mid-1970s. Government analyses, however, indicate that there has been a rise in public expenditure on education in the last two years and as a proportion of GDP it may be returning to the level of the early 1980s.[2] We welcome this recent trend, but note that this measure tends to rise during recessions due to a combination of falling GDP and education expenditure being boosted by rising post-16 participation rates.

There is, however, a further explanation for the perception of cuts in education spending in the UK. Salaries form a large component of education expenditure: they account for over 70% of current expenditure[3] and rise faster than the general level of prices. Using the GDP Deflator to calculate real changes in education expenditure ignores the fact that costs in the education world have risen and continue to rise faster than prices in the economy as a whole. This is clearly shown in Figure 14.1 (although capital costs are an exception).[4]

Figure 14.1 Costs in education and the overall economy, 1980–81 to 1990–91, United Kingdom.

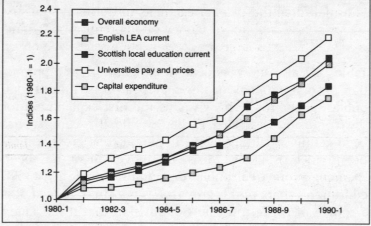

Sources: See Note.[5]

Adjustments using the GDP Deflator do not, therefore, allow us to examine what the money will buy in terms of goods and services, in other words, to view expenditure in *volume* terms. We have analysed education spending by deflating the figures for the costs of the different components of education spending.[6] In these terms, spending on education rose by only 0.4% between 1980–81 and 1990–91 (as compared to 12.6% when the GDP Deflator is used). In other words, resources were only made available for a tiny increase in the number of teachers, books, buildings and suchlike during this period.[7]

How does public expenditure on education in the UK compare with our competitors? Unfortunately, very up-to-date figures are not available. The most recent are shown in Table 14.2. They need to be viewed with caution, since a given percentage for a rich country or one with relatively few young people means more abundant funding than in a poor country or one with a larger proportion of young people. Even allowing for these qualifications, the UK fares worse than the table suggests, since many of the countries also have much more substantial *private* expenditure on education than the UK. For example, in Germany industry spends a large amount of money on apprenticeships,[8] and in Japan there is a large private education sector, mainly at higher, upper secondary and pre-school levels.[9]

Table 14.2 Public expenditure on education, 1988, international comparisons.

	Japan	Germany	UK	US	France	Sweden	Netherlands
% of GDP	3.8	4.3	4.7	5.0	5.1	5.7	6.3
% of total public expenditure	11.7	9.1	11.4	13.7	10.2	9.6	10.9

Source: Centre for Educational Research and Innovation, 1992.[3]

Capital expenditure

The figures above relate to overall (both current and capital) expenditure on education. Table 14.3 shows capital expenditure alone in cash and real terms over the last twenty-five years.[10] The last figure in the table is almost wholly explained by a real rise in capital expenditure in 1989–90 of 36.2%.[11]

Table 14.3 Capital expenditure on education, 1965–66 to 1990–91, United Kingdom.

	1965–6	1970–71	1975–6	1980–81	1985–6	1990–91
Cash terms (£m)	273	406	728	763	737	1,359
Real terms (1990-1 prices)	2,412	2,781	2,637	1,399	994	1,359
Average annual change over 5 year period (%)	-	3.1	-1.0	-9.4	-5.8	7.3

Source: Government Statistical Service.[12]

Expenditure by phase

Unit costs show how much is spent on each pupil or student. A rise in unit costs, far from showing a loss of efficiency, as might be the case in the commercial world, can be seen to indicate a rise in quality of provision due to the smaller classes and improvement in resources that it allows. Table 14.4 shows unit costs in volume terms (i.e. adjusted by our education price deflators) in the different phases of education over a recent three year period.[13] Unit costs for primary pupils remain well below those of secondary pupils.[14] Unit costs for HE students fell in 1989–90 and 1990–91, dropping by nearly 10% between 1985–6 and 1990–91.[15]

Table 14.4 Unit costs in volume terms, 1988–89 to 1990-91, United Kingdom.

	1988–89	1989–90		1990–91	
	Unit cost (£, 1990–91 prices)	Unit cost (£, 1990–91 prices)	% change from previous year	Unit cost (£, 1990–91 prices)	% change from previous year
Pre-primary	1,591	1,636	2.9	1,639	0.2
Primary	1,479	1,527	3.2	1,531	0.3
Secondary	2,430	2,479	2.0	2,420	-2.4
Special	10,733	11,500	7.1	12,223	6.3
FE	2,650	2,681	1.2	2,626	-2.1
HE	6,644	6,449	-2.9	6,339	-1.7

Source: Department for Education communication.

Figure 14.2 shows unit costs for primary and secondary schools in England, both in the maintained and independent sectors.[16] The gap between the primary and secondary phases in the maintained sector is apparent throughout the period, widening particularly in the middle of the decade. In both phases, the gap between the maintained and independent sectors widened dramatically over the same period. By 1990–91, unit costs in independent secondary schools (£3,206) were 66% higher than in maintained secondary schools (£1,926). Unit costs in independent primary schools (£2,317) were 84% higher than in maintained primary schools (£1,262), and even 20% higher than in maintained secondary schools.

Figure 14.2 Unit costs in volume terms, 1983–84 to 1990–91, England.

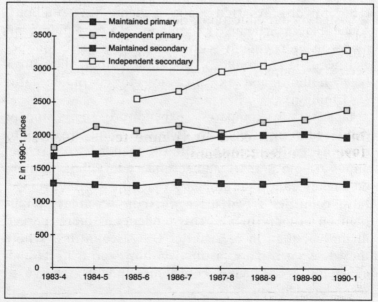

Sources: See Note.[17]

Why has this gap been increasing? The main explanation is the fact that, unlike maintained schools, independent schools have been able to cope with rising costs by increasing their fees well above the rate of inflation. For example, school fees in schools covered by the Independent Schools Information Service (educating 80% of independent school pupils) increased in 1991–2 by 12.0%, having gone up in the previous year by 12.6%.[18] Average termly fees in January 1992 were thus £1,258 for day pupils and £2,875 for boarders, varying from £350 to £3,850.[19] Money for independent schools does not come only from private individuals, but also from public expenditure and this has also been increasing. It is difficult to estimate the total cost to the tax-payer of subsidies to independent schools but six important categories (figures given are for England in 1990–91) are City Technology Colleges (£56 million), Assisted Places Scheme (£76 million), Aided Places Scheme (£7 million), LEA spending on places in independent schools including those for special needs (£174 million), Boarding School Allowances (£115 million), and tax concessions for charitable status (£41 million).[20]

Table 14.5 compares expenditure per student expressed in equivalent US dollars in some OECD countries.[21] It can be seen that the UK spends less on school pupils at both primary and secondary level but far more on higher education students than the OECD average. Most countries spend more on their secondary pupils than on primary pupils. This tendency is more marked in the UK than in most other OECD countries. Where the UK is even more distinctive, however, is in its high expenditure on higher education students relative to secondary school pupils.

Table 14.5 Unit costs, 1988, international comparisons.

$ using purchasing power parities

	France	Germany	UK	Japan	US	Nether-lands	Sweden	OECD Average
Primary	1,885	2,101	2,105	2,550	3,566	1,913	4,423	2,711
Secondary	3,073	2,659	2,763	2,325	4,370	2,263	5,146	3,150
Tertiary (higher)	3,780	5,085	7,960	2,504	4,301	9,542	6,334	5,534

Source: Centre for Educational Research and Innovation, 1992.[3]

Variations within the UK

Levels of education expenditure vary greatly within the UK. There are substantial differences between the four countries of the UK. Table 14.6 shows expenditure per young person. Grants to universities (but not to students) are excluded from these figures because Scotland's universities educate so many students from the rest of the UK.[22] In these terms, expenditure per young person in Scotland was 21% higher than in England and Wales and expenditure per young person in Northern Ireland was 4% higher. Some of these differences are accounted for by higher participation rates in Scotland and Northern Ireland and also by the fact that more Scottish students take four-year degrees than their counterparts elsewhere in the UK.

Table 14.6 Public expenditure on education per young person (aged 4–20) in the population, 1990–91, countries of the UK.

£

	England	Wales	Scotland	N. Ireland
Expenditure per young person	1,876	1,882	2,278	1,953

Sources: Department for Education communication; *Population Trends*, HMSO.

There are also wide variations *within* England, although it should be noted that these partly reflect variations in the cost of living. Figure 14.3 shows unit costs for primary and secondary school pupils by English region.

Figure 14.3 Unit costs, 1990–91, English regions.

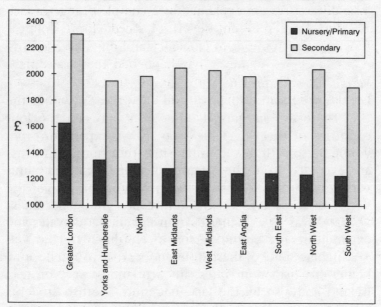

Source: Department for Education communication.

In both cases, Greater London was the highest spender and the South-West the lowest, with a 28% difference for nursery and primary schools and a 21% difference for secondary schools. Some of this variation might be accounted for by differences in costs. The order of the regions was different for the two phases, with Yorkshire and Humberside and the North spending relatively generously on primary schools but not on secondary schools, and the North-West spending relatively generously on secondary schools but at the lower end on primary. The differentials between regions, although still significant, have narrowed since the mid-1980s.

Even wider than regional discrepancies are differences between local authorities. In 1990–91, Westminster spent 113% more on its nursery and primary pupils than Kent and 91% more on its secondary pupils than Bradford. The large differences are explained by a complex range of factors including different levels of need, local political imperatives, variations in efficiency and different patterns of provision.[23] Whatever has happened to these differences over time,[24] it remains the case that authorities set different priorities for phases, and that primary and secondary unit costs differ greatly.

Specific expenditure

A further reason for the perception of decreasing funding for schools lies in recent trends in expenditure on specific visible items, in particular books and buildings.[25] In England in 1990–91, spending per pupil on books and equipment was £57 and on repairs and maintenance was £79. The price of books has risen more rapidly than general inflation; indeed school books cost nearly three and a half times more in 1990–91 than in 1979–80. Taking this into account, expenditure per pupil on books fell by around 17% over this period. Spending on repairs and maintenance has also been constrained. Expenditure per pupil fluctuated but was no higher in volume terms in 1990-91 than in 1980–81, despite the fact that reductions in capital expenditure in the 1980s increased the need for expenditure on repairs and maintenance. The trends in spending on both books and school buildings have had an adverse effect on the quality of learning, much to be regretted.

Private expenditure

Tightly defined figures for private expenditure on education are not available. We estimate private expenditure in the UK as £2.7 billion in 1991, around £50 per person and around 0.45% of GDP. This expenditure is spread across the different phases of the education system and includes expenditure on private institutions. However, in recent years, the assumption that statutory education provision in the maintained sector should be provided by government funds has been challenged. HMI reports have shown clearly that maintained schools, particularly primary schools, are under-funded and that repairs and maintenance, books and other essential teaching and learning materials have particularly suffered.[26] One of the most important consequences is that maintained schools are increasingly relying on financial and other contributions and donations from parents, charities, business and industry. There have been numerous reports of schools running fund-raising activities to prevent teacher redundancies or asking charities such as Children in Need and Telethon for money to cover basic educational requirements.

It was estimated in 1991 that each year parents and trusts contribute between £80 million and £100 million towards the support of the maintained system, with a further £50 million to £130 million coming from industry and commerce.[27] Many schools use this money for essentials such as teachers' salaries, buildings and equipment and there is evidence of an inequitable distribution of these funds in favour of schools in richer areas. It is possible that this trend is reducing the psychological distinction for parents between paying for education in independent schools on the one hand and in maintained schools on the other.

Expenditure on training
Table 14.7 shows recent trends in public expenditure on training in the UK (central government programmes such as Employment Training and Youth Training).[28] Between

1987–8 and 1992–3 expenditure rose by 4% in real terms. During a period in which the unemployment rate almost doubled (1989–90 and 1992–3) expenditure actually fell by 28%.

Table 14.7 Public expenditure on training, 1987–88 to 1992–93, United Kingdom.

	1987–8	1988–9	1989–90	1990–91	1991–2	1992–3
Cash terms (£m)	1,390	1,829	2,296	2,179	2,099	1,996
Real terms (1992–3 prices) (£m)	1,913	2,346	2,765	2,431	2,189	1,996
% change from previous year	-	23	18	-12	-10	-9
Unemployment rate (%)	9.5	7.6	5.8	6.0	8.8	10.2

Sources: See Note.[29]

Figures for total expenditure on training, including private expenditure, are hard to come by. A one-off survey showed that the country was devoting £33 billion to training in 1986–7.[30] Of this, £18 billion was contributed by employers (£11 billion by the private sector) and the rest shared by individuals (£8 billion, mostly in wages forgone) and Government (£7 billion).

International comparisons of public expenditure on training are not available, but a 1984 survey of average expenditure on training as a proportion of labour costs in five EC countries showed the UK ahead of Italy but behind Denmark, Germany and France.[31]

The Future Pattern of Resources

The level of spending
The figures in the previous section confirm the message that has emerged from earlier chapters: that as a nation we need to spend more on education and training. We believe that in order to move towards our vision, extra resources will be required from both public and private

sources. Finance for improvements to the compulsory phase of education, to pre-school provision and to training for the unemployed should come mainly from government. Putting the entitlement to post-compulsory provision into practice and improving on-the-job training should draw mainly on finance from individuals and companies.

We believe that by the turn of the century, both public and private expenditure on education as a proportion of GDP should rise. Government and society may decide to make this shift sooner rather than later and indeed may be beginning to do so already.

It is our conviction that in the long term the improvements in education and training that will result from this increase in expenditure will lead to improvements in the economy and benefits to society with consequent improvements in government finances. The most important of these will be flowbacks in taxes and savings in benefits. These would result from increases in employment as more people qualify to take on skilled work and others are able to enter the labour market due to increased pre-school provision for their children, assuming, that is, that there are jobs for them to go to. Other savings will result from the more stable and well-informed society that will stem from benefits to indivdiuals from quality education and training provision. Reduced expenditure on crime and health care is to be expected.

Cutting the education cake
We have seen that the way in which public expenditure on education is distributed across the phases of the system in the UK is like a pyramid turned upside down, with much more money being spent on each higher education student than on each secondary pupil, and in turn more on each secondary pupil than on each primary pupil. The

Commission's recommendations require a reduction in these differentials, which will bring them more in line with our competitors. We have seen in the previous section that in the UK the cost of higher education to the tax-payer is a great deal higher than in most other countries. Through contributions from the direct beneficiaries, the students, to the cost of their higher education, some of the burden of public expenditure on higher education will be relieved. This will in turn allow government to redress the imbalance within the education budget in favour of the underfunded parts of the system.

It is also clear that public expenditure on education is not distributed fairly across different parts of the country. We would wish to see a much fairer distribution of resources for education across the whole of the UK to put all parts of the country on a more even footing, taking account of needs and costs alone, rather than letting political considerations have such a great influence as they do at present. Expenditure on education in every part of the UK should be brought up to a level that can provide high quality, whatever its circumstances. Our proposals for the funding of ETBs (see Chapter 13) will contribute towards this goal.

Who pays?

Our target is that the costs of education provision for all 3–18-year-olds before they enter higher or continuing education will be funded by government. During the compulsory phase of education (5–16) particular attention will be needed to ensure that schools are fully funded for statutory provision. Schools may wish to attract extra funding for non-statutory provision from individuals and companies in the community. We would encourage education/business partnerships, which open up schools more to the outside world. It is important that disadvantaged localities do not lose out. For this reason, we welcome the efforts of some companies to target particular deprived areas, especially when resources are provided for schools in these areas to counteract their disadvantage.

We have argued for a shift in the balance of funding in post-compulsory education so that the costs will be shared between the private and public sectors. The benefits of high quality education and training beyond compulsory schooling that accrue to individuals and companies are such that they can be expected to make a personal contribution, especially if a large-scale national expansion is to take place. Research by the London School of Economics into the benefits of qualifications to individuals already mentioned in Chapter 9 found that: 'Those who leave school with no qualifications can look forward to no increase, in real terms, in net earnings throughout their lives beyond their late twenties. At the other extreme, university graduates can expect to see their net earnings rise steadily up to their mid-forties.'[32]

Those with vocational qualifications have some economic benefits compared to those with no qualifications. But these compare unfavourably with the returns from academic qualifications. The LSE found that: 'Males with NVQ 2 qualifications can expect to earn significantly less over their lifetime than their counterparts with GCSEs, though these are often regarded as being roughly equivalent qualifications.' All employers should recognise increases in productivity that ensue when their workforce is better educated and trained and hence should encourage their employees to train for qualifications, contribute to the cost of this and offer staff with qualifications enhanced pay prospects. Many, of course, already do so. The Investors In People award is increasing awareness amongst businesses of the competitive edge which a well-trained workforce can give. However, there is still considerable scope for improvement.

Our recommendations for funding post-compulsory provision in Chapters 9 and 10 take into account the costs and benefits of education and training to individuals, companies and government. What is proposed is a clearer notion of partnership. The government will fund young people on traineeships to go to college one or two days a week; companies will provide 'trainee wages'. The government will fund 80% of the tuition costs of HE courses; students will secure loans to pay for the remaining 20% and for maintenance. Beyond this, government may continue to provide funds to stimulate participation and to encourage provision to move in desirable directions.

Opportunities for greater efficiency

Most industries and services can expect to improve productivity over time and thus to produce a given level of output from a decreasing level of input. Productivity is a difficult concept to define in education, where outputs in particular cannot easily be quantified in economic terms. Nevertheless, we do not believe the current system is as efficient as it could be. A Minister, using Audit Commission figures, estimated the cost of maintaining surplus places in schools as £300 million.[33] Perhaps half this could be saved through reducing surplus provision. Another Audit Commission report suggested that in relation to failure rates and drop-out rates in courses for 16–19-year-olds, 'the value of improvements resulting from a reduction of one-third in the number of pupils who do not succeed would be worth some £150 million each year'.[34] Another report estimated improvements in efficiency in school transport at £20 million a year.[35] A National Audit Office study looked at university purchasing and estimated that more efficient spending, including some centralised purchasing, could lead to savings of £40 million.[36]

Eliminating wasted resources such as these will result in valuable savings. Several of our proposals exploit these opportunities: Chapter 4 outlines a modular post-14 qualification which allows students to be certificated on a cumulative and continuous basis; surplus places in primary schools, if suitably adapted, might contribute to the expansion of nursery education proposed in Chapter 6. Other chapters suggest that it might also be possible to make savings from newly introduced efficiencies, for example, more extensive usage of the buildings of schools, colleges and universities and better use of information technology to save administrative and other costs. In sum, these represent a potentially significant improvement in productivity. It is difficult to quantify this with accuracy but a conservative estimate of all of these improvements to efficiency would be in the region of £500 million a year.

Paying for our proposals

Many of our recommendations may be seen as cost-neutral, either because our new suggestions will cost the same as existing practice, or because any increase in costs could be compensated for by consequential savings.

The figures set out below are for those of our main proposals which will require extra resources, and give estimates of annual costs. The figures are in current prices but relate to targets to be attained by around the end of the century.

Proposals for expansion of pre-school provision (recurrent costs)	£860m
Traineeship scheme	£180m
Improvements to teacher training	£150m

and development
Extra expenditure on part-time   £240m
  HE students
Paying for our proposals in primary schools   £1,450m
Paying for our proposals in secondary schools   £310m

The last two sums listed above would be distributed to schools using appropriate national and local funding criteria. On a per pupil basis, an extra £375 would be spent on an average primary school pupil outside Scotland and £100 on one in Scotland. An extra £100 would be spent on an average secondary school pupil outside Scotland. Schools will clearly differ in the way in which they deploy these extra resources. What are the implications of this for two typical schools?

School A is a primary school in England with 200 pupils and 8 teachers.

Under our proposals, this school might receive an extra £75,000 a year. It might use this to:

- employ an extra qualified teacher to allow the school to reduce its larger classes to 30 or below and allow more non-contact time;
- appoint an administrative assistant to relieve the headteacher and deputy of some of their more mundane tasks and to allow them to do more teaching and to exercise their management role;
- give accelerated pay rises to two mid-career teachers who have been at a standstill for some years;
- buy two extra computers for the school complete with up-to-date educational software;
- redecorate the more run-down classrooms and provide armchairs and a coffee-maker in the staff room;
- introduce a reading recovery scheme for five pupils;
- buy the equivalent of a book for every pupil.

School B is a secondary school in England with 800 pupils and 50 teachers.

Under our proposals, this school might receive an extra £80,000 a year. It might use this to:

- appoint two guidance co-ordinators;
- employ a learning support specialist;
- give accelerated pay rises to five mid-career teachers;
- offer one teacher a secondment for a term to work for a large company;
- give another teacher a year away from school to do a masters degree;
- buy five extra computers;
- buy the equivalent of a book for every two pupils.

There are other miscellaneous recommendations in the report which have not been costed above but which will have implications for additional resources (e.g. special attention to deprived urban areas, setting up of new bodies, new buildings and training of new teachers for nursery education). We estimate that these will cost no more than £250 million a year.

So what is the net overall impact of our proposals? Extra expenditure amounts to £3.2 billion a year. But by the end of the century, annual savings from improved efficiency could amount to £500 million, and from our proposed higher education contribution scheme to £1,300 million.

This means that the net additional overall annual expenditure required by our proposals to the end of the century in current prices will be around £1.4 billion.

What would the implications of this extra expenditure be for taxation? Total tax revenue in 1992–3 was estimated at £207 billion, so it would need to be increased by 0.5% to yield £1 billion and a 1% increase in all tax revenue would yield £2 billion. In order to get a feel for the scale of the tax increase that would be required to pay for our proposals, Table 14.8 gives examples of changes in tax rates based on estimates for the current financial year, 1993–4.

Table 14.8 Illustrative changes in taxes, 1993–94, United Kingdom.

Tax	Measures to yield £1 billion	Yield of 1% rate rise/allowance cut
Income tax, all rates	0.5% increase in all rates	£1,960m
Income tax, basic rate	0.7% increase	£1,400m
Income tax allowances	5% cut in all allowances	£200m
Corporation tax	2.5% increase in all rates	£405m
VAT	0.6% increase in all rates	£1,675m

Source: HM Treasury, November 1992.[37]

National Insurance contributions are widely regarded as a form of tax. Employers' contributions are forecast to bring in £23.6 billion, and employees' contributions £14.6 billion in 1993–4 – a total of £38.2 billion. Thus a 1% increase in National Insurance revenue would bring in nearly £400 million and a 2.5% increase would be needed to raise £1 billion. The effect of a 1% rise in National Insurance contribution rates is harder to calculate. It would bring in something like £2 billion from employers and £1.5 billion from employees.

Other sources of revenue could be reductions in tax reliefs. The potential yield of removing some of the main tax reliefs are as follows (figures are for the UK in 1992–3): mortgage interest relief (£5.2 billion), married couples' allowance (£4.6 billion), Inheritance Tax nil band (£4.5 billion) and Capital Gains Tax exemption on housing (£1 billion).[38]

In any proposals for increases in public expenditure it is necessary to be conscious of their impact on the Public Sector Borrowing Requirement (PSBR) which in 1993–4 is expected to be about £50 billion, or 8% of GDP. Each extra expenditure of £1 billion adds 2% to the PSBR and additional interest charges of about 8% on the PSBR must also be taken into account.

Conclusions

The bulk of our recommendations could thus be funded by any one of the following:

- a 0.7% rise in all three income tax rates;

- a 1% rise in basic rate alone;

- a 0.8% rise in the VAT rate;

- a 0.4% rise in National Insurance contribution rates;

- a 3.5% rise in corporation tax.

We do not wish to propose which, if any, of these mechanisms for increasing public expenditure on education is preferable nor, alternatively, to suggest cuts that might be made in other public spending programmes. These are matters for government. After two years of inquiry and detailed assessment of the present position of education and training in the UK, we are wholly satisfied that, if our vision is to be realised, additional spending from both public and private sources is essential.

Notes

1 Sources:
    (i) Government Statistical Service. Education Statistics for the United Kingdom. HMSO.
    (ii) Public Expenditure Analyses. HMSO.
    (iii) *Population Trends*. HMSO.
2 HM Treasury, 1993. Public Expenditure Analyses to 1995–6. HMSO.
3 Centre for Educational Research and Innovation, 1992. Education

at a Glance. OECD Indicators. Organisation for Economic Co-operation and Development.

4 Different revaluation factors are used in Scotland, since their teachers are on a separate pay scale.

5 Sources:
(i) Public Expenditure Analyses. HMSO.
(ii) Local Authority Repricing Factors. Cleveland County Council.
(iii) Local Authority Revaluation Factors. Convention of Scottish Local Authorities.
(iv) Universities Pay and Prices Index. CVCP.
(v) UK National Accounts. HMSO.

6 We used an education deflator which specifically relates to education rather than the general economy, derived from repricing factors reflecting geographical, sectoral and specific price variations.

7 The two series are appropriate in different circumstances. If a government is spending more on education when using the GDP Deflator but the same in volume terms, the government can in one sense be said to be spending more. It is still diverting funds from other programmes or raising more in tax revenues in order to increase that spending, despite the fact that there is no increase in volume terms due to education being more expensive. To sustain volume levels and hold overall public expenditure constant may require the transfer of funds to education from other programmes. However, if one is looking at education spending in terms of numbers of teachers and other resources, then the series using the education deflator is the more relevant.

8 Green, A. and Steedman, H., 1993. Educational Provision, Educational Attainment and the Needs of Industry: A Review of Research for Germany, France, Japan, the USA and Britain. NIESR.

9 Her Majesty's Inspectorate, 1991. Aspects of Upper Secondary and Higher Education in Japan. HMSO.

10 Net of expenditure funded by capital receipts.

11 This sudden increase in 1989–90 is largely explained by local authorities rushing to increase capital expenditure in anticipation of the new system of capital controls introduced in 1990. It should also be mentioned that LMS makes budgetary freedoms available to schools for the improvement of their buildings through 'non-structural maintenance'. There is evidence that this has resulted in a marginal increase in capital expenditure in at least some authorities.

12 Government Statistical Service. Education Statistics for the United Kingdom. HMSO.

13 These unit cost figures have been calculated on a standardised basis to allow international comparisons. The unit costs for pre-school pupils should be viewed with caution due to the high proportion of part-time provision. Only education expenditure on nurseries is covered (not additional expenditure by social services). The unit

costs for higher education are not directly comparable with those for schools, since the former include Government expenditure on maintenance grants for students.

14 This gap reflects significant differences in staff ratios between the two phases and also some differences in curriculum costs, for example in science, technology and modern languages.

15 It should be noted that there are huge variations in costs between HE institutions and even more so between subjects.

16 The unit cost figures for the maintained sector are lower than in Table 14.4, partly because they exclude unspent balances held by schools at the end of the year under local management schemes, and partly because unit costs in England are much lower than those in Scotland.

17 Sources:
(i)   Department for Education, July 1992. Statistics of Schools in England – January 1991. *Statistical Bulletin* 13/92.
(ii)   Department for Education, May 1993. Education Expenditure from 1979–80. *Statistical Bulletin* 13/93.
(iii)   MacIntyre and Co. Independent Schools Cost Surveys.

18 Source: ISIS Annual Census. NB: The Retail Price Index for those years rose by 4.1% and 9.1% respectively.

19 Using these fees to compare expenditure on pupils in private and state schools is not advisable. It does not take account of the substantial endowment funds possessed by some schools, support from the Government through APS and suchlike. Nor does it take account of profits enjoyed by the schools and whether they are directed towards shareholders or towards reinvestment in the fabric of the school.

20 Sources for these figures: DFE, 1993. Government's Expenditure Plans. HMSO; MoD communication; Independent Schools Information Service communication.

21 Purchasing power parities (PPPs) are the most commonly used units for eliminating differences in price levels in international comparisons of expenditure. They are the rates of currency conversion that equalise the purchasing power of different currencies, so that a given sum of money will buy the same basket of goods and services in all countries.

22 Maintenance grants are not excluded since each country pays for its own inhabitants. It should be noted, however, that most degree courses in Scotland are four years as opposed to three years, which is the norm in the rest of the UK.

23 For example, authorities differ in their arrangements for post-16 provision.

24 There is no hard evidence of any increased divergence or convergence of spending across authorities in recent years. Since 1988, the existence of need assessments and capping relating to them has narrowed the differentials between individual authorities. The DFE

in its consultative document on the Common Funding Formula (18/12/92) says that 'there is clear evidence that individual LEA budgets and education Standard Spending Assessments (SSAs) are converging'. However, this trend is complicated by the area cost adjustments and additional expenditure needs adjustments which work to the benefit of the South-East and inner cities respectively. It is also complicated by the break-up of ILEA in the same year as the introduction of SSAs since the differentials amongst the constituent boroughs are now even greater than those previously between ILEA and other LEAs.

25 Sources for figures in this section are: DFE, 1993. Departmental Report. HMSO; Local Authority Repricing Factors, Cleveland County Council.

26 HMI, 1992. Education in England 1990–91. The Annual Report of HM Senior Chief Inspector of Schools. Department of Education and Science.

27 Mountfield, A., 1991. State Schools: A Suitable Case for Charity. Directory of Social Change.

28 The GDP Deflator is used to show the real year-on-year changes. It should be noted that this does not give us any sense of the *volume* of the provision of training by Government and in this sense exaggerates increases, since rapidly rising staff costs are such a large component of training expenditure.

29 Sources:
(i) Public Expenditure Analyses. HMSO.
(ii) *Employment Gazette.*

30 Training Agency, 1989 *Training in Britain: A Study of Funding.* HMSO.

31 EEC Labour Cost Survey quoted in *OECD Employment Outlook,* July 1991.

32 Bennett, R. and others, 1992. Learning Should Pay. London School of Economics.

33 Hansard, 11/11/92. Question asked by Nigel Spearing and answered by Eric Forth.

34 OFSTED and Audit Commission, 1993. Unfinished Business: Full-Time Educational Courses for 16–19-Year-Olds. HMSO.

35 Audit Commission, 1991. Home-to-School Transport: A System at the Cross Roads. HMSO.

36 National Audit Office, 1993. University Purchasing in England. HMSO.

37 HM Treasury, November 1992. Autumn Statement 1992. HMSO, Cm 2096.

38 All figures in this section are derived from HM Treasury, 1992. Autumn Statement. HMSO, including its statistical supplement (Public Expenditure Analyses).

15
No Time to Waste

We are filled with a sense of the importance and urgency of achieving the seven goals which we set out in Chapter 3. Only if those goals are achieved can our vision for the future be made a reality.

The emphasis on urgency may at first seem surprising. After all, we emphasise that our vision is for the long term, that much change is already in hand and that hasty action is almost certain to mean slower progress in education and training.

The sense of urgency comes in the first instance from our belief, which we hope the reader will feel is fully justified by this report, that there is much to do in order to assure this country's well-being in tomorrow's world. It is reinforced by the knowledge that careful planning, full consultation and sensitive implementation are all essential and all take time. There is therefore no time to waste if good progress is to be made at the pace which the present situation demands.

Our first hope is that our vision will be very widely shared: by political parties, by teachers and educationalists, by parents and students, and by the public at large. A wide consensus will be the best possible basis for action.

We would like to think that the Government will speedily indicate that it shares our vision. Decisions about implementing our recommendations will follow. Many of these do not require significant expenditure and action can be put in hand quickly. We hope in particular that the Government will implement without delay the proposal for a new Department for Education and Training for England. That would provide the key to unlocking many of the problems that have for too long beset both pupils and school-leavers in this country.

It is essential, we believe, that a new national target for foundation learning should be adopted as recommended in Chapter 10. This would provide that by AD 2000 90% or more of young people will be working for nationally recognised educational qualifications at least until they are 18 years old.

Much of the extra funding required by our recommendations relates to nursery education and primary schools. We are very conscious of the present constraints on public expenditure, but we believe that any significant postponement of action on these recommendations for short-term financial reasons would be most regrettable. We have been careful to propose a progressive and well-planned phasing in of extra provision and improvements over a period of years.

We consider that the new entitlements to learning which we recommend should follow the compulsory phase of education will redress long-standing imbalances in provision. They will do much to promote in our society those positive attitudes to learning which will become the hallmark of all successful countries as the next century unfolds. In order to finance these entitlements, we consider that high priority should be given to implementing our recommendations for seeking a bigger contribution to the cost of higher education from those who benefit from it.

We emphasise, in conclusion, the necessity of a high level of public interest in education and training. Well-informed and lively discussion should provide the essential basis for future progress.

We believe that the Department for Education and Training should commit itself to publishing once a year a report reviewing progress in education and training. This should cover the whole field and should aim to create widespread understanding as well as provoke debate. The nearer that this annual report can approach to objectivity, demonstrated not least by quality of the evidence that it adduces in support of its assertions, the more useful it will be.

Finally, we make a suggestion not made earlier in our report. We believe that a very valuable role could be performed by an independent institution which assumed the task of regularly carrying out a comprehensive review of developments and progress in education and training. There are several independent institutions with this kind of mission elsewhere, and they clearly play an important part in raising the quality of public debate. Any such institution in the United Kingdom would likewise need to be able to demonstrate its independence from any political party and from any other influence which might cloud its objectivity. It would not merely be concerned with the overall scene, but would necessarily have to look more closely from time to time at particular aspects of education or training. It might also wish to conduct pilot projects of its own. Such work would increase its ability to speak authoritatively.

We conclude our report, then, by expressing the hope that the idea of establishing an institution of this kind will attract support. We believe that the opportunity given us to look independently at the whole field of education and training has been invaluable. A new institute doing so on a continuing basis could, over the years, make an outstanding contribution to raising the quality of British education and training.

16
Summary of Recommendations

Introduction

We provide in this chapter a summary of the recommendations in this report. Chapter 3 sets out our vision and the seven goals which we recommend should be adopted in order to turn it into reality. We summarise our recommendations under each of these seven goals.

Goal No 1: High-quality nursery education must be available for all 3- and 4-year-olds.

The Commission recommends a national strategy for improving early childhood education and care in Chapter 6.
  The following targets are recommended:

- within 5 years at most, there should be nursery education places meeting nationally agreed standards for children in deprived areas within each local authority;

- within the present decade, there should be nursery education places meeting nationally agreed standards for a minimum of 60% of all 3- and 4-year-olds in every local authority area;

- within 5 years thereafter, sufficient nursery education places meeting nationally agreed standards

should be provided to cater for 95% of 4-year-olds
and 85% of 3-year-olds in every local authority area.

The Commission recommends that Education and
Training Boards (for ETBs see Chapter 13) develop and
publish plans, no later than 1995, for improving under-
5s provision. These should be based on reviews of current provision and wide consultation with providers and
others.

Central government funds for nursery education
should be based on an assessment of the number of 3-
and 4-year-olds in the population, the amount of local
provision already in existence and additional needs created by local targets for expansion and improvement.

Goal No 2: There must be courses and qualifications that bring out the best in every pupil.

The Commission makes recommendations on the curriculum, assessment and qualifications in Chapter 4.

The Commission proposes that there should be five
basic areas in the national curriculum, within which there
should be a wide choice of specific subjects. The areas are:
language, mathematics, natural science and technology,
expressive arts (including physical education), and
humanities (including social science).

The Commission wishes a voluntary fifth stage – Key
Stage 5 – to be added to the curriculum. Education for
young people aged 14–18 should be planned as a single
whole. To help this, the National Council for Vocational
Qualifications should be merged with the School
Curriculum and Assessment Authority to form a single
body entitled the Education and Training Development
Authority.

The Commission recommends what should be included

in the curriculum, but seeks to reduce the amount of time that should be compulsorily pre-empted by the national curriculum at each Key Stage. Young people who leave full-time education at age 16 or 17 will be able to work for a qualification within the proposed framework as trainees in formal traineeships.

The Commission recommends that the national curriculum should be made compulsory for independent schools.

The Commission recommends the establishment of an Educational Achievement Unit for the United Kingdom to monitor the nation's progress in educational achievement. It hopes that such a unit might also take a leading part in a world-wide network of units concerned with international comparisons.

The Commission recommends the introduction of a new General Education Diploma (GED). This will be awarded at two levels: Ordinary level, normally reached at age 16; and Advanced level, normally reached at age 18. It will replace the existing range of qualifications, including GCSE, 'A' levels, BTEC and existing vocational qualifications.

Courses at Key Stages 4 and 5 will be on a modular basis, and achievement will be assessed at the end of each module and credit points for the achievement awarded accordingly.

The GED will be a 'grouped' award, that is to say that achievement in a range of subjects will be required both at Ordinary and at Advanced level. The requirements are set out in Figure 4.1; and examples of studies for the Advanced level of the GED are set out in Figure 4.2.

A separate section discusses the position in Scotland. It notes in particular the widespread endorsement of the Howie Committee's analysis of current weaknesses in Scottish secondary education and the almost unanimous rejection of that Committee's proposed 'two-track' qualification system starting at age 15. The Commission endorses the idea of a one-track solution suited to Scottish circumstances, as the proposed GED is for those of England. Scottish awards must have a status at least as high as the GED and as awards elsewhere in Europe.

The Commission recommends in Chapter 10 that a new national target should be set for foundation learning, namely that, by AD 2000, 90% or more of young people will be working for nationally recognised educational qualifications at least until they are 18 years old.

The Commission recommends requirements which should govern traineeship agreements, entrants to which will normally be 16 or 17. Where there are not enough employers to provide high-quality traineeships, colleges should be enabled to offer education-based traineeships. The Commission recommends that there should be compulsory further education for $1^1/_2$ days a week for all 16- and 17-year-olds not in full-time education.

Goal No 3: Every pupil in every lesson has the right to good teaching and adequate support facilities.

Every pupil should be entitled in each lesson to be taught by a teacher with the knowledge, training, competence and commitment to teach that lesson well.

In Chapter 8, the Commission says that the quality of a significant minority of teachers is unsatisfactory and the overall quality of the profession needs to be raised. It discusses the means for doing that.

The Commission recommends that teaching should continue to be an all-graduate profession. There should be rigorous selection for training.

All primary teachers should have a GCSE qualification (at grades A–C or the equivalent) in English, mathematics, science and a modern foreign language.

A carefully managed induction programme for new teachers is recommended before Qualified Teacher Status is awarded.

The Commission endorses the view that in-service training is a 'high and permanent priority'. It recommends that:

- all schools should have a policy for staff development;

- all teachers should have a personal development plan, which should be used in teacher appraisal;

- every teacher should be entitled to 2 days each year for training outside the school for personal development.

The Commission favours further expansion of the use of classroom assistants, always under the supervision of a qualified teacher.

The improvement of the working environment of schools should be seen as a major priority for resources. All staff should be helped to become computer literate.

The Commission recommends improvements to secure better senior management in schools. In particular, it says that there needs to be a more professional approach to the selection of heads. Selection panels should have 5 members, 3 from the governing body, an adviser or inspector from the Education and Training Board and an external professional assessor from outside the area, all with equal voting rights.

The Commission recommends a measure of statutory self-regulation of the teaching profession through a General Teaching Council for England and Wales and suggests what its initial powers should be. (Scotland already has its own General Teaching Council.)

In Chapter 5 the Commission gives detailed consideration to innovation in learning. It concludes by recommending the establishment of a Council for Innovation in Teaching and Learning. The Commission places emphasis on the need for better implementation of new approaches, once tried and proven to be effective. The new Council would advise the relevant Secretaries of State on innovation policy.

In Chapter 7, the Commission recommends a determined drive to raise performance in literacy and numeracy, and lists eight measures which should be included.

The Commission recommends substantial reductions in primary school class sizes. Within five years no primary school pupil should be taught in classes of over 30; and, in deprived urban areas and in schools with high proportions of pupils whose mother tongue is not English, classes in the first two years of primary school should be reduced to a maximum of 20 pupils.

A maximum class size should be set for all primary school classes; the Commission suggests a provisional target of 20.

The Commission recommends a programme to ensure that every school pupil receives continuing guidance throughout schooling. The Commission also recommends (in Chapter 13) the establishment of Community Education and Training Advice Centres to provide independent and impartial advice about education, training and careers.

The Commission refers in Chapter 7 to the need for adequate learning support provided by trained teachers. The Commission proposes measures to improve the capability of schools to respond to special educational needs.

The Commission wishes to see links between school

and community strengthened.

The Commission recommends measures for securing improved performance by all schools. It discusses the problem of raising achievement in deprived areas and advocates measures to improve the situation. These will be assisted by the approach to funding Education and Training Boards and schools proposed in Chapter 13.

The Commission examines (again in Chapter 7) the question of diversity and choice between schools. The Commission commends the trend towards collaboration and sharing of facilities between schools in the independent and maintained sectors. The Commission's vision is that the improvements which it proposes for maintained schools will allow all pupils to make the best of themselves; as this vision comes to be translated into reality, there will be no need for an Assisted Places Scheme; accordingly it should be phased out in appropriate stages.

The Commission proposes a system, as regards school choice, which responds to the individual needs of children and also addresses wider issues of equity, the efficient use of resources and the difficulties faced by less popular schools.

Goal No 4: Everyone must be entitled to learn throughout life and be encouraged in practice to do so.

The Commission considers participation and entitlement after 16 in Chapter 9.

The Commission recommends a new system of awards to assist families with low incomes in which children wish to stay in full-time education from 16 to 18.

Turning to adults, the Commission considers that high priority should be given to the introduction of a right to one day a week off work, without loss of pay, for anyone under 25 who wishes to complete the General Education Diploma or obtain a qualification at equivalent level; and that by AD 2000 employers should provide, for all employees over 25, a minimum of 5 paid days' leave per year for recognised off-the-job education or training, whether offered as part of an internally based initiative or taken through an external organisation.

There should be an immediate entitlement for anyone under 35 to the payment of fees for completing the General Education Diploma (or the equivalent); eventually this entitlement should be extended to all adults.

The Commission recommends early introduction of allowances for incidental (non-fee) expenses of education or training at basic or intermediate levels.

The Commission puts forward recommendations for a new system of student support which will apply to all students in higher education, whether full-time or part-time.

The Commission proposes, in Chapter 11, new arrangements for progression in higher education. This requires a framework of qualification levels building directly on those established by the General Education Diploma. This will be developed in association with credit accumulation and transfer arrangements and also with the accreditation of prior learning.

The Commission sees increasing diversification of the mission of universities and other higher education institutions as crucial. It regrets that no Humanities Research Council has yet been established.

The Commission discusses problems relating to professional staff both in higher and in further education. It considers that a permanent appointment in either sector should require the holder to have a qualification which attests his or her competence as a teacher.

The Commission says that the time has come when the Government should join with the higher education sector in a joint examination of the financial basis on which future expansion can be secured without putting quality at risk. The need for capital investment is discussed.

In Chapter 12, the Commission underlines the need to persuade and enable adults with weak basic skills to take appropriate training. For unemployed people the '21-hour rule' should be waived so that they can draw unemployment benefit while undertaking a full-time course. The Commission urges the Government to give greater recognition to the potential contribution which adult education can make to promoting learning which is of economic and social value.

Goal No 5: The management of education and training must be integrated, and those with a stake in them must have this recognised.

The Commission devotes Chapter 13 to the management of education and training.

It recommends the establishment of a Department for Education and Training (DET) for England, formed by merging the DFE with those parts of the Employment Department which are responsible for training. There would be parallel changes in the Welsh Office.

There would be a Teachers' Management Board within the DET to assist the Secretary of State with his management responsibilities. This would be composed of members with substantial experience in the management of the education service, together with members with senior executive and personnel management experience in industry.

The Office for Standards in Education would assume responsibility for inspecting training provided under publicly-funded programmes, and its title would be amended to the Office for Standards in Education and Training

(OFSET).

The Commission considers it essential that there should be an intermediate tier of locally accountable bodies between the DET and individual schools: these it terms Education and Training Boards. The constitution of these bodies is discussed. Under this arrangement there will be no place for the new funding agencies for schools and they should be removed.

The ETBs will be formally required to operate on an arm's-length or purchaser-provider basis in relation to schools. The Commission proposes that all schools will enjoy benefits similar to those available to grant-maintained schools but within a framework which promotes local co-operation where that is desirable and makes support available when it is needed. City Technology Colleges should also be brought within the aegis of ETBs.

The Commission proposes arrangements whereby responsibility for school inspection is shared by ETBs and OFSET.

The Commission says that the Government should give high priority to designing better arrangements for the funding of schools. It must embody two features: a reconciliation between central allocation based on statistical indicators and assessment by each ETB of what it needs to reach a given level of quality; and freedom for ETBs to raise (or lower) the contribution of council tax to education (with some proportionate response by central government).

ETBs will assume responsibility for programmes of education and training for unemployed people. Training and Enterprise Councils will concentrate on promoting enterprise and training among employers.

The Commission discusses at length how the principles which underpin its recommendations on the management of education and training will apply in Scotland.

The Commission hopes that the model proposed for

England could eventually be applied to Northern Ireland, but recognises that this may be achievable only in the context of a broader political settlement.

Goal No 6: There must be a greater public and private investment in education and training to achieve a better return.

The Commission makes recommendations on the funding of education and training in Chapter 14.

It considers that at a conservative estimate the implementation of measures to cut out waste and improve productivity will yield £500 million a year. (This is without taking credit for improvements resulting from implementation of the innovation policy proposed in Chapter 5.)

Many of the Commission's proposals are cost-neutral. The main proposals requiring extra resources are listed. Their implementation would eventually require additional spending of £3.2 billion a year. Against this must be set the Commission's proposed higher education contribution scheme, which by AD 2000 could be producing savings of £1.3 billion a year. This means that the net additional overall annual expenditure required by the Commission's proposals by the end of the century would be around £1.4 billion.

The Commission illustrates tax changes which might be needed to raise this amount; it says that this is a matter for the Government to decide. It does however emphasise that the additional spending is essential if its vision for the future of education and training is to be realised.

Goal No 7: Achievement must constantly rise and progress be open for all to examine.

The Commission discusses the implementation of its

report in Chapter 15.

Its first hope is that its vision for the future will be very widely shared.

The Commission would like to think that the Government will speedily indicate that it does share the vision. Many recommendations do not require significant expenditure and can be put in hand quickly, and the Commission hopes in particular that the Government will implement the proposal for a new Department for Education and Training.

The Commission believes that it is essential that a new national target for foundation learning should be adopted. This would provide that by AD 2000 90% or more of young people will be working for nationally recognised educational qualifications at least until they are 18 years old.

The Commission would regret any significant postponement of action on its recommendations relating to nursery education and primary schools.

High priority should be given to implementing the Commission's recommendations for seeking a higher contribution to the cost of higher education from those who benefit from it.

The DET should commit itself to publishing once a year a report reviewing progress in education and training.

Finally, the Commission hopes that an independent institution will be established to carry out regularly a comprehensive review of developments and progress in education and training. It could over the years make an outstanding contribution to raising the quality of British education and training.

Appendix 1 (See Preface)

National Commission on Education

Terms of Reference

'In the light of the opportunities and challenges that will face the United Kingdom in a changing world over the next 25 years, to identify and consider key issues arising from:

- the definition of educational goals and assessment of the potential demand for education and training, in order to meet the economic and social requirements of the country and the needs and aspirations of people throughout their lives; and

- the definition of policies and practical means whereby opportunities to satisfy that demand may be made available for all, bearing in mind the implications for resources and institutions and for all of those involved in the education and training system;

and to report its conclusions and recommendations in such manner as it may think fit.'

Membership

Lord Walton of Detchant, House of Lords (Chairman)

Mr John Raisman CBE, formerly Chairman, Shell UK Ltd
   (Deputy Chairman)

Sir John Cassels CB, formerly Director General, National
   Economic Development Office (Director)

Mrs Averil Burgess, Head, South Hampstead High School

Mrs Betty Campbell MBE, Head, Mount Stuart Primary
   School, Cardiff

Dr David Giachardi, Director of Research, Courtaulds plc

Mr Christopher Johnson, formerly Economic Adviser,
   Lloyds Bank

Ms Helena Kennedy QC, Barrister

Prof. Alistair MacFarlane FRS, FEng, Principal and Vice-
   Chancellor, Heriot Watt University

Ms Margaret Maden, County Education Officer,
   Warwickshire

Sir Claus Moser KCB, CBE, FBA, Warden, Wadham
   College, Oxford

Ms Jenny Shackleton, Principal, Wirral Metropolitan
   College

Mr Richard Staite, Head, Beeslack High School, Penicuik,
   Lothian

Professor Jeff Thompson CBE, Professor of Education,
   University of Bath

Professor David Watson, Director, Brighton University

Mr Peter Wickens, Director of Personnel, Nissan Motor
   Manufacturing (UK) Ltd

Associate Commissioners

Research Committee
Professor A. H. Halsey, Nuffield College, Oxford University
Professor Andrew McPherson, Centre for Educational

Sociology, Edinburgh University
Professor Peter Mortimore, Deputy Director, Institute of
  Education, University of London

Working Group 1 – Effective Schooling
Mrs Pat Clark, Headteacher, Peterborough Primary
  School, Fulham
Mr Michael Duffy, Headteacher, King Edward VI School,
  Morpeth, Northumberland
Professor Desmond Nuttall, Professor of Curriculum &
  Assessment Studies, Institute of Education, University
  of London

Working Group 2 – Schools, Society & Citizenship
Mr Richard Holmes, Business Development Manager,
  Citibank N.A.
Professor Bob Moon, Professor of Education, School of
  Education, Open University

Working Group 3 – The Teaching Profession & Quality
Mrs Ruth Collins, Deputy Headteacher, Kineton High
  School, Warwickshire
Professor Richard Pring, Director, Department of
  Educational Studies, Oxford University
Ms Anne Watts, Equal Opportunities Director, Midland
  Bank plc

*Working Group 4 – Higher & Further Education in the Twenty-
First Century*
Mr Mike Austin, Principal, Accrington & Rossendale College
Dr John Daniel, Vice Chancellor, Open University
Dr Bernard McManus, Vice Chancellor, Bournemouth
  University
Mr Trevor Thomas, National Personnel Manager, Unilever
  plc
Mr James Wright, Vice Chancellor, University of
  Newcastle upon Tyne

Working Group 5 – Preparing for Work Today and Tomorrow
Dr Clive Booth, Director, Oxford Brookes University
Ms Sheila Drew-Smith, Partner, Coopers & Lybrand
　Deloitte
Mr Chris Hayes, Chairman, The Prospect Centre

Working Group 6 – Better Ways of Learning
Dr Eurfron Gwynne Jones, Director of Education, BBC
Mr Stuart Hamer, Director, Education and Training, Ford
　of Europe Inc.
Mr Stan Hughes, Headteacher, Lord Grey School,
　Bletchley, Bucks

Working Group 7 – Resources
Mr Tony Travers, Research Director, London School of
　Economics
Professor David Ulph, Head, Department of Economics,
　University College, London

Commission Staff

Sir John Cassels, Director
Mr Barry Wakefield, Deputy Director (Research)
Ms Sue Taylor, Research Officer
Mr Josh Hillman, Research Officer
Mrs Janice Robins) Joint Secretaries
Ms Denise Eacher) to the Commission
Ms Gwynneth Rigby, Consultant, Higher Education
Mr Philip Dale, short-term secondment from Unilever plc
Mr Norman Brand, Reporter
Miss Louise Priestley, Office Manager
Ms Andrea Hill, Personal Secretary to the Director
Miss Ann Rowe, Administrative Assistant
Miss Sarah Banks) short-term administrative
Ms Claire Gontier) appointments

We are indebted to very many people who have given time and effort to supporting the work of the Commission in a variety of ways – for example by helping to organise events, chairing seminars, speaking at conferences, providing expert advice, and commenting on early drafts of reports.

We are particularly grateful to our Associate Commissioner, Professor Andrew McPherson, for his outstanding contribution on all matters relating to Scotland, and to Dr Robert Osborne of the University of Ulster and Dr Anthony Gallagher of Queens University, Belfast, who acted as consultants on all matters relating to Northern Ireland.

List of Events Run by the Commission and its Working Groups

Quality in the Teaching Profession
30 January 1992, Shrewsbury: in association with Shropshire LEA and Shrewsbury College of Arts and Technology.

Quality in the Teaching Profession
12 March 1992, Birmingham.

The Next 25 Years
3–5 April 1992, Oxford.

Quality in the Teaching Profession
13 May 1992, Newcastle upon Tyne.

Roles, Rights and Responsibilities
16 June 1992, Glasgow: in association with Strathclyde Regional Council and Jordanhill College.

Dropping in and Out at 16
30 June 1992, Gloucester: in association with Gloucestershire LEA.

Towards a Well-Qualified Workforce
2 and 22 July 1992, London

A 13-Year-Old's Experience of Education
7 July 1992, Manchester: in association with Manchester LEA.

Multicultural Issues and Educational Success
1 October 1992, London: in association with the Runnymede Trust.

Future Framework for the Governance of Schools
7 October 1992, Birmingham.

Primary Education
13 October 1992, London.

A Framework for Learning in the Twenty-First Century
23 October 1992, London: in association with the Institute of Education, University of London.

Effective School Governance for Staff, Governors and Parents
11 November 1992, London.

Technical and Vocational Education (16–19) in France and Britain
1 March 1993, London: organised in association with the Franco-British Council.

Seminar on Education in Northern Ireland
3 March 1993, Belfast: organised in association with the University of Ulster.

Lecture Series – Universities in the Twenty-First Century
A series of six lectures at the Royal·Society, London, run jointly with the Council for Industry and Higher Education.

Other Events

Commissioners took part in an international symposium at Leeds Castle, Kent, on 19–21 March 1993. The symposium was organised by the America-European Community Association Trust.

Individual Commissioners visited many education and training establishments in the United Kingdom and also in Denmark, France, Germany and the United States.

List of Oral Evidence to the Commission and Working Groups

Action for Governors' Information and Training; Jane Arden (Education Officer of the London Diocesan Board), Joan Sallis, Ada Fordham, Ann Holt.

Adult Literacy and Basic Skills Unit; Mr Alan Wells (Director), Ms Lesley Morphy.

Association of County Councils; Ken Watson (Vice Chairman, ACC Education Committee and Chairman of Devon Education Committee), Councillor Fred Riddell, Ian Langtry.

Association of Metropolitan Authorities; Councillor Graham Lane (Deputy Chairman, Newham Education Committee and Vice Chairman), Councillor Mrs Marlene Newman, Alan Parker.

Association of Teachers and Lecturers; Mr Harry Isaac (Senior Vice President), Mr Peter Smith (General Secretary), Ms Judith Rowley, Ms Mary Rodgers, Ms Meryl Thompson, Miss Gillian Wood, Ms Anne Keeble.

Balcarras School; Mr Mike Hughes (Head of Geography).

Bristol University, Centre for Assessment Studies; Ms Gillian Squirrel (Director of Prison Education).

British Academy; Sir Anthony Kenny (President), Professor Michael Thomson, Professor Brian Tate, Mr

Peter Brown.

British Association for the Advancement of Science;
Professor Rosalind Driver (Vice President for Education
& Youth), Professor Paul Black.

Centre for Education and Industry, Warwick University;
Dr David Finegold.

Church of England; The Rt. Revd Michael Adie – Bishop
of Guildford (Chairman of the Church of England
Board of Education), Geoffrey Duncan, David
Lankshear.

Commission for Racial Equality; Jean Cousins (Director,
Social Policy Division), Maureen Fraser, Phil Barnett.

Committee of Vice-Chancellors and Principals of the
Universities of the United Kingdom; Dr David Harrison
(Chairman), Dr Clive Booth, Professor David Dilks,
Professor Derek Burke, Mr Tom Burgner, Dr Roger
Brown.

Confederation of British Industry; Ian Dixon (Chairman,
Willmott Dixon, Chairman of the CBI's Education
Policy Panel), David Ayres, Tony Webb, Mrs Margaret
Murray, Roy Harrison.

Department of Trade and Industry; Mr Bob Dobbie.

Educational Institute of Scotland; Mr Fred Forrester
(Deputy General Secretary), Mr George MacBride.

Employment Department; Roger Dawe (Director General,
Training, Enterprise and Education Directorate), Derek
Grover, John West, Lester Parker (Senior Psychologist).

Engineering Employers Federation; Vivien Marshall.

Equal Opportunities Commission; Brenda Hancock
(Director of Social Policy), Anne Madden.

Free Church Federal Council; The Revd Professor H.W.
Marratt (Consultant, Education Committee), Mr Derek
Robson.

Further Education Funding Council; Mr Bill Stubbs (Chief
Executive).

General Teaching Council for Scotland; Mr Ivor
    Sutherland (Registrar), Miss Mary Rose Caden.
German Federal Institute for Vocational Training; Dr
    Hermann Schmidt (Director).
Girls' Schools Association; Miss Joan Jefferson
    (President), Miss Elizabeth Diggory, Miss Ann Parkin.
Headmasters' Conference; Father Dominic Milroy
    (Chairman), Mr Vivian Anthony, Mr Tony Evans.
Incorporated Association of Preparatory Schools; Mrs
    Elizabeth Prichard (Chairman), Mr Robin Peverett, Mr
    R.S. Trafford.
Institute of Education, University of London; Professor
    Peter Mortimore (Deputy Director).
Kentish Town School; Mrs Elizabeth Owens (Headteacher).
King's College; Mr Philip Adey (Centre for Educational
    Studies).
National Association of Governors and Managers; Peter
    Morris (Chairman, NAGM), Tom Hinds, Walter Ulrich.
National Association of Headteachers; Mr David Hart
    (General Secretary), Mr R Hewins (Chairman of NAHT
    Primary Advisory Committee), Mr George Varnava, Mr
    Jeff Holman.
National Association of Schoolmasters/Union of Women
    Teachers; Mr Peter Cole (Chair of NASUWT National
    Education Committee), Mr Graham Terrell (National
    Executive member for Greater London), Mr H. Iven
    (Assistant Secretary, Education).
National Children's Bureau Early Childhood Unit; Gillian
    Pugh (Director), Dorothy Rouse, Mary Jane
    Drummond, Wendy Scott, Iram Siraj-Blatchford.
National Confederation of Parent Teacher Associations;
    Larry Goodband (Chairman), Margaret Morrissey, Judy
    Moylan.
National Council for Educational Technology; Mr Peter
    Avis (Director, Development of the IT Curriculum), Mr

Stuart France (Programme Manager).

National Council for Vocational Qualifications; Mr Tim Oates (Principal Adviser).

National Union of Teachers; Janet Sturgis (Executive Member and Vice Chairperson), Michael Barber (Assistant Secretary), Kathy Baker (Professional Assistant), Anne Moran, Marion Darke, John Bills.

Northumberland Supported Self-Study Unit; Mr Chris Boothroyd (Education Manager).

Nottingham University, Department of Psychology; Professor David Wood.

Office for Standards in Education; Mr Gabriel Goldstein (Assistant Director of Inspection).

Open University; Ms D. Laurillard (Programme on Learner Use of Media).

Policy Studies Institute; Dr Michael White (Senior Research Fellow).

Professional Association of Teachers; Mr Nicholas Griffin (National Chairman), Mr John Andrews (General Secretary), Mrs Joyce Watts, Mr Bob Smith, Dr Roger Taylor, Dr David Jones, Miss Jackie Miller, Mr Peter Kairis, Mr John Andrews.

Royal Academy of Engineering; Brian Manley (Chairman of the Education, Training and Competence to Practise Committee), Professor John Sparkes, Professor Geoffrey Hall, Miss V.E. Budd.

Royal Society; Professor Roger Blin-Stoyle (Chairman of the Royal Society's Education Committee), Robert Rees.

School Examinations and Assessment Council; Ms Kate Seager (Professional Officer).

Scottish Consultative Council on the Curriculum; Mr Cameron Harrison (Chief Executive).

Secondary Heads Association; Mr John Sutton (General Secretary), Mr R. Clarke (Assistant General Secretary), Mr Mike Pugh, Mr Roger Haslam, Mr M. Hewitt.

Society of Education Officers; Keith Anderson (President and Chief Education Officer for Gloucestershire), Peter Coles, Brian Slater.

United Synagogue Board of Education; David Lerner (Administrative Secretary).

University of Warwick; Professor John Tomlinson, (Director, Institute of Education).

List of Written Evidence

Adult Literacy and Basic Skills Unit; Mr Alan Wells.

Advisory Centre for Education (ACE) Ltd.

Ainley, Patrick; University of Kent.

Allen, Dr Michael.

Allied Lyons; Richard Martin.

Anderson, Mr Eric.

Assistant Masters and Mistresses Association.

Association for Science Education.

Association for Spina Bifida and Hydrocephalus.

Association of Accounting Technicians.

Association of British Chambers of Commerce; Mr Alan Bartlett.

Association of British Correspondence Colleges.

Association of Colleges for Further and Higher Education (Scotland).

Association of Colleges in Further and Higher Education.

Association of London Authorities.

Association of Metropolitan Authorities.

Association of Polytechnic and College Teachers.

Association of the British Pharmaceutical Industry.

Automobile Association.

Ayles, Rosemary; University of Reading.

Ball, Sir Christopher.

Banking Information Service.

Baring Foundation; Mr Barry Till.

Barnardos; Janice Funnell and Mike Hughes.
Bartley, Mr David.
BBC Education; Mr Brian Wright.
Bolton, Professor Eric CB
Boyle, Alan; Knowsley Metropolitan Borough.
BP Educational Affairs; Mr C.L. Marsden.
Brent Council Education.
British Aerospace; Sir Graham Day and others.
British and Foreign School Society.
British Association for Commercial and Industrial
    Education.
British Association for Early Childhood Education; Janet
    S. Dye.
British Educational Management and Administration
    Society; H. Tomlinson.
British Educational Research Association; Professor J.
    Elliott.
British Furniture Manufacturers.
British Library.
British Medical Association; Dr Ian Field.
British Medical Association Foundation for AIDS.
British Nuclear Fuels plc.
Burrows, Professor C.R.; University of Bath, School of
    Mechanical Engineering.
Business and Technician Education Council; Diane Billam.
Butterfield, Lord.
Cadbury Schweppes.
Cademuir International School.
Callaghan, Lord.
Campaign for Equal Access to Primary Education for All
    (CEAPEA); Mrs P.E. Nicholas.
Campaign for the Advancement of State Education;
    Margaret Tulloch.
Careers Research and Advisory Centre.
Central Regional Council (Scotland); Ian Collie.

Centre for Studies on Integration in Education; Mark
  Vaughan.
Chemical Industries Association.
Children's Legal Centre.
Church of England General Synod Board of Education.
Church of Scotland Department of Education; Very Revd
  D.R. Davidson.
Citizenship Foundation.
City and Inner London North Training and Enterprise
  Council; Peter Box.
City of Salford, Education Department; H. Pickles.
City of Sheffield, Education Department.
Comino Foundation; Dr Eric Bates.
Commission for Racial Equality.
Commission of the European Communities.
Committee of Vice-Chancellors and Principals.
Commonwealth Secretariat.
Community Service Volunteers.
Confederation of British Industry; Mr A.J. Webb.
Confederation of British Industry Education Foundation.
Congress of University Convocations & Graduate
  Associations.
Consumers' Association.
Council for Education in World Citizenship; Patricia
  Rogers.
Council for Environmental Education.
Council of Subject Teaching Associations.
Cowan, Bryan J.
Cranfield Institute of Technology; Professor F.R. Hartley.
Dahrendorf, Sir Ralf.
Daycare Trust; Marion Kozak.
Department for Education.
Derbyshire College of Higher Education; Professor J.
  Powers.
Devon County Council; Dr P.L. Gray.

Dolton, Professor Peter; University of Newcastle upon Tyne.

Duke, Professor Chris; University of Warwick.

Dyer, Gordon; (Open University, East Anglia Regional Centre).

Early Childhood Unit, National Children's Bureau; Gillian Pugh.

Education 2000; Mr John Abbott.

Education for Development; Professor Alan Rogers.

Elton, Professor Lewis, Higher Education Adviser; Employment Department.

Engineering Council.

Engineering Employers Federation; Vivien Marshall.

Equal Opportunities Commission; Anne Madden.

Esperanto Teachers' Association; P. Gubbins.

Fellowship of Engineering.

Finegold, Dr David.

Ford of Europe Inc.

Frazer, Dr Malcolm.

Free Church Federal Council.

Freeman, Dr Joan; European Council for High Ability.

Fulton, Professor Oliver.

Further Education Campaign Group.

Further Education Unit.

Futures Information Associates; Brian Burrows.

General Electric Company plc.

General Teaching Council (England and Wales).

General Teaching Council for Scotland.

Girls Public Day School Trust.

Girls' Schools Association.

Gordon Cook Foundation; William Robb.

Grampian Enterprise.

Gray, Harry.

Gray, Dr P.L.; Devon County Council.

Greenhead College; Dr J.K. Conway.

Hammersmith and Fulham Education Authority.
Hatfield Polytechnic.
Headmasters' Conference.
Headteachers' Association of Scotland.
Hickman, Mr B.M.; Sonic Code Research.
Howie, Professor J.M.
Hubbard, Dr S.R.
Hurst, Victoria.
IBM.
Imperial College of Science, Technology and Medicine;
   Sinclair Goodlad.
Incorporated Association of Preparatory Schools.
Incorporated Society of Musicians.
Independent Panel for Special Education Advice.
Independent Television Commission.
Information Centre for State Schools; John Dunford.
Institute of Careers Guidance; Paul Chubb.
Institute of Electrical Engineering; B.W. Manley
Institute of Manpower Studies.
Institute of Physics.
Institution for School and College Governors.
Investors In People.
Irving, Dr Ann; Loughborough University.
Jones, Professor Anne.
Kent Training and Enterprise Council; Gerald Baker.
Kibel, Regina.
Kidscape; Ms Michele Elliott.
Kobiernicki, Leszek.
Korda & Co Ltd; Ms Carolyn Hayman.
KPMG Peat Marwick; D.W. Westcott.
Learning from Experience Trust; Norman Evans.
Leask, Marilyn; Bedford College of Higher Education.
Library Association.
Lifespan Consortium.
Lincolnshire County Council, Education Department.

Lister, Councillor Edward; Wandsworth Council.

London Borough of Barnet.

London School of Economics and Political Science; Dr J.M. Ashworth.

London Study Centre and Greenfields School.

Lord Silkin School; D. Lewis.

Loughborough University of Technology, Department of Geography; W. Hamley.

Lucas Open Learning; M.C. Dickins.

MacFarlane, M.J.

Maclure, Mr Stuart.

Manchester Polytechnic; J. Hogbin.

Marshall, Mr Alan R.

Methodist Church Division of Education and Youth.

Miliband, Mr David.

Morton, Dr C.N.

Morton, Dr Greteli.

Napier Polytechnic; Professor William Turmeau.

National Alliance of Women's Organisations.

National Association for Design Education; David Buchan.

National Association for Educational Guidance for Adults.

National Association for Gifted Children; Dr E. Chitham.

National Association for Special Educational Needs; Mike Hinson.

National Association for Staff Development in Further and Higher Education.

National Association of Advisory Officers for Special Education.

National Association of Governors and Managers.

National Association of Head Teachers; David Hart.

National Association of Schoolmasters/Union of Women Teachers.

National Association of Schoolmasters/Union of Women Teachers (Scotland).

National Association of Teachers in Further and Higher

Education; Derek Betts.

National Confederation of Parent Teacher Associations.

National Council for Voluntary Youth Services.

National Deaf Children's Society.

National Extension College.

National Foundation for Educational Research.

National Health Service Training Directorate.

National Institute for Adult and Continuing Education.

National Institute for Careers Education and Counselling;
Tony Watts.

National Institute of Adult Continuing Education; Mr
Peter Clyne.

National Toy Libraries Association.

National Union of Students.

National Union of Teachers.

National Youth Agency; Janet Paraskeva.

Newhofer, Frank.

Norfolk County Council.

North Yorkshire County Council.

Northumberland County Council.

Nottingham Polytechnic; Professor G.H. Bell.

O'Brien, Sir Richard.

Organisation Mondiale (OMEP).

Paisley College; Professor John Woodward.

Partnership Trust; Dr D.M. Brancher.

Pearce, Richard; International School of London.

Pearson, Mr Richard.

Peers School; Bernard Clarke.

Plaskow, Mr Maurice and colleagues.

Polytechnic of Wales.

Porter, Lord, of Luddenham.

Prior, Lady (Jane).

Professional Association of Teachers.

Publishers Association.

Putteridge Bury Management and Conference Centre;

Professor P.T. Wilson.

Raffe, Mr David.

Reading Reform Foundation; Mona McNee.

Root, Ms Betty.

Round Square Conference.

Royal Academy of Engineering; Mr B.W. Manley.

Royal Association for Disability and Rehabilitation; Paul Simpson.

Royal Institute of British Architects.

Royal National Institute for the Blind; Paul Ennals.

Royal National Institute for the Deaf.

RSA (Royal Society for the Encouragement of Arts, Manufactures and Commerce).

RSA Examinations Board; Mr Martin Cross.

Saferworld.

School Library Association; Valerie Fea.

Scottish Consultative Council on the Curriculum.

Scottish Examination Board; H.A. Long.

Scottish Forum for Development Education in Schools.

Scottish Parent Teacher Council.

Scottish Secondary Teachers Association.

Scottish Vocational Education Council; Mr T.J. McCool.

Scout Association; Derek Twine.

Secondary Heads Association.

Sex Education Forum; Rachel Thomson.

Shaw, Mr Colin.

Sheffield City Polytechnic.

Snell, Ms Patricia.

Society of Education Officers.

Society of Headmasters and Headmistresses of Independent Schools; I.G. Templeton, Dr R.A.S. Atwood.

Solomon, Dr Joan.

Special Educational Needs – National Advisory Council.

Spoonley, Neil.

St. Michael's Catholic School; Len Smith.

Standing Committee for the Education and Training of Teachers; R. Beardsworth.

Standing Conference on Schools Science and Technology.

Stewart, Ronald.

Stubbs, Mr William H.

Sunderland, Borough of.

Sunderland Polytechnic.

Sunderland Polytechnic; Mrs Y. Stewart-Smith.

Taylor, Matthew, MP.

Teesside TEC; John R. Howell.

Thompson, Professor Sir Michael.

Tomei, Mr Anthony.

Trades Union Congress; Norman Willis.

TUC; Roy Jackson.

Turvey, Professor Ralph.

Understanding British Industry.

United Kingdom Central Council for Nursing, Midwifery and Health Visiting.

United World College of the Atlantic; Mr Colin Jenkins.

Universities Council for Adult and Continuing Education; Professor D.J. Johns.

Universities Council for the Education of Teachers; Professor A. Edwards.

University College London; Dr D.H. Roberts, Provost.

University College of Ripon and York St. John; Ken Ridley, David Sellick, K.R. Oley.

University College of Swansea.

University of Cambridge.

University of Dundee MicroCentre; Professor A. Newell.

University of Edinburgh, Centre for Continuing Education; Tom Schuller.

University of Exeter, School of Education; Professor E.C. Wragg.

University of Keele; Professor Tim Brighouse.

University of Lancaster; Professor Oliver Fulton.

University of London, Institute of Education; Professor P. Mortimore, Sir Peter Newsam, Professor G.J. Whitty.

University of London Observatory; D. McNally.

University of Manchester, School of Education; Professor P. Mittler, Professor G. Verma.

University of Newcastle upon Tyne, Faculty of Medicine.

University of Newcastle upon Tyne, School of Education; Professor C.T. Fitz-Gibbon.

University of Newcastle; Professor Peter Dolton.

University of Reading, Department of Education Studies and Management.

University of Sheffield.

University of Southampton; Sir Gordon Higginson.

University of St Andrews; Professor J.F. Lamb.

University of Strathclyde.

University of Warwick; Professor J.R.G. Tomlinson, Professor T. Brighouse, Dr F. Inglis, Professor J. Campbell, Dr S. Neill, Ms L. Evans, Dr E. Keep, Alan Sanday (Centre for Educational Development, Appraisal and Research (CEDAR), Dr C. Pole (CEDAR), Professor Burgess, Mr C. Hughes, Ms S. Moxon (CEDAR).

Voluntary Council for Handicapped Children.

Voluntary Organisations Liaison Council for Under Fives.

Volunteer Reading Help; Charles Martineau.

Warren, Dr R.C.

Wells, David.

Wessex Project.

White, Graham.

White, Mr Michael.

William Ellis School; Michael Wheale.

Williams, Professor R.J.P.

Wolverhampton Polytechnic; Professor G. Doherty.

Worcester College of Higher Education; Professor

Christine Pascal, Tony Bertram, Peter Heaslip.
Wright, Dr Peter.
Young of Dartington, Lord (Michael).

Appendix 2 (See Chapter 9)

New arrangements for the support of students in higher education

How Will the System Operate?

For students
Students will either make their contribution (HECON) direct to their institution at the time of registration, or contract, through their institution, with an intermediary body (see below) to repay after the period in higher education has been completed. Repayments will start once the student's post-course income has reached the specified level (say 25% above the average wage), and will vary in relation to income. Collection will be by the PAYE mechanism for those in employment, and through the tax system for the self-employed.

Those students who wish to receive a maintenance allowance (HEMA) will use the same procedure, with their institutions acting as the administrative interface. There will no longer be a requirement for a means test, so administration will be simplified, the student will no longer be dependent on parental income, and the LEA will no longer have a role. There will be a need for a transition period during which the old-style grant is phased out.

The interest rate for deferred payments could be fixed by the Government at an economic rate sufficient to attract the financial institutions. In this case, tax relief could be granted as under the present MIRAS arrangements. Interest for the period while the student is studying will be rolled up into the overall amount due and will not be collected until repayments are triggered.

For educational institutions

Each institution will keep a record of all registered students indicating whether they have paid the HECON in advance, or wish to defer payment. The record will also indicate whether or not they have claimed HEMA. The record will be used by institutions to claim payment in respect of contributions from the intermediary body, which will reimburse both the deferred contributions and the discount element of advance payments. The record will also provide the basis upon which the intermediary body issues HEMAs to students. The cash flow of institutions will benefit as the present problems of dealing with a large number of local authorities, many of which make late payment of student tuition fees, will be removed, and the intermediary body will provide a single interface. Student debtors will not be a problem for institutions as registration will not be allowed unless either an advance payment is made or a contract signed.

There are a number of options for fixing the level of HECON. In our view, it should be a flat rate contribution, applicable to any course at the specified level. To introduce a contribution which is a percentage of the differential costs in different subject areas would be to introduce financial considerations into the choice by students of their subject area. We consider this inappropriate. On present costs, a course in medicine or engineering will cost three or four times as much as one in history or law. Similarly, we do not wish institutions to have discretion to introduce top-up fees for home students. While we approve of competition between institutions for students, we wish academic quality rather than the cost of courses to the student, to be its source.

For the intermediary body

Government will need to establish an intermediary body to act as its agent in operating the scheme. This could either be the present Student Loan Company, the Higher Education Funding Councils, or some entirely new body.

The intermediary body will go out to financial institutions to raise loan funding, which will be paid into a specially constituted fund. It will make payments from the fund to institutions in respect of the contributions due from their registered students and pay HEMAs to students via their institutions. It will inform the Inland Revenue of the payments due from students and will pay those collected back into the loan fund to service repayments to the financial investors.

For the financial institutions

Banks and other financial institutions will make a loan to the intermediary body in return for interest at market rate plus an agreed margin of, say, 0.5%. Government will guarantee against an agreed level of expected default. Repayments to financial institutions will be by the intermediary body which will receive its payments from the Inland Revenue. The loan fund will, therefore, represent a risk-free investment. The rate of return will be low, in comparison to some other forms of investment, but will, nevertheless, be attractive as a secure base within a mixed portfolio, and will not require capital backing in bank balance sheets because its risk-weighting will be zero. It will, moreover, be 'securitised', that is, institutions will be able to sell on the loan in the form of a bond, should they so wish. We are confident that a loan fund set up in this way will secure investors.

How Much Income Will the Scheme Make Available?

The scheme will produce a number of different income streams.

The introduction of HECON should be the first stage in a phased transition programme. The following assumptions have been made in order to assess income from HECON: 25% of students pay in advance; the rate for full-timers is £1,000, discounted by 15%, and pro rata for part-timers; the scheme starts in 1994–5; student numbers are as projected in Government expenditure plans. The immediate annual income to the system will be around £260 million for the UK.

Deferred payments will not start to flow back in significant amounts until about the year AD 2000. Potentially, the amount recoverable, using the same assumptions as above, is around £950 million per annum, but the scheme will take about twenty years to build up to that full amount.

As the amount payable via the maintenance grant gradually reduces, the funds currently devoted to that purpose will be freed for other uses. The amount estimated for 1994–5 for this purpose is about £1.5 billion, including the cost of the student loan scheme.

How Much Will Need to be Raised From Financial Institutions?

Using the assumptions above, the amount which will need to be raised from institutions to cover deferred payments of the HECON will be £950 million.

The following assumptions have been made to assess how much will be needed to cover HEMAs for full-time students once present grant and loan arrangements have been entirely phased out: 1994–5 estimates are used; the

HEMA is 20% higher than previous payments; the amount required to compensate for parental contributions is 66% of the former grant element; take-up of the HEMA is 75%. The total amount to be raised will be roughly £2.2 billion. This will, however, be a phased requirement.

What Will Be the Cost to Government?

The charges on Government will be as follows.

The amount of the agreed default will need to be charged against the PSBR. A low level of default is crucial if the scheme is to be acceptable to financial institutions. Actual default is likely to be very low if the NIC/PAYE machinery is used as the collection mechanism. However, the linking of the scheme to ability to pay will mean that some people will never complete their payments. Nicholas Barr estimates that under his proposals the default rate is likely to be around 13% as opposed to 23% on the present Government scheme. In costing our scheme we have assumed that Government will guarantee a default of 20%.

Under present accounting rules, Government requires that the full amount of any loan is set against the PSBR. We argue that only the level of default needs to be provided against in this way. The Government has also always resisted the use of the tax or National Insurance machinery to collect other funds. Again, we see no justification for maintaining this position. Government has the power to change both practices and should do so in the interests of creating a workable scheme.

If we assume the 20% default rate, the guarantee on the contribution fund will be £190 million and on the allowance £440 million.

If interest is to be charged to students, the Government will need to meet the cost of tax relief.

By extending the payment of fees to part-time students, the public purse will forgo the difference between fees previously paid and the fee contribution. Part-time student numbers for 1994–5 are estimated at 480,000. If the Government forgoes, say, £500 per student then the cost will be £240 million. However, the cost will undoubtedly be higher since the purpose of the scheme is to stimulate an increase in part-time student numbers.

What Will Be the Cost to the Individual?

All students will be required to pay the HECON, which will be in the region of £1,000 per annum. All will be eligible to claim the HEMA, but need not take the maximum permissible. A student following a three-year course will therefore face a bill repayable over, say, twenty years, of about £12,000, plus any interest. Interest will attract tax relief at the basic rate. The present means-tested maintenance grant will be phased out. In future, the level of support higher education students receive from the public purse will be linked to their own future earnings rather than their parents' present income.

Glossary

AAP	Assessment of Achievement Programme
ABRC	Advisory Board for the Research Councils
ALBSU	Adult Literacy and Basic Skills Unit
APL	Accreditation of Prior Learning
APU	Assessment of Performance Unit
BBC	British Broadcasting Corporation
BP	British Petroleum
BTEC	Business and Technician Education Council
CASE	Cognitive Acceleration through Science Education
CATE	Council for the Accreditation of Teacher Education
CATS	Credit Accumulation and Transfer Scheme
CBI	Confederation of British Industry
CETAC	Community Education and Training Advice Centre
CHE	College of Higher Education
CIHE	Council for Industry and Higher Education
CITL	Council for Innovation in Teaching and Learning
CNAA	Council for National Academic Awards
CRE	Commission for Racial Equality
CSE	Certificate of Secondary Education
CVCP	Committee of Vice-Chancellors and Principals
DENI	Department of Education in Northern Ireland
DES	Department of Education and Science
DET	Department for Education and Training
DFE	Department for Education
EAU	Educational Achievement Unit
EC	European Community
ED	Employment Department
EHE	Enterprise in Higher Education
ELB	Education and Library Board

ESRC	Economic and Social Research Council
ETB	Education and Training Board
ETDA	Education and Training Development Authority
FE	Further Education
FEFC	Further Education Funding Council
FEU	Further Education Unit
GCE	General Certificate of Education
GCSE	General Certificate of Secondary Education
GDP	Gross Domestic Product
GED	General Education Diploma
GHS	General Household Survey
GNVQ	General National Vocational Qualification
GTC	General Teaching Council
HE	Higher Education
HECON	Higher Education Contribution
HECS	Higher Education Contribution Scheme
HEFCE	Higher Education Funding Council for England
HEFCW	Higher Education Funding Council for Wales
HEMA	Higher Education Maintenance Allowance
HEQC	Higher Education Quality Council
HMI	Her Majesty's Inspectorate
HND	Higher National Diploma
ILEA	Inner London Education Authority
IMS	Institute of Manpower Studies
INSET	In-Service Education and Training
IT	Information Technology
ITT	Initial Teacher Training
LEA	Local Education Authority
LEC	Local Enterprise Company
LMS	Local Management of Schools
NAEGA	National Association for Educational Guidance for Adults

NASUWT	National Association of Schoolmasters/Union of Women Teachers
NCE	National Commission on Education
NCET	National Council for Educational Technology
NCVQ	National Council for Vocational Qualifications
NFER	National Foundation for Educational Research
NHS	National Health Service
NIACE	National Institute of Adult Continuing Education
NIC	National Insurance Contribution
NIESR	National Institute of Economic and Social Research
NVQ	National Vocational Qualification
OECD	Organisation for Economic Co-operation and Development
OFSET	Office for Standards in Education and Training
OFSTED	Office for Standards in Education
OST	Office of Science and Technology
PCAS	Polytechnics Central Admissions System
PCFC	Polytechnics and Colleges Funding Council
PDP	Personal Development Plan
PES	Public Expenditure Survey
PGCE	Post-Graduate Certificate of Education
PSBR	Public Sector Borrowing Requirement
PTR	Pupil Teacher Ratio
QTS	Qualified Teacher Status
RSA	Royal Society of Arts
SAT	Standard Assessment Task
SCAA	School Curriculum and Assessment Authority
SCOTVEC	Scottish Vocational Education Council
SEB	Scottish Examination Board
SEN	Special Educational Needs
SHEFC	Scottish Higher Education Funding Council
SOED	Scottish Office Education Department
STRB	School Teachers' Review Body

SVQ	Scottish Vocational Qualification
TASC	Teaching as a Career
TEC	Training and Enterprise Council
TGAT	Task Group on Assessment and Testing
UCCA	Universities Central Council on Admissions
UFC	Universities Funding Council
UGC	University Grants Committee
UPPI	Universities Pay and Prices Index
YMEI	Younger Mature Entry Index
YT	Youth Training
YTP	Youth Training Programme
YTS	Youth Training Scheme

Index

Also available as a Heinemann hardback

Briefings
The Paul Hamlyn Foundation
National Commission on Education

This volume contains the widely acclaimed series of Briefing papers published by the National Commission on Education between January 1992 and October 1993. The Briefings enabled authoritative writers to inform the work of the Commission during the two years of preparation of its report *Learning to Succeed*. They also, as intended, stimulated public debate in some of the more controversial issues that the report addresses.

Each Briefing draws together, analyses and discusses a vast range of statistics and research findings and suggests ways forward. They are short and written in clear language. The series is unique in that while instantly accessible to the lay reader it has also become a vital source for academics and policy-makers.